Kings
OF THE
COURT

Kings
OF THE
COURT

LEGENDS
OF THE
NBA

A L A N   M I N S K Y

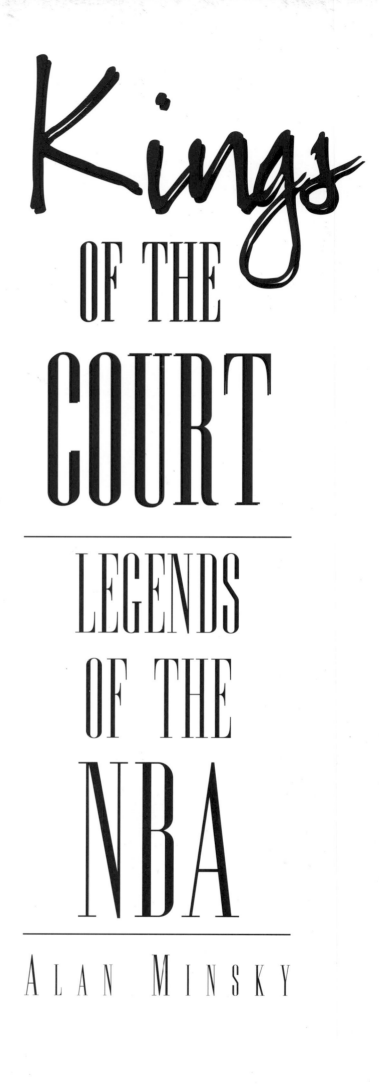

MetroBooks

MetroBooks

An Imprint of Friedman/Fairfax Publishers

Library of Congress Cataloging-in-Publication Data

Minsky, Alan,
    Kings of the court : legends of the N.B.A. / Alan Minsky.
        p.   cm.
    Includes bibliographical references and index.
    ISBN 1-56799-177-7 (Hardcover)
    ISBN 1-56799-220-X (Paperback)
    1. Basketball players--United States--Biography.   2. National
Basketball Association--History.   I. Title.
GV884.A1M56   1995
796.323'092'2--dc20
[B]   95-8214
                                      CIP

Editor: Nathaniel Marunas
Art Director: Jeff Batzli
Designer: Kevin Ullrich
Photography Editor: Wendy Missan

Color separations by Bright Arts (Singapore) Pte. Ltd.
Printed in China by Leefung-Asco Printers Ltd.

For bulk purchases and special sales, please contact:
Friedman/Fairfax Publishers
Attention: Sales Department
15 West 26th Street
New York, NY 10010
212/685-6610 FAX 212/685-1307

DEDICATION

This book is dedicated to the memory of my
grandfather, Cesare DePardo

ACKNOWLEDGMENTS

Special thanks to Nathaniel Marunas, Wendy Missan,
and Kevin Ullrich; Jessica K.; Susie and Michael;
Nora, Sara, and Paul, who kept me crazy when sanity
was a vice; Julie Pilliter and Kelly Smith, who got the
ball rolling; my parents, always; and Kareem Abdul-
Jabbar, for doing it all with dignity

Contents

INTRODUCTION

The forty-five-year history of the National Basketball Association, the world's premier professional basketball league, is dominated by its legendary superstars. The game's first great big man, George Mikan, led his Minneapolis Lakers to five titles during the league's infancy. Bill Russell was the backbone of the Boston Celtics' dynasty that won eleven titles in thirteen years (from 1957 to 1969) and continually frustrated the era's most dominant player, Wilt Chamberlain. The seventies was a decade of relative parity, though Kareem Abdul-Jabbar stood out as the NBA's premier star. Larry Bird's Boston Celtics battled for supremacy with Magic Johnson and Jabbar's Lakers throughout the eighties. Michael Jordan lifted the Chicago Bulls to three consecutive titles in the early nineties before retiring prematurely. Then Hakeem Olajuwon led the Houston Rockets to two titles. Of course, these roundball legends all had strong, complementary supporting casts, but it is unlikely that any of their teams could have won an NBA title without them.

Individual excellence stands out in basketball more than in such other team sports as baseball, football, hockey, or soccer. With only five men on the court per team, all of whom have to play offensively and defensively, a player who can dominate on either end of the court can control a basketball game. A player who performs in this manner over a whole season becomes a star; if he can maintain that level of play throughout an entire career in the NBA, he merits consideration as one of the greatest players of all time. Competitive college teams consist of players who were all-stars in high school; NBA players all excelled in college. A star in the NBA is truly the best of the best; to be the league's greatest star for a generation is tantamount to becoming a national treasure. This book looks at the careers of such legends.

Which players deserve inclusion among the NBA's all-time elite and which players, as great as they were, fail to make the short list is a tantalizing dilemma. Although it is true that certain players make larger contributions than others, organized basketball is not a one-on-one sport and therefore does not provide clear criteria for declaring one player better than another. Because basketball has evolved so rapidly, one thing that assists in selecting the all-time greats, oddly enough, is the inherent difficulty in comparing players across generations. Therefore, *Kings of the Court* is organized into five main chapters, representing five generations of NBA players: the Mikan era,

the Celtic dynasty, the seventies, the Bird and Magic years, and the age of Michael. Each chapter consists of an introductory section, which discusses the way the game was played during that era and the teams that dominated the league, followed by essays on the greatest players of that generation. A short sixth chapter discusses the contemporary players who may be destined for NBA greatness. The appendix cites the career statistics of the players featured in the book and several NBA records. The afterword features the ultimate argument starter, a discussion of who belongs on the all-time NBA starting five and who deserves the appellation of the "greatest player of all time."

Initially, this book was going to feature essays on ten players selected as the top echelon of superstars from throughout NBA history and include shorter essays on ten runners-up. This well-balanced organization, however, was determined arbitrarily, and upon closer inspection it seemed that only seven players belonged in the highest category ("Gold Medal"): Bill Russell, Wilt Chamberlain, Oscar Robertson, Kareem Abdul-Jabbar, Larry Bird, Magic Johnson, and Michael Jordan. Three players—George Mikan, Elgin Baylor, and Julius Erving—who had been in the top ten were relegated to a middle group ("Silver Medal"), also occupied by Bob Pettit, Jerry West, and Moses Malone. A third rung ("Bronze Medal") of NBA superstars consists of Dolph Schayes, Bob Cousy, John Havlicek, Rick Barry, Elvin Hayes, Hakeem Olajuwon, and Charles Barkley (the only player selected who was never part of a championship team).

George Mikan certainly dominated the NBA as much as any player in league history, and he proved to be a great innovator, but he played in an era before Russell introduced shot blocking to the game, and it seems unlikely, given Mikan's skills, that he could have dominated in the same way after Russell. Nonetheless, Mikan's impact on NBA history was so

The great Kareem Abdul-Jabbar waits for a pass in the low post while being guarded by Celtic center Robert Parish. Few opposing centers played Kareem as well as the seven-foot (213.3cm) Parish, a potent combination of size, strength, and quickness. Jabbar, however, usually responded to the challenge of facing the Celtics, in particular when he led the Lakers to their first playoff triumph over Boston in the 1985 NBA finals. Kareem was the playoff MVP that year, at the age of thirty-eight. Parish, although in his early forties, continues to play, currently for the Charlotte Hornets. Jabbar and Parish rank first and second on the all-time list for most NBA games played.

Celtic Sam Jones shoots a baseline jumper during the 1969
NBA finals against the Lakers. In
the background are all-time
greats Wilt Chamberlain (Number
13) and Elgin Baylor (Number
22) of the Lakers and Bill
Russell (Number 6) and John
Havlicek (Number 17) of the
Celtics. The 1968–69 season was
Chamberlain's first in Los
Angeles, and the Lakers were
consequently favored to win
against the aging Celtics, even
though Boston had won all six
finals between the two teams
over the past decade. Alas, 1969
was no different: it came down
to the last few seconds of Game
Seven in Los Angeles. The previously huge Celtic lead was down
to just 1 point, 103–102. On
defense, West knocked the ball
loose but it went right to
Boston's Don Nelson, who—with
just seconds left on the shot
clock—launched a jumper from
around the free throw line that
hit the back rim, went straight
up in the air about two feet
(0.6m), and fell through the
middle of the basket. The Celtics
held on to win 108–106. It was
the last game for both Sam
Jones and Bill Russell; the Celtics
had clinched their eleventh
championship in Russell's thirteen years with the team.

great that he merits as much attention as any player in league history. Elgin Baylor and Julius Erving were the game's two greatest aerial innovators, but their accomplishments as professional basketball players do not clearly outshine those of Jerry West and Bob Pettit and are not on par with the top seven. Oscar Robertson did not collect as many championship rings as the other top-tier players, but his overall impact on the game was so tremendous (a fact reflected in his statistics) that it seems impossible not to place him in the same grouping as Magic Johnson and Larry Bird.

Contemporary fans and players often gripe that stars from previous generations could not compete in today's game because its rapid pace and above-the-rim pyrotechnics require more athleticism than the old school ever exhibited; but imagine what high-flying Elgin Baylor might have accomplished had he benefited from today's improved conditioning. And perhaps it's worth considering whether today's players would fare well in yesterday's slower game, which placed greater emphasis on working for a good shot (if Jerry West had played for either the Knicks or the Rockets in the 1994 final, the team with West and his outside shot probably would have swept the series in four games). The longevity of certain players also suggests that the old-timers would more than hold their own against today's best. Kareem Abdul-Jabbar learned his basketball in the sixties and was an NBA superstar into the eighties; Wilt Chamberlain learned to play in the fifties and led his team past Kareem's and into the NBA finals twice during Kareem's prime; Bill Russell's Celtics were winning championships over Chamberlain right up until Abdul-Jabbar entered the league.

The 1963 Celtics versus the 1993 Bulls? The prevailing opinion, of course, is that the Bulls would romp. Perhaps. Because basketball is so much more popular now than ever before, logic suggests that the best players of today must be better than the best of an earlier era since today's superstars have ascended to the top of a larger group. But the NBA had only nine teams in 1963, so each team consisted exclusively of elite players. If the Celtics got a month to prepare and adjust to the evolution of the game, it would probably be close.

Public interest in the NBA has soared over the past decade. As recently as the early eighties, television ratings and attendance were slumping and many franchises were in dire financial straits. Today, the league's popularity in America is comparable with professional baseball and football for the first time in its history.

Many factors contributed to the NBA's turn-around, but the key ingredient was the public's familiarity with the league's stars. There was the epic struggle between Larry Bird and the Celtics and Magic, Kareem, and the Lakers; then the Lakers' successful campaign to become the first team to win consecutive titles in two decades; then the dominance of Isiah Thomas and the well-balanced, hard-nosed Detroit Pistons over the Celtics in the East and even-

tually over the Lakers as well. In the early nineties, the whole world marveled as Michael Jordan led the Bulls over the Pistons and toward three NBA championships. Today, NBA stars are the most renowned and celebrated athletes in the world. However, many NBA fans are recent converts and know little about yesterday's heroes of the hardwood, men whose accomplishments rival those of today's NBA superstars and laid the groundwork for the basketball of today and tomorrow.

If a common thread runs through the essays on the players featured in *Kings of the Court*, it is that these men all shared something beyond their great basketball ability, something more than a strong desire to win, something more basic. Basketball is a physical game played in a small, restricted space; each player is almost continually face to face with his opponent. The legends of the game celebrated in this book conquered their foes, many of whom are great basketball players in their own right, night after night throughout their careers. They defeated men who were focused specifically on the task of stopping them. What the greatest players in NBA history share is an unshakable confidence, not just in their basketball ability, but in their strength as men, as people.

Houston's Hakeem Olajuwon drives against Orlando's Shaquille O'Neal during the 1994–95 regular season. While Olajuwon has already established himself as one of the NBA's all-time greats, O'Neal is well on his way to joining the Rocket center in the NBA pantheon. One of the dominant centers in the league for the past decade, Olajuwon has never stopped refining his game, and in recent years his array of low-post spin moves and short jumpers has been almost unstoppable. Likewise, O'Neal's short jumper has improved each of his first three seasons in the league, and he stands poised to be one of the league's dominant players for the next decade. Olajuwon's Rockets swept O'Neal's Magic in the 1995 NBA finals.

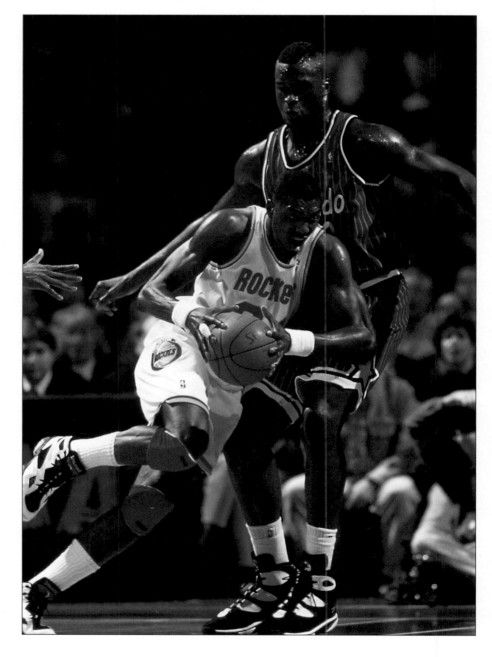

Chapter 1

GEORGE MIKAN AND THE BIRTH OF THE NBA

Thanks to a bespectacled giant named George Mikan, the NBA became America's premier professional basketball league by the early 1950s. Mikan was already the sport's dominant player when his champion Minneapolis Lakers left the National Basketball League (NBL) to join the Basketball Association of America (BAA) for the 1948–49 season. Although the quality of play in the BAA, founded in 1946, was the same as that of the older NBL, the BAA had succeeded in establishing franchises in the nation's largest cities, while the NBL consisted of teams from small midwestern cities. Mikan was the sport's biggest draw, and with his defection, the NBL's days were numbered. Sensing the inevitable, the NBL's four remaining strong franchises followed the Lakers. When the resultant league was organized for the 1949–50 season, it was named the NBA. By the mid-fifties, the NBA was synonymous with pro basketball.

Invented by Dr. James Naismith in 1891 as a recreational exercise for restless youth in the wintertime, basketball flourished in high schools and colleges. As it spread in the early decades of the century, professional teams and leagues were formed. The early pro game was rugged; played inside a chain-link "cage," pro basketball featured many brawls, which attracted a roughhouse audience. Soon barnstorming teams with national reputations toured the land, playing local teams. Before World War II, regional leagues prospered in the East and the Midwest. Then, basketball became tremendously popular among American GIs during the war.

By the late forties pro basketball had mellowed somewhat, but it was still a rough game. The offensive strategy of the day was dominated by constant ball and player movement, and these motion offenses resulted in countless bone-jarring picks. Inside position was won by wrestling in the paint, and referees blew the whistle only if physical contact directly affected the person with the ball. The team with the ball would spread out on the half-court and look for cutters heading toward the basket. There was no 24-second clock until 1954–55, so if the offense did not have the shot it wanted, it would wait until it did. Outside shots were lofted from a set position—both feet on the ground, both hands on the ball—and often very far from the basket. Players rarely left their feet except to battle for rebounds. The two great innovations of the day were the dominant center, exemplified by Mikan, and the fast break, pioneered by Boston Celtic Bob Cousy, who mesmerized players and audiences alike with his spectacular open-court play.

Among the notables of the NBA's first generation were Joe Fulks, who had led the Philadelphia Warriors to triumph in the BAA's first season; Dolph Schayes (the thinking man's forward who personified the gritty NBA game of the day) and Johnny Kerr, who led the Syracuse Nats to a 1-point, seventh-game finals victory over George Yardley and the Fort Wayne Pistons in 1955; and Paul Arizin, who led the Warriors to their second title in 1956. Chuck Cooper, Earl Lloyd, and Nat "Sweetwater" Clifton became the first three African-Americans to play in the NBA, in the fall of 1950, six years before Bill Russell joined the Celtics and pointed the way to the next decade. But it was Mikan who redefined basketball in the fifties.

Minneapolis Laker George Mikan, the NBA's first superstar, tosses up one of his unstoppable hook shots against the Anderson Packers in the semifinals of the 1948 World Tournament. The Lakers defeated the Packers and went on to win the World Tournament.

GEORGE *Mikan*

In the late forties and early fifties George Mikan was far and away basketball's leading celebrity, a veritable ambassador for the game. Recognizing his stature, Mikan sought to emulate his childhood hero, Babe Ruth, whose warm personality had endeared him to the whole nation. However, Big George was soft-spoken and lacked the Babe's flair. Nevertheless, Mikan was tremendously popular and his thoughtful demeanor served basketball and the NBA well. A relentless warrior on the court, Mikan was always amiable—a true gentleman—after the final buzzer had sounded.

Standing at six feet ten-and-a-half inches (209.5cm), weighing 245 pounds (111.2kg), and wearing thick glasses, the lumbering, hulking George Mikan did not resemble the agile, muscle-bound big men of today's NBA. Yet in his day, the late 1940s and early 1950s, Mikan revolutionized professional basketball by dominating the sport from the center position like no man before him. A disciplined team player of brute force who nonetheless had a masterful soft shot, Mikan remade professional basketball in his own image, carrying along the fledgling NBA in the process. The Mikan-led Minneapolis Lakers won five championships in six years in the NBA, becoming the league's first dynasty and transforming pro basketball into a game dominated by big men.

●●●

George Mikan was born into a devoutly Catholic family on June 18, 1924, in Joliet, Illinois. By age thirteen, he was six feet four inches (193cm), but was

uncoordinated and had bad eyesight. Yet friends advised George to play basketball, because the newly popular sport could earn him a scholarship to continue his studies at Notre Dame University, the nation's leading Catholic college, in nearby South Bend, Indiana. So come freshman year, Big George tried out for the basketball team at Joliet High; he was unceremoniously cut. However, George transferred to Quigley Preparatory Seminary in Chicago for academic reasons, and he made the team there. His basketball progress, however, was stalled when he broke his leg. George graduated from Quigley a determined scholar, but an unaccomplished basketball center.

After George received no scholarship offers, he enrolled at DePaul, a Catholic university in Chicago. It was 1942, however, and the Notre Dame basketball program was hard-pressed to find able-bodied young men not in the armed services. Since George was too tall for active military duty, he was offered a tryout. Catholic schools still dominated organized college ball, so Notre Dame was the big time. George trekked down to South Bend during winter break, but Coach George Koegan was unimpressed. "Koegan told me to return to DePaul, that I'd make a better scholar than a basketball player," Mikan recalled. So George Mikan retreated to Chicago, prepared to follow Koegan's advice.

However, during the spring of Mikan's freshman year, DePaul's young coach, Ray Meyer, noticed big George on campus. Meyer was young, very ambitious, and, it turned out, ingenious. He persuaded Mikan to commit to a rigorous and unique training program. Meyer hired a coed to give George dancing lessons to improve his agility. He had George play one-on-one against short, quick opponents to improve his defensive positioning. Mikan's regimen also included jumping rope, playing hours of catch with tennis and medicine balls, and taking 250 hook shots with each hand. Meyer recognized that Mikan was a determined young man willing to work hard to discipline his body—though Meyer could not have envisioned that the results would be so superlative.

Basketball in the early forties was still about five guys, often six feet (182.8cm) or shorter, moving constantly on offense, looking for backdoor passes or the open set shot. In Mikan's junior year, DePaul and Oklahoma A&M, which had seven-foot (213.3cm) center Bob Kurland (who never played pro ball), dominated college hoops. Mikan led DePaul to the 1945 National Invitational Tournament crown, college basketball's most coveted trophy in those days. In one tournament game, Mikan scored an amazing 53 points. Playing in the middle, close to the basket, the two skilled big men not only overwhelmed smaller opponents on the offensive end, but also clogged the lane, shutting down players cutting in for layups, and controlled the defensive boards. Mikan and Kurland were so adept at reaching up and swatting away shots at the last second that the goaltending rule was devised. A revolution was beginning.

Under Meyer's tutelage Mikan had developed into an almost unstoppable force near the basket. While other centers had nifty, quick moves, Mikan relied on his brute strength to gain position near the basket, where he would employ a simple drop-step move followed by his soft, accurate hook shot, which he shot equally well with his left or right hand. In other words, Mikan would post up with his back to the basket, receive an inlet pass, take a step back, pivot toward the basket, and release his hook or, if he was close enough (and he often was), a layup. As he moved to the basket, Mikan would lead with his elbow, but since he had both hands on the ball he could not be called for an offensive foul.

Battles for position beneath the basket were brutal in Mikan's day, and no one could dish it out like George. On defense, Mikan used his broad frame to clog the middle, and his height gave him the ability to block shots regularly. The bespectacled giant could control the boards at both ends of the floor. Number 99 was truly the center of attention.

Mikan graduated from DePaul in the spring of 1946, a three-time All-American and the biggest star of the hardwood. George went straight into the pro ranks, which were especially rough, and fans wondered if Mikan would be able to dominate with his rugged style. George quickly settled the issue when his team, the Chicago American Gears, won the NBL in his first full season.

A new league, the Basketball Association of America, began in the fall of 1946. The BAA included some old Eastern franchises like the Boston Celtics and the New York Knickerbockers that previously had no league affiliation. Yet the focus of the pro basketball world remained the NBL, which consisted mainly of teams from small midwestern cities, because George Mikan played in the NBL. In the 1946–47 season Mikan averaged 16.5 points per game, and the Gears struggled, finishing third in their division. But the team came alive during the playoffs and went on to defeat the powerful Rochester Royals in the finals.

When the Gears' owner, hoping to exploit Mikan's immense popularity, tried unsuccessfully to start a third league in the autumn of 1947, the Chicago team was disbanded and its players, Mikan included, were placed into a dispersal draft. The team with the worst record in the league the previous season, the Minneapolis Lakers, who had moved from Detroit in the off-season (as the Detroit Gems the team was a pathetic 4–40 in 1946–47), had the first

pick and naturally chose George Mikan. Suddenly, Mikan was on a team that would provide him with little support beyond first-round pick Jim Pollard, a sharpshooting six-foot-four-inch (193cm) forward. Mikan would have to raise the level of his game, and to the thrill of Minneapolis, he did. George averaged 21.3 points per game and led the upstart Lakers to first place in their division with a 43–17 record. Once again, Mikan's team conquered the hard-luck Rochester Royals in the finals. As if the NBL championship were not enough, the Lakers played in and won the 1948 World Tournament.

Having established his dominance over the NBL, Mikan and the Lakers (and their archrivals, the Royals) jumped to the BAA for the 1948–49 season. The big-city BAA promised larger road gates for the Lakers. Together in the western division, the Lakers and Royals compiled the league's two best records. Mikan brought new excitement to the BAA, attracting the largest crowds of the season wherever he played. George responded by scoring a spectacular 28.3 points per game. The Lakers disposed of the Royals in the Western Conference finals and went on to win the BAA championship.

When a few more teams jumped from the NBL in the off-season, the National Basketball Association was officially formed. It was an unwieldy seventeen-team organization. Mikan led the league with a 27.4 scoring average, and the Lakers, who now had star point guard Slater Martin and power forward Vern Mikkelsen to complement Mikan and Pollard, posted their best regular season record of the Mikan era, 51–17. The Royals, of course, had the same record, though they were upset in the first round of the playoffs. The Lakers breezed into the finals, where they met and defeated young Dolph Schayes and the Syracuse Nats.

The Laker offense revolved around big George; in contrast to the standard motion offense, it was very deliberate. The Laker point guard would bring the

George Mikan reaches for a rebound against Hamlin star Howie Schultz in Mikan's junior year at DePaul. Whether battling for position on the low post or under the boards, big Number 99 was a master at using his tremendous height and wide body to maximum advantage. By all accounts, Mikan absolutely dominated the defensive glass and also grabbed numerous offensive boards while at DePaul and early in his pro career. The NBA did not begin compiling rebounding statistics until the 1950–51 season, by which time Mikan was joined on the Lakers by another great rebounder, Vern Mikkelsen. Still, Mikan averaged 14 boards per game over his last four seasons and won the league rebounding title in the 1952–53 season.

RIGHT: Mikan jumps out to block a shot by the Rochester Royals' Bob Davies in the 1951 playoffs. Mikan's interior defense was often just as devastating to opponents as his offense. Most teams in Mikan's era ran a motion offense, in which picks were used to free players for layups. Mikan could single-handedly frustrate this strategy, either by playing off his man and clogging the lane or by moving over to challenge the layup, forcing an altered shot. The Royals eliminated the Lakers from the playoffs in 1951 and went on to win the NBA title, the only time in Mikan's pro career that his team failed to win its league's title. OPPOSITE: Big George about to score against the Fort Wayne Pistons in January 1956 during his attempted comeback. Like Michael Jordan, Mikan retired after leading his team to three consecutive championships and then, a year later, decided he wasn't through yet. Unlike Mike, George could not recapture the old glory—his aging body was too worn. A proud champion who won three NBA scoring titles and five NBA titles in six years, Mikan could not accept being a role player on a mediocre team. Rather than tarnish his glorious reputation, he retired permanently at midseason.

ball up slowly and the team would methodically work the ball around the perimeter until Mikan established position just outside the narrow six-foot (1.8m) foul lane. No player could stop Mikan, and most opposing centers were overwhelmed. Often, as a point of pride, George would challenge the double-team—and he would usually succeed. Sometimes when he was doubled up, Mikan would use his sharp passing skills to find a free teammate cutting to the basket or an open man for a set shot. Occasionally, other Lakers, especially Pollard, would object to Mikan's apparent self-ishness on offense. But Lakers Coach John Kundla was an expert at restoring order among his players, and no one could complain about the results. "The thing about Mikan, everything revolved around him, and he got too much publicity," Pollard said. "But he was a hell of a competitor. We'd get through a game and his question was, 'Did we win?' That was his idea of the whole game. That made us all on George's side, because he was a winner."

The success of the fledgling NBA represented an end to the era of many disparate leagues, and George Mikan's dominance was the primary unifying force in the organization of the pro game. The NBA was the league that Mikan built.

One barrier, however, still existed between Mikan and absolute dominance of the professional ranks—and by association, the NBA's status as the world's top league—the legendary Harlem Globetrotters. In later years, the Trotters would devolve into a comedy troupe, but before and during World War II, they were revered as the greatest basketball team on earth. An average Globetrotter season would consist of 150 victories against, maybe, ten losses. Trotter owner Abe Saperstein could always smell a promising spectacle, and the Globetrotters versus Mikan's Lakers was just that. So in 1948, the two teams played a two-game series, a tradition that would last five years. In 1948, the Trotters took both games, and they also won the first matchup of 1949.

The games were followed so closely in the black communities in the American North that a Trotter victory was cause for huge celebrations. However, the Lakers finally broke through in the second game of early 1949, defeating Harlem 68–53 before a packed house in Minneapolis. In 1950 the Lakers, with Mikkelsen, Martin, and Harrison now alongside Pollard and Mikan, beat the Globetrotters by 16 and 15 points. The Laker domination continued in 1951 and 1952 before Saperstein put an end to the series. Mikan and the Lakers had established the primacy of NBA basketball over the best touring team in the world; it was a serious rite of passage and legitimization for organized professional basketball.

It is fair to say that at the beginning of the 1950s, George Mikan ruled the basketball universe. College ball was still followed more closely by more people than was the professional game, but Mikan was recognized as the sport's premier star. One time the marquee at Madison Square Garden read "George Mikan vs. the Knicks." As basketball's leading man, Mikan kept a surprisingly low profile. What most fans knew about him was that he was huge, strong, agile, skilled, and a fierce competitor. Even against lesser opponents, George was unrelenting: "It was constantly a test as to whether or not I was able to beat the other guy," Mikan recalled. "It was a day-to-day type of competition. Every time I played, they wanted to beat me. But being stubborn and determined, I wouldn't let them."

Mikan was brilliant throughout the 1950–51 campaign, scoring 28.4 points and pulling down 14.1 rebounds per game. The extreme lengths that teams would go to defeat Mikan was vividly displayed on November 22, 1950, when the Fort Wayne Pistons employed stalling tactics against the Lakers, resulting in a 19–18 victory for the Pistons. The Lakers seemed destined for another title when Mikan injured his ankle just before the playoffs. George played through the pain as he always did (he once estimated that he received 166 stitches during his career, and yet he rarely missed a game), but he was not himself. With Mikan hobbled, the Rochester Royals finally defeated their arch-nemesis Minneapolis in the semifinals and went on to capture the league crown. Mikan hated the idea that someone else had won one of his championships.

It would never happen again. Even though the league widened the lane to twelve feet (3.6m) for the 1951–52 season in an effort to curtail Mikan's dominance, George and his Lakers swept the next three NBA seasons, a feat accomplished only by the Celtic dynasty of the sixties and Michael Jordan's Bulls. Mikan and the Lakers were in a contract dispute before the 1954–55 season; rather than hold out, bruised and battered from years of low-post combat, Mikan decided to retire and pursue a law degree. Some thought it was just as well, since the NBA adopted the 24-second shot clock that season, not only to speed up the tempo of the game, but also to disrupt the Lakers' slow-developing, Mikan-oriented half court offense. Without Mikan the Lakers floundered, so he staged an ill-advised comeback in the fall of 1955. Mikan was a shadow of his former self and retired permanently after 37 games. He went on to coach briefly and later became the first commissioner of the American Basketball Association (ABA).

However, Mikan will always be best remembered as pro basketball's first superstar and household name. Basketball fans of today casually dismiss Mikan, claiming that he would not have succeeded against later generations of NBA big men, that Number 99 did not possess the physical skills necessary to star in the modern NBA. Mikan, they say, would be little more than a backup center today. But Mikan possessed an unquenchable desire to be a champion; who's to say that he could not have raised his game to another level? Mikan never displayed skills that would make him a contemporary superstar, but he didn't have to; he only perfected his game to where he could dominate all comers in his day. He led his team to three straight NBA titles, seven league championships in eight years as a pro, and eight crowns in ten years going back to his days at DePaul—a record of success rivaled only by Bill Russell in the annals of basketball history. Not bad for an uncoordinated hulk with glasses.

THE LOWEST-SCORING GAME IN NBA HISTORY
Fort Wayne Pistons 19, Minneapolis Lakers 18

The Pistons traveled to Minneapolis to face the Lakers on November 22, 1950. It was early in the season and Fort Wayne Coach Murray Mendanhall was willing to employ a radical strategy to try to derail George Mikan and the defending champions. The Pistons knew the Lakers well, having squared off against them in the previous season's Central Division Final. The Pistons had a strong year up until that playoff series, having finished 40–28 and upsetting powerful Rochester in the first round of the playoffs. But the Lakers ended the Pistons' season abruptly, sweeping the series. During that playoff Mendanhall learned that it was futile to play Minneapolis at a fast pace, since Mikan usually made a higher percentage of his shots than anyone else and also dominated the rebounding. Thus, Mendanhall told his troops to hold on to the ball as long as possible and only take shots at the end of the quarter or if the shot was extremely easy. The league would not institute a shot clock until the 1954–55 season, so the Pistons planned to take their time.

Keeping the game at a snail's pace, the Pistons, led by their star Fred Schaus, were ahead 8–7 after the first quarter. The second frame was less successful for Fort Wayne, however, as the defending champions took a 13–11 lead to the locker room. The Pistons regained control of the contest in the third quarter by doubling the Lakers output, 6–3, to take a slim 17–16 advantage into the final quarter. Fort Wayne held on to the lead and the ball and escaped Minneapolis with a 19–18 victory. Considering that the Pistons would win only four other road games during the 1950–51 season, and that the Lakers would only drop two other home games that year, Coach Mendanhall's strategy was apparently a stroke of pure genius.

Actually, the Pistons only pulled off the upset because of Laker failures from the free throw line. Each team managed only 4 field goals. But the referees called the game closely, providing both teams with opportunities to score from the charity stripe. Fort Wayne buried 11 one-pointers to the Lakers' 10, though Minneapolis had more free throw attempts (17) than the Pistons (15). Mikan missed 4 free throws, but made 7—below his exceptional 80% ratio for the season, but acceptable. The real goat was guard Slater Martin, who had a passable .684 free throw percentage for the year but missed all of his 3 attempts in a game that magnified such errors. Mikan was the only Laker with any success scoring from the field, hitting on 4 of 11 shots. His Minneapolis teammates went 0 for 7. Thus, Mikan tallied 15 of his team's 18 points, a miraculous 83.3% of the Lakers total and most definitely an NBA record. Guard John Oldham led the Pistons' more balanced attack with 5 points. Many prominent coaches and officials in the NBA community castigated Coach Mendanhall for his ingenuity. After the 19–18 "debacle," NBA teams never again tried a complete-game stall, though teams frequently employed slow-down tactics to try to preserve leads late in games, a practice that ceased with the advent of the 24-second clock in 1954–55. Mikan and the Lakers won the NBA title in the three years preceding the adoption of the shot clock; perhaps someone should have tried the strategy successfully deployed by the Pistons once upon a time in Minnesota.

DOLPH Schayes

DOLPH Schayes

BELOW, RIGHT: Native New Yorker Dolph Schayes dribbles around Knick Connie Simmons in Schayes' pro debut in the Big Apple during the autumn of 1949. Schayes became a hometown hero while playing for New York University. After graduating in 1948, Schayes signed with the Syracuse Nationals of the NBL, a league without a New York City franchise. However, the Nats joined the NBA for the 1949–50 season and Schayes returned to his old stomping grounds, Madison Square Garden, amidst considerable fanfare. Syracuse won the game 77 to 74.

OPPOSITE: Dolph Schayes grabs a rebound against the Knicks in early 1958. Not the most physically gifted athlete, Schayes compensated with hustle and intelligence. Nowhere was this more evident than in his rebounding skills. Dolph was six feet eight inches (203.2cm) tall and had a solid body, but he had very little leaping ability. Yet when the ball came off the boards, Schayes usually found a way to grab it. Schayes led the league in rebounding in the 1950–51 season, was the first player ever to amass 10,000 rebounds in the NBA, and averaged 12 rebounds per game over his illustrious sixteen-year career.

In the days before the Celtics ruled the NBA with their fast-breaking offense, before the NBA became a league of expert jump shooters, long before the advent of "fan-tastic" dunks, the pro game was the domain of rugged, fundamental basketball. No player personified such a style more than, or played it any better than, the Syracuse Nationals' Dolph Schayes. At six foot eight inches (203.2cm) and 280 pounds (127.1kg), with virtually no leaping ability, Schayes was a textbook player, constantly moving on offense, seeking an open space to set up for his deadly two-handed set shot, always fighting for position to secure a defensive rebound, and a master from the free throw line. A model of consistency, Schayes led the Nats to the playoffs every year of his fifteen-year career, was the star of the 1954–55 championship squad, and retired in 1964 as the NBA's all-time leading scorer.

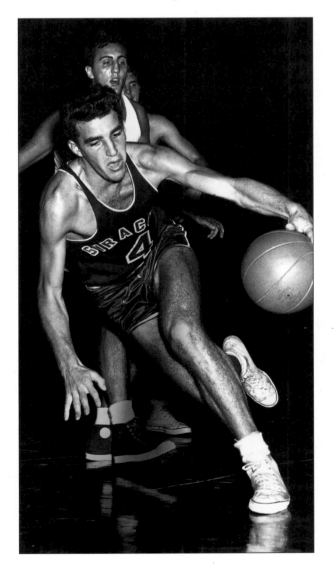

• • •

Dolph Schayes, who personified what was known as the "New York" style, was born, appropriately, in New York City on May 19, 1928. Dolph learned to play hoops in the gymnasiums of Gotham City, where he was taught that success relied on motion offense: movement without the ball, to cut to the basket or find an open space to take a set shot or get to the basket for an offensive rebound. Dolph was a hardworking student of the game who experienced an opportune growth spurt during adolescence. At the tender age of fifteen, Dolph was made the captain of a successful DeWitt Clinton High School team in the Bronx. Schayes attended college at New York University and was an All-American as a nineteen-year-old senior. He won the prestigious award as the top college player in New York for 1948. Schayes played center in college and he learned how to compete in the rugged terrain beneath the boards, but he averaged only 10 points per game. Schayes would not fully mature as a player until the pros.

Dolph joined the Syracuse Nationals in 1948–49, their final year in the NBL, and contributed 12.8 points per game to a team that improved 16 games over the previous year by going 40–23. The Nats joined the NBA for the next season and continued their rapid improvement, finishing with the league's best record, 51–13, and making the finals, where they lost to George Mikan and his Laker juggernaut in 6 games. Schayes' offensive skills began to blossom that year as he led the Nats with a 16.8 average per game. In two brief years the Nats had become winners and began a tradition that would last throughout the fifties. Dolph was both the catalyst and the backbone of that tradition; the Nats never failed to make the playoffs during his career. Accordingly, Syracuse Nats fans were the most fervent in the NBA.

In his prime, Dolph played an all-around game. He was among the league's top ten in scoring and rebounding his first twelve seasons in the NBA (a feat unmatched in league history), averaging 18 points and 12 rebounds per game over his career. Schayes was renowned for being constantly in motion and for possessing pinpoint, long-range shooting talent, which he displayed in the classic set shot style. Legendary coach Alex Hannum noted, "Schayes had legitimate 25 to 30 foot [7.6 to 9.1m] range. You could add 5 points to his career scoring [average] if they had the three-point shot back then, because he never failed to take a 30-footer." Whenever Schayes

made a shot he would raise his hands as he ran back
to play defense, a gesture that became Schayes' on-
court signature.

Dolph was also a tremendous rebounder, even
though he could barely jump. Dolph relied on establishing good position. A thinking man's star, Schayes
even used his inability to jump to his advantage.
Having boxed out his opponent, he would reach up
and tap the ball to an open spot nearby on the court
and run down the ball, which he could do quickly
because he had never left his feet.

Dolph's on-court ingenuity and skill were the
product of his tremendous work ethic and love for the
sport: "I was consumed by the game, especially what
I call true basketball, where you don't stand there
with your hand up, you move for the ball. You try to
get better, learn new shots and moves. That is why I
loved to practice." Dolph would continually challenge himself to expand his skills. When he came out
of New York University, he knew he had to develop
his game away from the basket since he recognized
he could not succeed in the low post as a pro. The
summer before he joined the Nats he discovered he
had a soft shooting touch from as far away as fifteen
feet (4.5m), so he moved back to twenty feet (6m),
then twenty-five (7.6m), then thirty (9.1m).
Throughout his career he would practice free throws,
telling himself that only swishes counted, even practicing on a special rim with a smaller circumference
(developed for rebounding practice). Schayes was
also fond of saying that an injury to his right hand
was the best thing that ever happened to him because
it forced him to learn to shoot with his left hand as
well. Over time, Schayes developed accurate running
shots with both hands from either side of the basket.

After losing to the Lakers in a dramatic seven-
game championship series in the final season of the
Mikan dynasty, 1953–54, Syracuse was poised to
claim the top spot in the NBA. Johnny Kerr, a highly
touted rookie, joined the Nats in 1954 and became
their star center. Schayes started at the "3" forward,
Paul Seymour and George King were the backcourt
tandem, and Earl Lloyd (one of the NBA's first
African-American stars) and Red Rocha split time at
power forward. The 24-second shot clock had been
put into effect at the request of Syracuse owner
Danny Biasone, who figured the quickened pace
would suit the up-tempo Nats. However, the team the
Nats met in the 1955 finals, the Fort Wayne Pistons,
also had an extremely quick team. The final proved
to be one of the most closely contested in history.
The Pistons led three games to two as the series
moved back to Syracuse for Game Six and, if necessary, Game Seven. Game Six was nip-and-tuck all the
way, and by the fourth quarter it was a shoot-out
between the two stars, Dolph Schayes and the
Pistons' George Yardley. In the end, Yardley
outscored Schayes 31–28, but the Nats prevailed
109–108. Game Seven was equally scintillating. The
game was tied 91–91 with 10 seconds left when the
Nats' George King buried a free throw and stole the

ABOVE: Schayes shoots from the perimeter against the Warriors on November 9, 1961. It was the 682nd consecutive game in which Dolph played, tying the previous NBA ironman record, set by Harry Gallatin. Schayes' streak, which began in February 1952, extended another 24 games and is the third longest in NBA history, behind Randy Smith (906) and Johnny Kerr (844), who was Schayes' longtime teammate on the Nats. **RIGHT:** Schayes drives to the basket against Bill Russell. In his prime, Schayes could score from anywhere on the court: under the basket on a tip-in, from either side of the lane with a running shot, from the charity stripe (which he visited frequently), or from long range with his signature set shot. When Schayes broke George Mikan's career scoring record in 1957 he noted, "It came just the way I hoped it would, on a long set shot." Dolph Schayes remained atop the NBA's list of all-time scorers for the rest of his playing days. He retired in early 1964 with 19,249 points.

ball from the Pistons to lift the Nats to their only NBA title. Dolph Schayes and the Syracuse Nationals were the national champs.

The Nats franchise moved to Philadelphia in the 1963–64 season and became the 76ers, filling the void left by the departure of the Warriors for San Francisco. Schayes became the player-coach of the 76ers, but retired as a player before the end of the season; at the time he was the NBA's all-time leading scorer. Schayes coached the 76ers into the playoffs for three

straight years, but a stormy relationship with superstar Wilt Chamberlain forced Schayes to step down following a division crown and a 55–25 record in 1965–66.

Dolph Schayes, however, will always be remembered as the quintessential Syracuse Nat in the hearts of NBA fans. Like Larry Bird, who was an NBA superstar at the time Dolph's son Danny played for the Milwaukee Bucks, Dolph Schayes got everything he could out of his talent, transforming limited physical gifts into transcendent basketball skill.

BOB Cousy

Whereas Dolph Schayes personified the disciplined, organized style of play that was the rule in the early years of the NBA, Bob Cousy was the exception incarnate. In the fifties, no one did more to bring improvisation and excitement to the pro game than the point guard of the Boston Celtics. Cousy was a magician with the ball, dribbling behind the back, between his legs, and through defenses at breakneck speed or unleashing bull's-eye, no-look passes—all in an era when such flamboyance was not only rare but often frowned upon by coaches. The fans, however, loved it unequivocally.

When Bill Russell joined Boston in 1956, Celtic mastermind Red Auerbach organized the famed Celtic fast break into the NBA's most devastating weapon. Russell would rebound and then make an outlet pass to Cousy, who would use his speed and sleight-of-hand passing skills to rush the ball up the court for easy Celtic baskets. Boston won the NBA title six out of Cousy's last seven years, and by the time of his retirement, Cousy was beloved by basketball fans across America who knew him either as the Cooz or Mr. Basketball.

• • •

Bob Cousy was born on August 9, 1928, in New York City. The son of French-speaking immigrants, Bob learned to play basketball on the asphalt of St. Albans playground in Queens. He fell in love with the game. When he failed to make the junior varsity team at Andrew Jackson High, he traveled throughout the city to play in nonschool leagues. He practiced constantly, dribbling basketballs on the city streets wherever he went. Naturally right-handed, he became equally adept with his left hand. Cousy made his high school team as a sophomore and gained recognition for his exceptional skill with the ball. In the summers, he played at camps in the Catskill Mountains with such up-and-coming stars as George Mikan, Dolph Schayes, and Ed Macauley.

Cousy attended college at Holy Cross, the leading basketball school in the Boston area. Thus began a lifelong romance between Cooz and Beantown. Holy Cross won the NCAA tournament in Cousy's freshman season, and during the next three years Holy Cross basketball became one of Boston's most popular diversions and Cousy one of the city's greatest heroes. The college game had never seen anything like Cousy's open-court game, and his last-second heroics were legendary. In the final 90 seconds of a

game against Kansas during his senior year, Cousy stole a pass and made a layup, stole the inbounds pass for another layup, and then dribbled out the clock, adding 2 free throws for a 4-point victory. Kansas' immortal coach, Phog Allen said, "I see it, but I don't believe it." An NCAA official present at the game added, "I've seen all the college stars of this game, but Cousy is far ahead of anyone. He is so far out of this basketball world that it's hard to compare him to anyone."

Still, the NBA powers-that-be were uncertain about Cousy at the pro level. General managers were reluctant to draft the six-foot-one-inch (185.4cm), 175-pound (79.4kg) Cousy, because he could only do one thing on the basketball court: run the show. No one wanted to give their team over to a floor general whose style contrasted so sharply with everyone else's in the league; it seemed like a formula for catastrophe. The Celtics did not want Cousy but, to the delight of their fans, ended up with him nonetheless. Red Auerbach, Boston's coach, had made it known that he was wary of Cousy and his flamboyant style.

Bob Cousy tries to corral a loose ball for Holy Cross in a 1949 game versus Manhattan. Wherever the young Cousy went on a basketball court, excitement followed; no-look passes, steals, fast breaks, loose balls, and dribbling exhibitions were all part of his dizzying repertoire. College roundball had never seen anything like Cousy's spectacular, frenetic style. On the public courts of America's cities, basketball had been evolving into a wide-open, up-tempo game. Cousy learned his game on the streets, and introduced "playground" basketball to the big time.

ABOVE: Bob Cousy and Bill Russell, the Celtic dynasty's two greatest stars, embrace after the Celtics defeated the Lakers 112–109 to wrap up the 1963 finals and claim their fifth consecutive NBA title. It was Cousy's last game as a Celtic. Cousy and Russell admired one another deeply; not only were they good friends and brilliant teammates, but both men were outspoken advocates of the civil rights movement. BELOW: Cousy makes a behind-the-back bounce pass past Laker Jerry West to teammate Sam Jones (Number 24). With Cousy at the helm, the Celtics matured into the smoothest-running basketball machine ever assembled. Even though Cousy lost none of his flamboyance along the way, his fellow Celtics learned what to expect from him just as he could anticipate their moves; it often seemed like the Celtics could read each other's minds.

Nevertheless, Cousy slowly won over Auerbach during his rookie year and led the Celtics to their first-ever playoff appearance.

At first, the Celtics did not adjust well to their new point guard's style. Often, when Cousy was leading a fast break, an unsuspecting teammate would be hit in the head or shoulder with a pass. However, the other Celtics soon realized Cousy had an amazing court sense. If he could fool them, he could certainly fool an opponent; they had to expect the unexpected. As the Celtics adjusted, Auerbach recognized that Cousy was the perfect weapon for employing his fast-break strategy. Boston became one of the league's winningest teams. In Cousy's third season, he led the NBA in assists for the first time in his career and directed the Celtics to their best record to date, 46–25, and their first appearance in the league semifinals. During the next three seasons, Bob led the league in assists every year, and finished second in scoring one year, and the Celtics competed each season with the league's elite teams. Cousy's spectacular play also made the Celtics the NBA's biggest drawing card. Still, Boston never won a division title or made the championship finals. Auerbach openly questioned whether a Cousy-led team could triumph in the NBA.

In retrospect, it's clear that the Celtics were missing only one piece to the puzzle, Bill Russell, and that after he came along, Cousy the court general

would lead the Celtics' conquest of the NBA. Russell's presence changed the outcome of everything, of course, but he fit perfectly into Auerbach's fast-break, Cousy-led strategy. Thus was born the legendary, lethal Celtic fast break of the dynasty years. Russell would clear the defensive glass and find Cousy, who would push the ball upcourt and use his wizardry to set up an easy Celtic basket. Cousy won four more assist titles after Russell joined the team (bringing his record total to eight, earned in consecutive years), and the Celtics won the Eastern Conference each year and the NBA crown six of the seven years that Russell and Cousy played together.

Bob himself did not attribute his unbelievable passes to his great peripheral vision and large hands like many commentators did, but rather to his intense concentration. Success on the hardwood was a deep-rooted personal need for Cousy, and he would work himself into a near-trance before playing. Whereas many athletes try to avoid pressure when playing, Cousy preferred playing in an agitated state: "A lot of athletes...lose their cool and can't function. I always looked for that feeling." Intensely motivated, Cousy always sought to make the best possible play, whether it be spectacular or mundane.

By the time Cousy retired, he was by far the most popular player in basketball history. At his "farewell" game in 1963, the mayor and governor attended and President Kennedy sent congratulations. The public's affection for Cousy stemmed not only from his breathtaking style of play, but also from the profound admiration people had for him as a man. He spearheaded the fledgling NBA Players Association, even though he was one of the highest-paid players in the league, and he was an outspoken proponent of civil rights both during and after his career. Both on and off the court, Cousy used his unique abilities to the advantage of all those around him.

The Luck of the Irish

Based on the simplest criteria, the quantity of cloth hanging from his ceiling, Red Auerbach has secured a preeminent position in pro basketball history. During Auerbach's stewardship, the Boston Celtics have garnered an unprecedented sixteen banners. So what makes the franchise great? Is it Celtic Pride, the parquet floor, green high-tops, Kevin McHale, Bill Russell, JoJo White, the sixth man, and the vaunted Celtic fast break? Well, yes, but the more succinct, and complete, answer is: Red Auerbach's mind. As former Celtic Gene Conley puts it: "Let's face it, Red is the Celtics." Thus former Celtic Coach, General Manager, and current Club President Arnold Jacob Auerbach is not only an unrivaled basketball strategist, but he's also a world class wheeler and dealer; he's the NBA's "Genius Emeritus."

However, even a maverick mastermind like Red Auerbach can use a little luck every now and then (though "fate" seems more applicable to the story of how Auerbach tried his best to keep Bob Cousy off the Celtics, but failed). Success stories often result when circumstances conspire to produce something unexpected, which, in turn, inspires new perspectives. Bob Cousy was a marquee college star at Holy Cross, which played many of its home games at the Boston Garden. Boston fans wanted the Celtics' new coach to draft the local hero, but young Mr. Auerbach didn't think much of the flashy guard. Cousy specialized in dribbling pyrotechnics, and spectacular, often no-look, passes. Auerbach thought there was no place for such shenanigans in the disciplined pro game. The Celtics had the regional draft rights to Cousy, but they passed him up for seven-foot (213.3cm) Charlie Share from Bowling Green. Cousy was drafted by the Tri-City Hawks, but was then traded to the Chicago Stags. A few months later the Stags folded and Cousy's name was placed in a hat with two other players' names, and the Celtics were one of the teams drawing. Auerbach wanted Max Zaslofsky or Andy Phillip, but Celtic owner Walter Brown drew Cousy—to the delight of Boston fans and to the Redhead's dismay. Briefly, Auerbach tried to discipline Cousy's improvisational flurries. But as the brilliant guard got more playing time, it was the Celtic team and its coach who were forced to adjust. Soon Auerbach realized that fate had dealt him a beautiful hand—Cousy was precisely the talent the Celtics' fast-break offense needed.

In the 1956 draft Red knew who he wanted: the shot-blocking, rebounding machine who had led the University of San Francisco to consecutive NCAA titles, six-foot-nine-inch (205.7cm) center Bill Russell. Some pro scouts were not so high on Russell, but Auerbach saw him as the man to initiate his fast-break offense by clearing the defensive boards and sending off outlet passes or by tapping blocked shots to his teammates. To attain his dream center, Auerbach was going to have to make some deals. In order to acquire Russell, the Celtics had to make a trade to get a higher draft pick (they had finished the previous season with the league's second-best record). Rochester had the first pick, but Auerbach passed them by

to deal two of his high-quality players, Ed Macauley and Cliff Hagan, to St. Louis for the second pick in the draft. But how to ensure that the Royals would pass on Russell? Three things had informed the Redhead's decision to risk losing two stars, who were major contributors to the Celtics throughout a very strong 1955–56 campaign, without being absolutely assured of corralling Russell. First, the defense master had failed to impress many NBA people at postseason all-star games; perhaps the scouts had wanted Russell to have an outside shot. Red knew better, and was encouraged by reports from scouts, who mentioned a few players ahead of Russell. Second, the Royals had no immediate need for a big man because they had a great young center in Maurice Stokes (who was tragically paralyzed from encephalitis only two years later). Third, Auerbach was on good terms with Rochester owner Lester Harrison. Legend has it that Harrison, who owned the arena the Royals played in, was losing money on the building. and since the bottom line was most important here, he cut some deal with Red whereby Auerbach arranged for the Ice Capades, which always sold out, to play at Harrison's arena in exchange for an assurance that Rochester would not draft Russell. Over the years, Auerbach has denied the Ice Capades tale, but he has also asserted that he would never have traded Macauley and Hagan for anyone besides Russell. On draft day, the Royals selected West Virginia's flashy Hot Rod Hundley, the number one pick overall. The Celtics chose Russell, forever shifting the balance of power in the league. The Celtics squared off against the Hawks with Macauley and Hagan for the NBA title each of the next two years. Auerbach had used his backroom skills to bring Bill to Boston to anchor his fast break; and many years earlier a lot of luck had landed him the magical Mr. Basketball, Bob Cousy, to push the ball upcourt. Shortly he would have his dynasty, then a couple of Jones', countless victory cigars, a Green Running Machine, the Chief, a Bird, and a leprechaun.

Jubilant Celtic fans hoist their heroes Tom Heinsohn, Coach Red Auerbach, and Bill Russell onto their shoulders as they celebrate Boston's defeat of the San Francisco Warriors in the 1964 NBA finals. The Game Five victory sealed the sixth consecutive NBA title for the Celtics, the only team in the history of American professional sports to accomplish such a feat.

THE GLORY YEARS
OF THE CELTIC DYNASTY

Following the introduction of the 24-second clock in 1954, offensive production in the NBA skyrocketed; on average, teams scored 15 more points per game in the first year of the shot clock. Teams frequently cleared 100 points in a game. Basketball also took flight in the late fifties. Bill Russell introduced leaping to block shots, the jump shot replaced the set shot as the preferred method from the perimeter, and Elgin Baylor introduced the NBA to "hang time"—going airborne while driving to the basket.

Although the game evolved rapidly on the court, the NBA itself was stable from 1955 to 1969. The only rule change of significance was the implementation of team foul limits. The Celtics won the title almost every year. And whereas the size of the league fluctuated frequently in the Mikan era, it consisted of only eight, nine, or ten stable franchises during the Golden Years. The eight core teams were the Celtics, Knicks, Hawks, Royals, Lakers, Warriors, Pistons, and the Nats/76ers. By 1969, only the Celtics and Knicks played in their original hometowns.

From 1956–57 through 1968–69 the Celtics won eleven titles. Not coincidentally, Russell's career spanned those thirteen seasons; the only times he failed to add a new banner to the Boston Garden rafters was in 1957–58, when Bob Pettit and the St. Louis Hawks defeated the Celtics in the finals, and in 1966–67, when Wilt Chamberlain and a fine supporting cast of Philadelphia 76ers crushed the Celtics in the semifinals. The Lakers never won a championship in this era, but they reached the finals seven times. The Lakers and Celtics played three seven-game series during this period, and remarkably, the Celtics won each Game Seven (in 1962, 1966, and 1969) by 3 points or less.

As basketball continued to become more popular, the number of excellent college stars increased each year and competition heightened for the few openings on NBA annual rosters. Not surprisingly, the league overflowed with exceptional performers. Johnny "Red" Kerr was a star big man for the Syracuse Nats. Cliff Hagan brought his uncanny hook shot to St. Louis, where Lenny Wilkens became the smoothest of point guards. Jerry Lucas was a terror on the boards for Cincinnati. Forward Billy Cunningham and guard Hal Greer were a lethal tandem for the Philadelphia 76ers. Nate Thurmond matured into a great rebounder and defensive center for the San Francisco Warriors. And, of course, Russell's whole supporting cast on the Celtics deserves special mention: sixth man Frank Ramsey, scorer Bill Sharman, Jim Loscutoff, Don Nelson, Tom Sanders, feisty Tommy Heinsohn, defensive wizard K.C. Jones, and perhaps the Celtics' most versatile star, Sam Jones.

The legends of the era include the greatest scoring duo in NBA history, the Lakers' Elgin Baylor and Jerry West. The Hawks' Bob Pettit terrorized the league with his crafty scoring and rebounding skills. But three men from this generation stand out as the greatest of their time: point guard Oscar Robertson and two giants whose rivalry is unmatched in the annals of basketball, Chamberlain and Russell.

The matchup that defined the NBA's Golden Age: Russell versus Chamberlain. Russell was a defensive specialist and the consummate team player; Chamberlain was a one-man offensive juggernaut. They were the two greatest rebounders in NBA history. Their teams stockpiled victories. They both dominated everyone in the league except, of course, one another. Their confrontations were legendary, and when the two titans went toe-to-toe, neither gave an inch.

BILL Russell

Bill Russell blocks a shot by Milt Scheurman of Iowa in the 1956 NCAA final. Russell's University of San Francisco Dons defeated Iowa handily for their second straight NCAA title and fifty-fifth consecutive win. The key to the Dons' dominance was Russell's revolutionary defense. In particular, Bill's shot-blocking technique, which he developed himself and refined to perfection, was unlike anything in the annals of organized basketball. Opponents had never encountered anyone who elevated so high to swat away their shots and invariably, they were dumbfounded.

Many superlatives can be used to describe Bill Russell the man and Bill Russell the basketball player, but three things stand out: one is a simple statistic, another is a historical fact, and the third is an observation about the man that underscores the first two. The statistic is that Russell led the Boston Celtics to eleven NBA titles in his thirteen seasons, an accomplishment unparalleled in the history of American team sports. The fact is that Russell invented modern basketball defense, bringing innovations to the hardwood that forever changed the sport. The observation is that Bill Russell possessed a will to win as great as any competitor in any field throughout history. Russell's defensive tenacity and skills would have amounted to very little—and the Celtic dynasty would not have happened—without Russell's drive to conquer.

An intelligent, proud, powerful, and complex man, Russell could focus and channel his energy and talents in an almost superhuman way. Once he stepped on the court, Russell was unflappable. Opponents had no business scoring over him or winning a rebound from him. For his entire career, the court was Bill Russell's kingdom; his Celtics ruled the NBA.

• • •

Bill Russell was born on February 12, 1934, in Monroe, Louisiana. Like most African-American families, the Russells had deep roots in the South. But the insults and dangers of Jim Crow racism were too much for a proud man like Bill's father, Charlie. The elder Russell went off to California, and when he landed a job in the naval shipyards on the San Francisco Bay, he sent for the rest of his family. Despite the fun nine-year-old Bill was having playing in the Louisiana countryside, he was glad to leave Jim Crow behind.

Not that Oakland was paradise: living conditions in the ghetto were often harsh. Bill's new peers were more hardened than Louisiana youth, and his height often made him the target of aggression. Things worsened for young Bill when his parents separated; then his mother died when he was twelve. In the face of this adversity, Bill went through a period of grave self-doubt. Then during his junior year of high school, the young loner who spent his days in the library had a simple revelation: "One day when I was walking down the hall from one class to another, by myself as usual, it suddenly dawned on me that it was alright to be who I was." From that day on, having struggled through a childhood fraught with trials, Russell became intensely confident and self-reliant.

Because of his height, Russell tried out for the junior varsity basketball team at Oakland's McClymonds High School. Sixteen kids tried out for fifteen spots, and by Russell's own estimation, he was number sixteen. But coach George Powles did not want to discourage an enthusiastic youth and refused to cut Bill. So Russell spent the season sharing a uniform with the team's other misfit; the boys alternated between sitting in the stands or on the bench during games.

Coach Powles became the varsity coach and Russell made the team his junior and senior years. McClymonds had a strong team, but not on account of the future legend in its ranks: Russell tried hard, but had few real skills. Most important, he grew into his body and had a strong physical presence. Coach Powles was a good man, but was a baseball coach and couldn't provide solid basketball instruction.

Fortunately for Bill, circumstances earned him a place on a traveling California high school all-star team. The team toured the West Coast in January, filling out its roster with quality players who completed their high school education after the fall semester. Bill, it turned out, had graduated at the right moment, and though he was never even a third-team all-league player (in a six-team league), he was suddenly a touring all-star. Young Bill was ecstatic; he would get to travel, which was a lifelong dream, play basketball every day, which he had come to enjoy very much, and he would avoid having to look for a job straight out of high school, which he was dreading.

It's safe to say that playing with the all-stars changed Russell's life. In those days, the early fifties, basketball was not a game played in the air; you only left your feet for a rebound. Offensively, the emphasis was on ball movement—looking for the open man for a set shot or layup or driving past your defender for a layup. Jump shots were discouraged, even though the new generation of players used them in the playgrounds. Coaches taught that if you have to leave your feet to shoot, you're not open enough to shoot in the first place. Defensively, leaving your feet to block a shot was considered bad form, because coaches taught that if you left your feet, your opponent would simply pivot around you. Defense was about keeping yourself between the basket and the man you're guarding, defending him closely, and denying him layups or open shots. However, the coach of the touring all-stars, Brick Swegle, was a fun-loving, freewheeling maverick who allowed his talented players to do as they liked on the floor, knowing that they would provide a good show (even though opposing coaches would complain about the "playground" tactics) and, invariably, a victory. Suddenly, Russell's innate physical gifts had an outlet.

Living and breathing this exciting brand of basketball, Russell was like a sponge on the trip, "soaking up whatever I could learn from the other players." The first thing he mastered was an aggressive offensive rebounding technique. Russell had seen the move before, but he had never been able to put it into practice. But by studying a teammate and playing the image over in his mind, he finally felt confident. To his amazement, it worked when he tried it. Bill's oncourt confidence was blooming, and "for the rest of the trip I was nearly possessed by basketball." When he saw a move he wanted to try himself, he would go over it in his mind repeatedly; and when he tried the move, if he messed up some part of it, he would know how he erred and try to correct it next time. He continued this practice throughout the trip and his game grew exponentially.

Then Russell had a breakthrough that would, in time, revolutionize the sport of basketball. Bill was learning the game at such a rapid pace that he was trying everything his skilled teammates were doing. He realized, however, that he would never be able to do certain things because of his size, such as dribble and weave through opponents and race full court for a

layup like teammate Bill Treu. Russell could practice and improve at jump shooting and rebounding, but he had to accept that Treu's open-court ability was something that, as a big man, Russell would never be able to do. A little guard would always be able to steal the ball on its long path from Bill's hand to the floor and back to his hand. Bill was frustrated by the discovery of this limitation. Then suddenly he realized that while he couldn't imitate Treu's moves, he could envision how to stop them. He imagined Treu spinning and weaving downcourt and knew he could anticipate exactly when Treu would release his layup. And he imagined himself leaping and blocking it perfectly: "When I saw him go up to lay the ball in the basket, I'd see myself go up and block the shot. I enjoyed the two-man show in my mind, so I expanded it. I sketched out scenes of Treu and me fast breaking together, pirouetting together, hanging in the air together. Any way he bent, I'd bend with him." When Russell first blocked one of Treu's shots, he was ecstatic—not only because it was a potent new weapon, but primarily because it was the first basketball skill of Russell's that was uniquely his own. Soon Russell was blocking shots on the tour.

Bill was excited that he was an innovator, but he also began to be upset. Why, he thought, had basketball come to him when he had only a few weeks left to play? Fortunately, Russell received a call from an alumnus of the University of San Francisco who wanted to arrange a tryout for Bill with Coach Phil Woolpert. To Bill's amazement, he was soon fulfilling a dream: attending college (and, thanks to basketball, doing it for free). While University of San Francisco provided Bill with the educational opportunities he had always sought, he experienced severe culture shock: Russell went from a 95 percent black high school to a 99 percent white Jesuit college.

Bill Russell scores a layup against Wilt Chamberlain and the Philadelphia 76ers. Throughout his career Russell provided the Celtics with steady, if unspectacular, offensive production. Of course, he regularly keyed the Celtic fast break with his outlet passes after grabbing a defensive rebound. Russell also grabbed more than his share of offensive rebounds. In the low post, Russell developed a reliable hook shot and was adept at finding the open man (he consistently finished second on the Celtics in assists). His best offensive season was 1961–62, when he averaged 18.9 points per game. Over the course of his thirteen-year career Russell averaged 15.1 points per game in the regular season and 16.2 points per game during the playoffs.

Bill Russell soars for a defensive rebound against the Lakers. Notice that Russell is already looking downcourt; the fifth Celtic is probably breaking for the basket, where Russell will hit him with a long pass. The Celtics were so confident about Russell's defensive rebounding skills that the players on the perimeter would break downcourt as soon as an opponent put up a shot. Red Auerbach's fast-breaking Celtic offense actually began before the team had possession of the ball. Apparently the Lakers also accepted that Russell controlled the boards under his basket; look how resigned the Lakers are about the rebound. No one even bothered to contest Russell for it.

Russell, however, soon adjusted to the environment. He also loved getting to practice basketball every day and conversing about the game with his otherwise introverted roommate, K.C. Jones.

Russell learned that the one thing that got K.C. talking was basketball. Together the two dissected every aspect of the game. In that era, basketball was not considered a strategic game. Players mostly went out and played hard, took their shots, and waited for the next game. But Russell and Jones both saw the complex geometry and dynamics of the court. Together they would discuss countless scenarios and discuss the nuances they observed. In the process, Russell's vocabulary expanded from one of individual possibility and innovation into one of total team integration. More often than not, Russell and Jones focused on defense. Most significantly, the two determined that when trying to block shots it was best to jump straight up, anticipate the arc of the shot, and use the length of your arms to full advantage. In other words, if you leap out toward the shooter, you are likely to make contact with the shooter and draw a foul. By jumping straight up, you not only avoid fouls but also have better body control in the air. The key, therefore, is to remain close to the defender, even taking a step closer to him before elevating. When Russell and Jones discussed offense, they focused on teamwork. On the court they tried their theories. The two young men were laying the groundwork for a revolution that would forever change the game.

Russell and Jones led the University of San Francisco freshman team to an impressive 19–4 record. Russell's defense had developed into something spectacular and his offensive contribution was considerable. Unfortunately, Jones had to sit out his sophomore year with appendicitis, and the Dons went only 14–7 in Russell's first year on the varsity. Russell's technique was new and some older players had no qualms about expressing their resentment toward him. Without support from Jones, Russell was unable to turn the team around. Thus, players and audiences alike were unprepared for what happened in the 1954–55 season.

The previously unheralded San Francisco Dons were like nothing anyone had seen before. Opponents began their games as they always had: they would try to work the ball around on offense, keep moving, look for the open shot, and crash the boards. But when an opposing player worked free for what looked like an uncontested layup, Russell would come "out of nowhere," time and again, to block the shot. Opponents, fans, and even teammates were amazed. Using his tremendous leaping ability as no player before him, Russell's sense of timing and his intuition about the flow of action allowed him to dominate the proceedings. Usually reliable scorers were rendered ineffective. Furthermore, Russell's control of the offensive and defensive boards was unprecedented. On offense the Dons would work for a good shot, and if they missed, Russell would win

the rebound more often than not. The Dons lost their third game of the year to University of California Los Angeles and then won 21 straight games to finish atop both wire service polls and enter the NCAA tournament. After two easy wins, Russell led the Dons past Oregon State University and their massive seven-foot-three-inch (220.9cm) center, Wade Halbrook, 57–56. University of San Francisco defeated Colorado in the semifinal, then easily disposed of defending champion La Salle, 77–63, to win the tournament. Jones scored 24 points in the final, while Russell added 23. Bill Russell, the tourney's high scorer with 118 points in 5 games, was named Most Valuable Player.

The next year San Francisco did one better. They became the first NCAA champion to go undefeated. During the tournament no team came closer than 11 points to the Dons. Russell closed out his college career with a 26-point effort in the final. But the key, of course, was Russell's defense; the Dons held opponents to a national low of 52.2 points per game. Russell and the Dons finished the 1955–56 season with a record 55 straight victories.

Strangely, Russell was not the first pick in the NBA draft. Rochester had the first pick, but they already had a young star center in Maurice Stokes, who led the Royals in scoring and the league in rebounding in his rookie year. (Tragically, Stokes contracted encephalitis and suffered severe paralysis two years later.) Still, the Royals would probably have drafted Russell, even though they were strapped for cash and Russell figured to be the highest-paid rookie that year (in part, because the Globetrotters wanted him), but Bill played poorly at postseason all-star games and failed to impress many scouts. But one man who wanted Russell was Red Auerbach, the coach of the Boston Celtics. He was confident that Russell's shot blocking and rebounding would revolutionize the NBA; but more important, he saw Russell as the missing ingredient he needed to carry out his theory of fast-break basketball. St. Louis, however, had the rights to the second draft pick, so Auerbach unloaded two high-quality players, Ed Macauley and Cliff Hagan, for the right to move up in the draft. The move was a tremendous risk since at this time no one was sure that the Royals would not select Russell. But after more backroom deals, Auerbach and the Celtics acquired Russell.

Bill intended to play for the Celtics, but would not sign with them until after the Olympics, which took place in November because they were in the Southern Hemisphere, in Melbourne, Australia. Russell led the U.S. team to a gold medal, crushing all opponents, and then signed with the Boston Celtics for $17,000.

In Russell's first pro game, the Celtics trailed the Hawks by 16 in the fourth quarter, but came back to win on a last-second jump shot; Russell blocked 4 of Bob Pettit's shots down the stretch. A couple of weeks later he held three-time league scoring champion Neil Johnston to 0 points. However, Russell

struggled a little his rookie year; he joined a Celtics team that was 16–8, and it went only 28–20 with Russell at center. Bill grabbed a record 19.6 rebounds per game and swatted away plenty of shots (statistics were not kept on shot blocking until the seventies). He also contributed offensively, though he struggled from the free throw line. Still, the league was not yet in awe of Russell. That didn't begin until the playoffs.

The Celtics had been contenders for five years; Cousy lead the running game, they played aggressive defense, and had fine shooters. But they never advanced to the finals. In recent years, their nemesis had been the Syracuse Nats. With Russell, the Celtics crushed the Nats in three straight lopsided games. Appropriately, they faced the Hawks, with whom the Celtics had traded in order to get Russell, in the finals. Ben Kerner, owner of the Hawks, recalls, "We began to realize the greatness of Russell was in the playoffs. In big games, no one was better. In the fourth quarter, he'd get every defensive rebound. How are you supposed to win when you get only one shot and there's Russell sweeping the backboards."

The 1957 NBA final was an all-time classic series. The Celtics were the favorites, but the Hawks came into Boston Garden and won the first game in double overtime. The games were all close; tension hung in the air. Ben Kerner and Red Auerbach actually got in a brawl before Game Three. In many ways, St. Louis was the most racist city in the NBA at the time. St. Louis had a reputation for rowdy basketball fans anyway, and in the finals the fans hurled racial slurs at the Celtics (the Hawks were all white). The Celtics regained home-court advantage with a close victory in Game Four; the series was tied after six games. In Game Seven Boston led 103–101 with 6 seconds left, when Bob Pettit was fouled. With the Garden crowd going crazy, Pettit sank both free throws. In the first overtime, the Hawks hit a shot in

Russell uses his wide wingspan to pull a rebound away from New York Knick Willis Reed. At only six feet ten inches (208.2cm) and 220 pounds (99.8kg), Russell did not win rebounds simply by virtue of his height or because of a large body, à la Moses Malone. Rather, Russell cleared all those boards due to a special blend of long arms, quickness, exceptional leaping ability, and secret Russell ingredients: intelligence and will. Russell wanted the rebound more than anyone and could usually figure out how to get it. And he did get those rebounds: 21,620 times during thirteen regular seasons, averaging 22.45 per game, and a record 4,104 times during the playoffs, for a miraculous 24.87 average.

CHAMBERLAIN VS. RUSSELL: CLASH OF THE TITANS

In the history of modern team sports no individual rivalry has captured the public imagination quite like the struggle between NBA legends Bill Russell and Wilt Chamberlain. Throughout the ten years that the two giants dominated the league, and up to this day a debate rages over which man was the greater player. Those who choose Russell cite his role as the backbone of the NBA's greatest dynasty, how he integrated his astonishing rebounding and defensive skills into the Celtics total team concept and emerged with an unparalleled eleven NBA championships in thirteen years. Chamberlain's advocates expound on the Big Dipper's unrivaled individual scoring and rebounding accomplishments. The Chamberlain people make a strong argument to support the claim that Wilt was his era's most dominant single player and that Russell did not have the offensive skills to carry a team to an NBA championship—that Russell's success was due to his marvelous supporting cast in Boston, and Chamberlain's failures stemmed from the otherwise weak teams that he played for. The Russell contingent scoffs at this criticism, noting that great teamwork consistently defeats individual brilliance and that Russell successfully molded his skills to produce championships while Chamberlain was not willing to make such a selfless gesture.

Chamberlain and Russell met a total of 162 times. In those games Wilt averaged 28.7 points and 28.7 rebounds per game, while Russell's averages were 23.7 points and 14.5 rebounds. Chamberlain's point production was below his career average and Russell's was well above his norm, but Wilt's rebounding totals were up against Boston, while Russell's dropped against Wilt and Company. Russell's Celtics won 88 and lost 74 of the contests, including a 59–54 regular season advantage. In the playoffs, Boston squared off against Chamberlain-led teams eight out of ten years, including six consecutive seasons from 1964 through 1969. Boston won seven out of the eight series and won all four Game Sevens (1962, 1965, 1968, and 1969), which were decided by an accumulative total of 9 points. Chamberlain missed a total of 24 free throws in those four games. Had Chamberlain been more accurate from the charity stripe it is possible that Russell's stature as the consummate champion and Chamberlain's reputation as a loser would never have been established.

Off the court, Chamberlain and Russell were as different as they were in the heat of competition. Russell was very serious and guarded except around his closest personal friends, whereas Chamberlain had a playful, joyous demeanor. Russell was reclusive, while Chamberlain was extremely generous with his time. Russell used his celebrity to focus attention on serious social and political issues; Chamberlain simply reveled in the limelight. Russell was a committed leftist and an outspoken radical; Chamberlain was a Republican, who was more outspoken about his romantic escapades and millionaire lifestyle than about politics. Ironically, the media consistently exalted Russell and denigrated Chamberlain, even though sports reporters in the sixties tended to be very conservative politically. Despite their many personal and political differences, however, Russell and Chamberlain always had tremendous respect for each other on the basketball court.

the final seconds to knot the score at 113. In the second overtime, the Celtics had a 2-point lead with 2 seconds left. The Hawks had the ball under their own basket. Hawks player-coach Alex Hannum called for a play in which he would hurl the ball the length of the court, have it hit the backboard, and have Bob Pettit there to grab the rebound and put up the tying shot. Amazingly, Hannum hit the backboard just as planned and Pettit jumped, got the rebound, and shot the ball before landing, but it rolled around the rim and came out. The Celtics won the most dramatic seventh game in history and claimed their first title.

The next year the Hawks exacted their revenge, defeating the Celtics in six games in the finals, winning the last two after Russell injured his ankle and was unable to play in Game Five and could only limp through 20 minutes in Game Six. In 1958–59, the Celtics sprang back and won their second championship in three years, the first of an amazing string of eight consecutive titles. Overall, the Celtics won eleven NBA championships during Russell's thirteen years in Boston.

Celtic Bill Sharman, a sleek swingman, assessed Russell's impact on Boston: "[Before Russell] we were probably the best in the league in execution, passing, and scoring baskets. Although we didn't have the size or strength to rebound...Russell's

tremendous skills in rebounding, defense, and shot blocking were exactly what we needed....[He] could control the boards; it allowed us the opportunity to take off early and gamble on the running attack, which was responsible for a lot of easy baskets. Therefore, with Auerbach's coaching, Russell's rebounding, and Cousy's playmaking, the first truly complete fast-break system was developed and refined."

Indeed, Russell's presence revolutionized the NBA in a number of ways. His shot blocking changed the strategy of the half-court offense, which was previously built around trying to work for layups; Russell would swat away soft inside shots, so outside shooting became a bigger part of the game. Also, other teams tried to copy the Celtic fast break, increasing the pace of the game spectacularly. By the late fifties the average time of a possession was down to 11 seconds. The faster pace placed a premium on good athletes. And, finally, Russell lifted the game above the rim with his willingness to take full advantage of height, long arms, and great leaping ability. He was even the first player to dunk regularly.

Shortly after Russell entered the league, his innovations were commonplace; but still no one could dethrone Bill and the Celtics. There were two reasons: one, Bill and the Celtics were exceptional at executing their game; and two, Russell was a master psychologist who found a way to conquer any foe. On the defensive side of the floor, Russell was, of course, a terror; but more importantly he harnessed his defensive talent into an offensive weapon. His presence in the middle allowed the rest of the Celtics to challenge for more steals. His timing in blocking shots was so exceptional that he regularly directed the blocks to a teammate; when the Celtics saw Russell go up for a block they prepared to dash for the other basket. The process was even more scientific when Russell grabbed a defensive rebound. Celtic forward and future coach Tom Heinsohn explained: "Russell had an effective rebounding range of eighteen feet [5.4m]. If he was nine feet [2.7m] off to one side of the basket, he could race over to pull down a rebound nine feet off to the other side! I saw him do it many times. That's the kind of athletic ability he had. So now all I had to do on defense was check my man, just hold him off until he was in no position to challenge for the rebound, then release him and take off....In effect, Russell was making me play faster...." Russell also became a master at long, accurate outlet passes. Auerbach built the Celtics around Russell in the middle, developing the concept of the role player in the process; the sixth man, the shooting guard, and the small and power forwards were all defined by Auerbach during the dynasty.

Russell realized that great defense required being able to get into the mind of an opponent. To block a shot, it is necessary to conceive exactly what another person is going to do and prevent him from doing it. Thus, Russell consistently demoralized the other team. Late in his career, unable to dominate as he had when he was young, Russell played selectively, blocking shots when they would most devastate an opponent's confidence. Russell consistently used this selective approach against Wilt Chamberlain. Russell knew he couldn't stop Chamberlain, but he knew he could guide the Celtics to a victory over Chamberlain's team. Russell also understood that his unparalleled record of championships, beginning at the University of San Francisco, had an impact on other players and that his proud demeanor let everyone know who was king. Russell frequently played in pain, and his mere presence could inspire the Celtics to victory. In his final year he tore ligaments in a knee and missed five games, all of which the Celtics lost. So he wrapped his knee, went out, hobbled around the court, pulled down 23 rebounds, scored the basket that forced overtime, and guided the team to a victory.

Russell's sense of pride and regal countenance did not diminish away from the court. Although close friends found him to be a warm, even laid-back man, to the public he remained as intimidating and uncompromising a presence as he was on the court. Throughout his career, Russell used his celebrity to bring attention to the hypocrisies of American culture, especially concerning matters of race. When asked for an autograph by a child, he told the child to ask that of his teachers because they were truer heroes than athletes. In 1964, he wrote an article titled "I Owe the Public Nothing," in which he said: "I'm not going to smile if I don't feel like smiling, and bow my head modestly. Because it's not my nature...I don't think it's incumbent upon me to set a good example for anybody's kids but my own." Russell was asserting the right of any man, black or white, to be his own person and not the image that others wanted to see. He continually pointed out the subtle and explicit forms of racism that existed in the NBA, even writing an article on it for *Sports Illustrated*. Through Russell's auspices the NBA hired its first black referee. And when Red Auerbach stepped down as head coach after the 1966 title, Russell took over as the Celtics' player-coach, becoming the first black man to coach a major American sports franchise. His success never interfered with his awareness of racism. Years before a congressional report declared the same thing, Russell decried the fact that even after the civil rights movement, the United States remained two countries, a white one and a black one, separate and unequal.

Russell's controversial words never interfered with the quality of his play; some have even suggested that the tension between him and white Boston fans gave him added motivation. Perhaps, but Russell never lacked motivation. Bill's style of play was built around intuition and intensity. The defensive moves that he developed while still an adolescent in the Bay Area revolutionized the sport, and while they became commonplace by the midpoint of his career, he remained the unrivaled master of basketball defense. It is unlikely that any player will ever have as large an impact on the evolution of the game—or win as many championships—as Bill Russell did.

With all the majesty, grace, and power of great dancers, the two giants hang suspended over the parquet floor in the heavy air of Boston Garden during a mid-sixties showdown between the 76ers and Celtics. Russell elevates and extends fully to try to flick a Chamberlain finger-roll away from the basket. Chamberlain had three inches (7.6cm) on (and was two and a half years younger than) Russell, yet Bill still manages to reach Wilt's shot.

WILT Chamberlain

Wilt Chamberlain, sophomore sensation at the University of Kansas, just manages to block a shot by California's Earl Robinson. Only twenty years old at the time, Chamberlain was already an awesome physical specimen, an unprecedented mix of size, coordination, and tremendous athleticism. Wilt dominated every game he played in, even though his basketball skills were unrefined. Opposing teams concocted all sorts of strategies to try to contain the young giant. Few of these schemes worked, as Wilt averaged 25.4 points in his first varsity season and led the Jayhawks to a 24–3 record, the Big Eight title, and a legendary showdown in the NCAA finals.

Twenty years after his retirement, the myth of Wilt Chamberlain is still deeply imbedded in the American cultural unconscious. Chamberlain was, so goes the myth, a regal giant: agile, powerful almost beyond imagination, indomitable—a veritable force of nature—and, yet, doomed continually to fall like Goliath to some heroic David.

Needless to say, the popular myth errs. Wilt Chamberlain was the single most dominant player in NBA history. To play a Chamberlain team was to go against Wilt. Unlike Russell in Boston, Chamberlain rarely had a complementary supporting cast. So Chamberlain scored more points and grabbed more rebounds than seemed humanly possible and led his teams to winning records, but come playoff time opponents were able to exploit his team's deficiencies. It wasn't until Wilt joined a strong Philadelphia 76er team midway through his career that he conquered the Celtics and captured an NBA crown. Long

before that, Chamberlain's individual achievements, his trials and tribulations, and his awe-inspiring strength and size captured the public's imagination as no basketball player had before him.

• • •

Wilton Norman Chamberlain was born in Philadelphia on August 21, 1936. Wilt was the sixth of nine Chamberlain children, and the second of three sons. Mr. Chamberlain held an array of modest jobs, and was able to support his large family well; Wilt grew up in a fairly nice neighborhood in West Philadelphia. Wilt was always eight or ten inches (20.3 or 25.4cm) taller than his peers, and he used it to his advantage as a child, allowing people to think he was older than he was so they would hire him for odd jobs. Wilt was an enterprising child, coming up with numerous schemes to make money. No matter the job, whether it was selling junk, hawking watermelon, or painting houses, Wilt followed his mother's advice: "Whatever you do, large or small, do it well, or don't do it at all." Wilt lived by this creed his entire life.

Track, not basketball, was Wilt's first athletic love. In fourth grade, he qualified to run the anchor for his school relay team; all the other guys on the team were in sixth grade. Track satisfied Wilt's desire to prove himself the best. When he was younger, Wilt was the best Monopoly player in his neighborhood. Then he had to show that he was the fastest runner in his school. He did not play basketball until junior high, but he would have to be the best at that, too.

Wilt did not think much of basketball, but many people told him that because he was so tall, he should give the game a try. Wilt began playing with his buddies in city playgrounds, and within a year the game was the most important thing in his life. When Wilt first played in organized leagues, he drew the attention of Philadelphia's Catholic high schools, which had strong basketball traditions. But Wilt chose to remain in public school, and attended Overbrook High with his childhood friends.

Wilt made the varsity at Overbrook in his sophomore year; he was already six feet eleven inches (210.8cm). He also already knew his way around a basketball court. Wilt averaged 30 points a game that year and Overbrook swept to the public school title, losing only one game. They faced West Catholic in the citywide championship game. West Catholic had spent the previous week preparing for Wilt by practicing against a player standing on a chair. Four defenders would collapse down on Chamberlain in the game, leaving the other Overbrook High players open, but no one could hit from the outside. West Catholic's strategy worked and Overbrook lost, 54–52. Chamberlain would encounter such defenses throughout his playing days.

During the next two years Wilt was virtually unstoppable; he even scored 90 points in a game during his senior year (and games were only 40 minutes long). Chamberlain averaged roughly 37 points per game each year and led Overbrook to back-to-back

public high school and city championships. In the process, he became a national phenomenon, attracting college recruiters, and reporters, from all over the country. More than two hundred schools recruited Wilt, an unprecedented number at that time. Red Auerbach, the coach of the Boston Celtics, tried to persuade Wilt to attend Harvard University so that the Celtics could claim him in the territorial draft. But Philadelphia Warriors owner Eddie Gottlieb actually selected Chamberlain as his territorial draft pick in 1955, before he left Philadelphia to attend college. He also encouraged Wilt to attend the University of Kansas so that no other club would have a territorial claim on Chamberlain.

Wilt decided to attend Kansas, not because of Gottlieb but because Kansas was a traditional powerhouse in both track and basketball. Dr. Forrest C. Allen, known as Phog Allen, who had been the basketball coach since 1920, was a living legend. In Wilt's first game at Kansas, the freshman team squared off against the varsity, a match the varsity had won every year since 1923. Wilt had the flu that day, but with the largest crowd ever to watch a Kansas game packing the auditorium, the Stilt did not disappoint. He scored 42 points, grabbed 29 rebounds, and lifted the freshmen to an 81–71 victory. In the spring, Chamberlain lettered in track, excelling in the high jump and shot put.

Unfortunately for Wilt and Kansas, Phog Allen was forced to retire (because of his age) before Wilt's

Russell and Chamberlain take to the stratosphere in unison as Wilt tries a short-range jumper over the outstretched arm of the Celtic center early in the 1961–62 season. Wilt developed this particular one-handed, fadeaway shot as an antidote for Russell's shot blocking. As great as Chamberlain was in his first two NBA seasons, he was still a raw talent. By his third NBA campaign, however, Chamberlain had added new weapons—which reflected a newfound knowledge of the game's nuances—to his offensive arsenal: shots like fadeaway jumpers and high-altitude finger-rolls, which he had learned were virtually impossible to stop.

Soaring above the rim and the mere mortals around him, Wilt grabs an offensive rebound and prepares to slam it home. The Big Dipper tallied 48 points, but the Lakers won the October 1961 contest, 118–111. While Chamberlain was an unstoppable offensive dynamo throughout the 1961–62 season, the Philadelphia Warriors were far from unbeatable. Wilt averaged 50.4 points per game during the season (the highest full-season average by someone besides Chamberlain is Michael Jordan's 37.1 in the 1986–87 season) and scored 60 or more points fifteen times (a feat accomplished only nineteen times by players other than Wilt throughout the NBA's entire history). The Warriors finished a distant second to the Celtics in the Eastern Conference.

sophomore season. His replacement, Dick Harp, was concerned with bringing home Jayhawk victories, whereas Allen was an educator who would have schooled Wilt in the nuances of the game. Unlike Bill Russell, who was self-motivated, or Kareem Abdul-Jabbar, who had John Wooden as his college coach, Wilt never studied basketball seriously before turning pro. Compared with Russell and Jabbar, Chamberlain entered the NBA as a raw talent.

In his sophomore season, Wilt's legend continued to grow. Chamberlain averaged 25.4 points and Kansas won the Big Eight title easily with a 21–2 record. The Jayhawks easily disposed of their next three opponents to reach the 1957 national championship game. Their opponent in the finals, North Carolina, had beaten Michigan State in the semifinals by 1 point, in triple overtime. North Carolina, which was 31–0 on the season, was coached by displaced New Yorker Frank McGuire and its entire starting lineup was from New York. The 1957 championship game was one of the most widely followed college games up to that point. Throughout the game, North Carolina collapsed its defense onto Chamberlain, leaving his teammates open, but they failed to hit their shots. At halftime North Carolina was shooting 64.5 percent from the field, while Kansas was hitting 27.3 percent. Nevertheless, Kansas moved ahead in the second half, behind Chamberlain's strong effort of 23 points and 14 rebounds, and led by 3 points with less than 2 minutes to play. But missed free throws and sloppy passing by Wilt's teammates allowed North Carolina to tie the game. After two overtime periods the game remained tied. In the third overtime, North Carolina hit the big clutch shot and Kansas failed to get Wilt the ball in the final seconds. University of North Carolina won the game 53–52, and with 2 consecutive triple overtime victories captured the national championship. After the 1957 NCAA final, the media began its long tradition of labeling Chamberlain a loser and blaming only him and not his teammates for their losses.

At seven feet one inch (215.9cm), Wilt was able to dominate opponents at Kansas because of his size and strength, but he also displayed an outside game that was rarely part of his repertoire in the pros. Footage of Chamberlain at Kansas shows him taking and making twenty-foot (6m) jumpers. Unfortunately Chamberlain got injured at the start of the Big Eight schedule his junior year, and Kansas, which was ranked number one before his injury, lost both their games while he was out. With Wilt not fully recovered, Kansas lost to archrival Kansas State, and their hopes for the Big Eight title, which they needed for a national title, vanished. Still, Wilt averaged 30 points and 16 rebounds per game. Chamberlain also excelled in track his junior year, winning the Big Eight indoor high jump contest.

However, Wilt decided that his days at Kansas were numbered. He had come to Kansas to concentrate on basketball, and the games he played in were often circuses. Frequently, opposing teams would

select a benchwarmer as their designated fouler; whenever Wilt got the ball, this player would foul him. Or the team would hold on to the ball for minutes at a time to shorten the game and lessen the effect of Wilt's dominance. After consulting with some friends, Wilt decided there must be a better place to prepare for the NBA, which he could not enter until his college class graduated.

Chamberlain chose the storied Harlem Globetrotters, and announced that he was leaving Kansas to tour with the Trotters. The Trotters allowed Wilt to continue to play hoops and fulfill his dream of traveling throughout the world. Considering the pressures Chamberlain encountered in Kansas and the scrutiny he would suffer in the NBA, it is understandable that his year with the Trotters was one of the most enjoyable in his life. And he got to play fun basketball: he even started at guard for the Globetrotters. And though the quality of the Trotters' play was no longer comparable to the NBA, they had some exceptional players. In the year Wilt played with them, they probably could have competed with anyone. By the summer of 1959, however, Chamberlain was ready to return to competitive ball. He joined the Philadelphia Warriors of the NBA.

The Warriors were a decent team in the mid-fifties, winning the league title in 1956 with a balanced attack that featured high-scoring Paul Arizin and center Neil Johnston. But the club declined rapidly and failed to make the playoffs in 1959. None of that seemed to matter when Wilt Chamberlain joined the Warriors in the fall of 1959, however: Eddie Gottlieb's team instantly became the biggest attraction in the history of the league and the fans' pick to win the championship. Unfortunately, Chamberlain's supporting cast was thin.

The Big Dipper, as Wilt was called, didn't disappoint in his rookie year. He played his first regular season NBA game against the New York Knicks in Madison Square Garden and led the Warriors to victory with 43 points and 28 rebounds. When he finally played in Philadelphia a week later against Detroit, it was a triumphant return home, with Wilt scoring 36 points and grabbing 34 rebounds as Philly triumphed 120–112. After winning their first three games, the Warriors traveled to Boston for a showdown the media had been hyping since 1955: "the unstoppable offensive force versus the immovable defensive object." Boston won and Russell held Wilt to "only" 30 points, scored 22 himself, and outrebounded the giant 35 to 28. The next time they met, Wilt destroyed Russell—45 to 15 in points, 35 to 13 in boards—and the Warriors won handily. There would be more to come.

Wilt led the Warriors to a 49–26 record his rookie year, the second-best mark in the league behind the Celtics. Wilt also established new records for points scored, rebounds grabbed, and minutes played. He was named Rookie of the Year and league Most Valuable Player, the first time anyone won both awards the same year. After dismissing Syracuse in

Wilt Chamberlain and 76er teammate Hal Greer celebrate over bottles of champagne after clinching the 1967 Eastern Division title with a 115–113 overtime victory over the Celtics. The 1966–67 Philadelphia 76ers were an awesome team, compiling the best regular season record up to that date: 68–13. And these 76ers accomplished something even more monumental when they ended the Celtics' string of eight consecutive NBA titles with a five-game triumph over Boston in the Eastern Division Finals; it was the only time a Chamberlain-led team defeated Russell's Celtics in the postseason. Philadelphia then defeated the San Francisco Warriors in six games to take the NBA title; Wilt was finally a certified champion.

the playoffs, the Warriors faced Russell and the Celtics. Boston won Game One, but Philly won Game Two in Boston. Chamberlain, however, bruised his hand badly in a brawl in that game, rendering him ineffective for the next two games, which Boston won. Healed by Game Five, he scored 50 points in a Philly victory, but Boston won Game Six by 2 points, ending Wilt's first season in frustration. Although the Celtics were the greatest team ever, journalists again squawked about Wilt the loser.

Chamberlain's second year furthered his frustration. Of course, he did break all nine of the records he set the year before and, in the process, became the first player in league history to make more than half of his shots from the floor. He set a still-standing record by grabbing 55 rebounds on November 24, 1960, versus none other than Bill Russell and the Boston Celtics; and his total rebounds record for the season also still stands as the best ever. But his troubles at the free throw line began to mount and his Warrior teammates continued to struggle. The team finished in second behind the Celtics in the East, but were upset by Syracuse in three straight games in the first round of the playoffs.

Things improved the next season, though the end result was familiar. In terms of individual scoring accomplishments, Chamberlain's third season is easily the greatest in the history of the NBA. Over the entire season Wilt averaged 50.4 points per game. Chamberlain possessed an awesome combination of power and finesse in the low post during his prime. He also had a soft touch and developed a nice short-range fallaway jumper just to combat Bill Russell's skill at blocking shots. But Chamberlain's jumper, though it was an effective and classic shot, left him far away from the basket; he preferred to spin past his defender and toss up a close-range shot so that he could follow up and slam the ball home if the first try missed. He broke Elgin Baylor's single-game scoring record by pouring in 78 points in a triple overtime

game on December 8, 1961, at home against Los Angeles. Then he added 73 points for a new regulation record on January 13 at home against Chicago. But he shattered all these marks when he scored 36 field goals and, miraculously, made 28 of 32 foul shots to score 100 points against the Knicks in a game at Hershey, Pennsylvania, on March 2. Wilt scored more than 60 points fifteen times that year.

The Warriors also fared better in the 1961–62 season under the leadership of Frank McGuire, the legendary coach who had led North Carolina in 1957. After another second-place finish, Philly got by Syracuse, three games to two, and then faced Boston. The first six games were all won by the home team, and Game Seven in the Boston Garden was close all the way. Philly led 56–52 at the half and 81–80 after three quarters, but Boston had been there so many times before. The Celtics led by 3 with only 10 seconds left when Wilt dunked over Russell and was fouled. He made the foul shot to tie the game, but Sam Jones buried a jumper—and the Philadelphia Warriors—with 2 seconds left.

Eddie Gottlieb sold the Warriors to a group of San Francisco businessmen in the off-season and the team moved west. Wilt contemplated quitting, but after his annual stint with the Globetrotters in the summer, he grudgingly reported back from Europe and the Globetrotters after the off-season. The Warriors had nine new players and Frank McGuire was gone, all of which made for a tumultuous and disappointing season. Wilt led the league in scoring again, but the team failed to make the playoffs. Things improved dramatically the next year as the Warriors won the Western Division in the regular season and again in the playoffs. Chamberlain had finally reached the NBA Finals and again faced the Celtics. This time, however, it wasn't close, as the Warriors managed only one victory.

The next season went from disaster to hope to heartbreak. Wilt started the season on the disabled list, and the Warriors tried to make amends with promising young center Nate Thurmond. It didn't work, but the team fared just as badly with Wilt in the lineup: the Warriors were 10–34 at the All-Star break. Then the Warriors shocked the sports world by sending Wilt back to Philadelphia for three journeymen and a load of cash. Formerly known as the Syracuse Nats, the Philadelphia 76ers had a strong cast of young and old players, including Hal Greer, Chet Walker, and Lucious Jackson. Instantly the team showed promise with Chamberlain in the lineup. In the playoffs, the 76ers dismissed Cincinnati and then challenged the Celtics to within an inch of their lives, only to lose by 1 point in Game Seven when John Havlicek stole an inbounds pass from Greer with 5 seconds left.

Finally, however, Chamberlain was on a promising team. The next year the 76ers added Billy Cunningham and Wally Jones to their nucleus and actually finished ahead of the Celtics in the regular season. Unfortunately the Sixers went flat in the playoffs and were crushed by the Celtics in five games. The next year the team jelled all season. Coaching great Alex Hannum took the reins for the 1966–67 season and guided the Sixers to the best regular season record in league history up to that time, 68–13. Perhaps the key of the team's transformation was Chamberlain's decision to concentrate more on passing and defense than scoring; he averaged 7.8 assists per game, but only 24.1 points. For the first time in his career he did not lead the NBA in scoring. Starting in 1966, he would lead the NBA in rebounding every year for the remainder of his career (Russell grabbed more boards than Wilt in 1963–64 and 1964–65). In 1967–68, Wilt became the only center in league history to lead the league in assists with an 8.6 average. Wilt later reflected, "The way I passed the ball in those years may have been the thing of which I am most proud, because people said Wilt Chamberlain was selfish, Wilt Chamberlain was one-dimensional, when the truth was that Wilt Chamberlain was finally with a team where he was allowed to show that he could pass the ball, and I give Alex Hannum credit for that." Chamberlain's overall effectiveness as a player was inhibited by the lack of high-quality coaching he received throughout his career. If Frank McGuire had been his college coach, or was allowed to coach him more than one year in the pros, Wilt might have been an even better team player. Instead, Wilt had weak coaching throughout high school, college, and his early years with the Warriors and again with the 76ers until Hannum, who had coached Wilt with the San Francisco Warriors, showed up.

The Sixers did not let up in the 1967 playoffs, defeating Cincinnati handily and whipping the Celtics in five games, ending Boston's string of eight consecutive titles. The series was never close as the Sixers won the first three games by an average of 10 points, lost Game Four in a squeaker, and then demolished Russell and Company by 24 points. Ironically, the 76ers faced the revamped Warriors in the finals. Behind Thurmond and the new reigning scoring champion, Rick Barry, San Francisco gave the Sixers more of a battle than expected, but Philadelphia won in six tough games. Wilt had finally won an NBA championship. Of course, the vultures in the press referred to it as a team victory, though all the previous losses to Boston were deemed Wilt's fault.

In the 1967–68 season the Sixers raced to the league's best mark again. In a game on February 2 against Detroit, Wilt set a new record for assists by a center with 21 and had more than 20 points and 20 rebounds—the only triple-double-double ever recorded. Wilt's career-long struggle with shooting free throws reached its nadir this year, as he sank only 38 percent from the charity stripe. In the playoffs, the Sixers ousted the newly competitive New York Knicks in six games and then jumped ahead three games to one against Boston. Then the wheels came off. Boston crushed the Sixers in Game Five, then won in the Boston Garden. Game Seven was close,

and ironically, the press would castigate Wilt for not scoring in the second half, but the Boston defense was collapsing on him and he was finding his teammates for easy eight-to-ten-foot (2.4 to 3m) jump shots, which they somehow kept missing. The Celtics won by 4, and the Sixers team was dismantled by the next season because of management infighting.

Wilt ended up in sunny Southern California with the Lakers. Wilt had enjoyed his short tenure in cosmopolitan San Francisco, and the bright lights of Hollywood also suited the Big Dipper more than his more mundane hometown of Philadelphia.

Wilt joined superstars Jerry West and Elgin Baylor, and the Lakers were heavily favored to win the NBA title. Once again they were frustrated by Bill Russell and the Celtics. This time the aging Celtics won Game Seven in Los Angeles after the home team had previously won every game in the finals. It was Russell's last game, and fittingly, he left the league having conquered his greatest foe, the man against whom he was always judged and against whom he always seemed to buck the odds and win. Compounding Chamberlain's frustration was that he sat out the final 5 minutes of Game Seven in Los Angelas because he injured a knee on a rebound. Chamberlain never fouled out of a game in his entire career, an amazing statistic of which he was extremely proud, even though he consistently led the league in minutes played, so he wasn't familiar with missing the stretch run of a game. After a few minutes he told Coach Butch van Breda Kolff that he was ready to go back in, but the coach ignored him. The Celtics had been ahead by 17 in the fourth quarter, but the Lakers had it down to 9 when Chamberlain was injured. But they continued to narrow the gap and had it down to 1 point when Don Nelson hit a desperation shot with

Chamberlain goes up against Knick Jerry Lucas in the 1972 NBA final. The story of the 1972 Lakers is eerily similar to the saga of the 1967 76ers. Both were great teams anchored by Chamberlain in the middle. Both the Lakers and Sixers had been championship contenders in recent years, but both shared a legacy of playoff frustration. Then for one magical season everything clicked. Both teams set new standards for regular-season success, compiling the highest winning percentages in NBA history (the Lakers' 69–13 record remains the best ever). And, in contrast to other years, neither team faltered in the playoffs. In fact, both the 1967 Sixers and the 1972 Lakers won playoff showdowns with the very teams that had defeated them in previous postseasons; both teams won the NBA title.

about a minute left that banged against the back of the rim, went straight up about two feet (0.6m), and fell into the basket. After that lucky bounce, the Celtics held on to win as Wilt fumed on the bench. Later, Russell would criticize Chamberlain, something he had never really done before, for leaving the game in the first place, saying he would have to be paralyzed to leave a seventh game.

The next year Russell was gone, but Chamberlain, West, and Company still got to play the role of the defeated overdog, this time for basketball-crazed New York City. In the three years after he finally broke through and won an NBA championship, Chamberlain had returned to his familiar role as the loser. In 1970–71, Kareem Abdul-Jabbar and the Milwaukee Bucks kept the Lakers out of the finals. But in 1971–72 the Lakers clicked, winning a record 33 straight games at one time and bettering the Sixers' record season by one game, going 69–13. Much like the Sixers of 1967, the Lakers of 1972 also steamrolled all comers in the playoffs, including the Knicks in the finals, and Wilt had his second NBA title. However, just as Russell fittingly got to leave the NBA with a final title, Chamberlain typically led his team back to the finals in 1973, his final season, where they lost again to the Knicks.

Chamberlain played fourteen seasons in the NBA and he won two NBA titles, but more significantly his teams were eliminated in the playoffs ten times by the eventual champion of the league. If the playoff loss wasn't in the final, it was still the toughest battle the future champion would face. During his career Chamberlain was not only the league's biggest star but also the measuring stick for greatness. From the early sixties to the early seventies the best teams knew they would have to square off against Wilt. Unfairly, the public always cast Chamberlain in the role of the heavy favorite, and he came out looking like a loser. In retrospect, Wilt didn't lose to Russell; the Celtics were clearly the best team in the league in the sixties. Take Wilt away from the teams he played on and they would have gone nowhere—even the Sixers of 1967 were only good at best. With this in mind it's clear that Wilt Chamberlain was the most dominant single player in the history of the NBA.

Chamberlain fights for a rebound against the Hawks. During Wilt's five-year stint with the Lakers at the end of his career, the man who had been the most prolific scorer in basketball history was content to let his teammates put the points on the board. Wilt averaged around 20 points per game his first three years with Los Angeles, but only 14 his final two seasons. The decline in scoring was not due to a decreasing role; Chamberlain played the second-highest number of minutes in the NBA in his final season. He led the league in rebounding for the eleventh time in his fourteen-year career. He also set an all-time record for field goal percentage, .727. Clearly Chamberlain decided that his role on the team was to control the boards and only take extremely high-percentage shots. Something was working: the Lakers won 80 percent of their games in Wilt's final two seasons and reached the finals each year. The Lakers dropped 13 more games in their first year without Chamberlain and exited the playoffs in the first round.

WILT SCORES 100!

Wilt strikes a pose only seconds after scoring his 100th point of the night. Once Wilt hit the century mark, the crowd poured onto the court even though 46 seconds remained in the game. Wilt made his way to the Warrior bench, took a seat amid the mayhem, and was handed a sheet of paper with a large "100" written on it in pencil. Wilt held up the number, a photo was taken, and the image entered posterity.

The record for the highest number of points scored in a game creeps one-by-one to 73, then jumps to 78; there is just one entry higher than that. The 78 has three asterisks beside it to connote the three overtime periods that were necessary to yield that score; still, it set a record of sorts at the time, December 8, 1961. Of the 73s, two were scored by Wilt Chamberlain and one was scored by the Denver Nuggets' David Thompson, who holds the single-game scoring record for non-Chamberlains; none of the 73s is blemished with any asterisks. Wilt first hit 73 on January 13, 1962, breaking Elgin Baylor's record total, 71, for a regulation-length game but failing to reach his own overtime total of 78.

So 73 and 78 were the single-game scoring records going into the matchup between the lowly New York Knicks and the Wilt Chamberlain–led Philadelphia Warriors on March 2, 1962. Nobody in the auditorium could have possibly imagined that they would witness the most celebrated regular-season game in NBA history. The setting was Hersey, Pennsylvania, where Warrior owner Eddie

Gottlieb had arranged a game because people everywhere were interested in Chamberlain, the Warriors' seven-foot-one-inch (215.9cm) scoring machine. Wilt was close to reaching an average of 50 points a game for the entire season. Chamberlain had perfected a fadeaway jumper to use against Bill Russell, the only player in the league who could slow him down. Non-Russells were virtually powerless against a tall, agile leaper such as Wilt; if he missed a shot he could usually win the rebound. In terms of the standings the game was virtually meaningless: it was late in the regular season and the Warriors were going to finish in second behind the Celtics and ahead of Syracuse, while their opponents, the Knicks, were hopelessly mired in last place.

Right from the start of the contest, it was evident that the Knicks lacked the means to slow down Wilt and the Warrior barrage. Philadelphia raced to a 42–26 lead after one period, behind 23 points from Chamberlain. Wilt made half of his 14 field goal attempts, which was barely below his average, but he managed to make all 9 of his free throw attempts, which was extraordinary since Chamberlain averaged just above 60 percent from the charity stripe. However, hopes for an exceptional night from Wilt were somewhat dampened in the second quarter when he managed only 18 points and broke his streak of consecutive free throws in the process. The Warriors led at the break, 79–68.

Chamberlain came out more aggressively after intermission, and soon it was apparent that he was on pace for a record. Once again, Chamberlain couldn't miss from the line, burying all 8 of his attempts in the third quarter. He also added 10 field goals. With 12 minutes left in the game Chamberlain already had 69 points. By this time all the Warriors were looking to do was help Wilt score. Knicks center Darrall Imhoff observed, "We'd shoot and Wilt would take off down the court like a lonesome end. It was like covering a receiver. It was the hardest I ever saw Wilt work." Soon the Knicks were getting embarrassed, and they tried to slow down the pace of the game; they even tried fouling Chamberlain's teammates to prevent Wilt from building on the new record he set every time he scored. Chamberlain reached 90 with 2:45 left. Warriors Coach Frank McGuire inserted substitutes to intentionally foul the Knicks to stop the clock and give Wilt more time to reach the century mark. Wilt buried his final 2 free throws of the game for points 91 and 92. Traditionally terrible from the line, Wilt knocked down 28 of his 32 attempts for a remarkable near–90 percent free throw average; it was clearly Wilt's night. Two fadeaway jumpers lifted Chamberlain's total score to 96; the crowd was delirious. Chamberlain dunked over all five Knicks to move within a bucket of what everyone (except the Knicks) wanted to see. With 46 seconds still remaining, Chamberlain slammed down a power dunk to bring his total to 100, and the crowd stormed the court. The final 46 seconds of this legendary contest were never completed—the referees declared the game over. The Warriors triumphed over the Knicks 169–147.

OSCAR Robertson

BELOW, RIGHT: Collegiate super-star Oscar Robertson takes a breather. By the time Robertson made his debut with the University of Cincinnati Bearcat varsity squad in his sophomore year, he was probably one of the best basketball players in the world. He led the nation in scoring as a rookie with a 35.1 average, shot an astounding 57 percent from the floor, controlled over 15 rebounds per contest, and was named Player of the Year. Everyone who saw the Big O knew he was the real deal; he not only came in an agile and powerful six-foot-five-inch (195.5cm), 220-pound (99.8kg) package, he also came complete with impeccable basketball skills, uncanny court sense, and the demeanor of a leader. OPPOSITE: The Cincinnati Royals' Oscar Robertson moves against Bill Russell, who tries in vain to knock the ball away; in the background K.C. Jones tries to anticipate Oscar's next move. Taking full advantage of his broad upper body, the Big O was the undisputed master at shielding the ball from defenders while dribbling. Robertson's signature move was dribbling backwards against an opponent, then deliberately moving closer to the basket while hiding the ball from the defender's eyes to keep him in doubt, thus turning medium-range jumpers into higher-percentage shots.

Sometimes basketball analysts speak of two categories when comparing great players: big men and all-around players. Big men, after all, play almost exclusively near the basket and therefore never have to develop dribbling skills or much of an outside shot. Whereas great small men not only have a complete perimeter game, they also know how to rebound, penetrate, and even post up; therefore, they are called all-around players. Before Larry Bird, Magic Johnson, and Michael Jordan came around in the eighties, there was a virtual consensus on who was the greatest all-around player. "No one," Ira Berkow wrote, "could perform on a basketball court with as much overall skill as Oscar Robertson." Bob Cousy, referring to Robertson, said, "He is the greatest all-around player to come down the pike in my lifetime." And Bob Pettit said, "Oscar gets my vote for the best all-around player ever."

How does Oscar stack up against the likes of Larry, Magic, and Michael? Consider this: a triple-double is when a player has double-digit totals in points, rebounding, and assists in one game. Basketball statisticians began to track the statistic in

the eighties because of Magic Johnson's ability to score, rebound, and pass. Those not familiar with NBA history probably assumed no player in history combined those skills like Magic Johnson. Oscar Robertson, however, was the only player in history to average a triple-double per game for an entire season (1962–63). In fact, Robertson averaged a triple-double per game over the course of his first five seasons in the NBA. Like Magic, Robertson was primarily a point guard, but he could play any position on the floor. More of a scorer than Magic, a better passer than Jordan, and more versatile than Bird, no one ever controlled the flow of a game like Oscar Robertson. The Big O still belongs in any meaningful discussion about the greatest all-around player in NBA history.

• • •

Oscar Robertson was born in Charlotte, Tennessee, on November 24, 1938. The Robertson family soon moved to Indianapolis, where Oscar grew up. There is no place on earth where basketball is as popular as the state of Indiana; thus, it should be no surprise that young Oscar grew up playing hoops. He didn't have to look far for a role model because his brother, Bailey "Flap" Robertson, was a high school basketball star.

But brother Bailey was more than just a cage star—he was a hero to the Indianapolis' African-American community. Indianapolis' public schools were segregated, and Bailey's school, Crispus Attucks (named for the black Revolutionary War hero), was the only black public high school in town. Indiana had a long-standing reputation as one of the most racist states outside the Deep South. When blacks migrated north to Indiana's industrial cities—for instance, Gary, Hammond, and Indianapolis—during the twenties, racist groups, including the Ku Klux Klan, grew in size and influence across the state. Until 1942, all-black schools were prohibited from participating in the state high school basketball tournament, which was followed religiously throughout Indiana. In 1946, a black star from Anderson led an integrated team to the title, but no all-black team had ever captured the vaunted title. In 1951, Flap Robertson led Attucks to the state semifinals. After every Attucks victory there were celebrations in Indianapolis' black neighborhoods (much like when Joe Louis won a bout), prompting conservative members of the black community to worry that an Attucks title would spark a racist backlash.

The same year that Flap starred at Attucks, his little brother Oscar led his eighth-grade team to the elementary school championship. At only thirteen years old, Oscar had already developed his signature style: he wanted the ball in his hands at all times. Little O was absolutely dedicated to the game: "I kept my basketball with me all the time. I was always being teased about it—about dribbling balls all over the neighborhood. I carried my basketball like a musician carries his trumpet."

Already the best player among his peers, Oscar Robertson fortuitously grew to a solid six feet three inches (190.5cm) in the summer before his sophomore year of high school. Not surprisingly, Robertson quickly established himself as the leader of the Attucks team, though his sophomore year ended abruptly when Attucks lost to the eventual state champions from tiny Milan High (the team that was the subject of the film *Hoosiers*).

In 1955, however, it was finally Attucks' year. Oscar led them to a 21–1 record. Ironically, the final was played against another all-black high school, from Gary, led by future pro star (and a hero of the New York Knicks' first NBA title) Dick Barnett. Attucks won 97–64 and Oscar led the way with 30 points. It was the first time a school from Indianapolis captured the state crown, yet the team was not allowed to have its victory celebration downtown. In 1956, Oscar led Attucks to another championship and the team was finally received at City Hall. Oscar was a hero to blacks across the state. Crispus Attucks' back-to-back titles no doubt played a role in the desegregation of Indiana schools, since whites feared the domination of their sacred sport by all-black schools.

By the time Oscar put on his varsity uniform at the University of Cincinnati during his sophomore year, he had come to full maturity as a basketball superstar. On January 9, 1958, Robertson had a coming out of sorts as he played in front of the New York media for the first time in a game against Seton Hall at Madison Square Garden. He made quite an impression, setting a new scoring record for the arena with 56 points. The terms *grace*, *precision*, *control*, *quickness*, *agility*, *effectiveness*, and *elegance* were used the next day to describe Oscar. Listed as a forward, Robertson was nevertheless the Bearcats' chief ball handler, leading the team in assists as well as rebounding. He led the nation in scoring each of his three years at Cincinnati and he won three consecutive Collegiate Player of the Year Awards. The national title, however, proved elusive as Oscar led the Bearcats to the NCAA Final Four both his junior and senior years, but failed to win the title on either occasion. Ironically, Cincinnati did capture consecutive national titles in the two years following Robertson's graduation with teams filled with players who flocked to play at the Big O's school. In the summer of 1960, Oscar cocaptained a potent U.S.A. squad that swept to the gold medal at the Rome Olympics.

When Oscar entered the NBA, his skills were already legendary. Robertson possessed great leaping ability, tremendous speed, and a lethal one-handed jump shot. The Big O could do it all offensively: drive, make pinpoint passes off the double-team, shoot from the perimeter, and use his leaping ability to garner offensive rebounds. But Oscar's signature move was to dribble the ball down one side of the court to an area below the free throw line and then dribble backward toward the basket while protecting the ball from the defender with his body; then, through a series of fakes, he would move closer and closer to the basket until he either was double-teamed or decided to shoot. He would free himself up by spinning around his defender, then try a short fade-

RIGHT: University of Cincinnati Bearcat superstar Oscar Robertson stages his hook shot for a photographer. The Big O was so dominant in his college days that Newsweek polled opposing coaches and players about how best to contain him. The consensus was that such a thing was impossible, although NYU Coach Lou Rossini did offer one novel suggestion: "Put your four best men on Oscar. Then tell your fifth man to cover his teammates. That might stop him." Robertson led the nation in scoring each of his three seasons with the Bearcats, averaging 33.8 points per game during his college career. OPPOSITE, TOP: Robertson beats Jerry West and the Lakers to score 2 points. West and Robertson were two of the marquee names on the celebrated 1960 U.S. Olympic basketball team that won the gold medal in Rome. Jerry West is canonized primarily as a great scorer whereas Oscar Robertson is heralded as an all-around player; as a result, Robertson's scoring skills are often forgotten. However, Robertson and West entered the league in the same year and played for fourteen seasons, but it was the Big O who retired as the NBA's second all-time leading scorer, behind Wilt Chamberlain. West was third on the all-time list. West (who was injured more than Robertson) did score slightly more per game than Robertson, but clearly Oscar was a great scorer as well. OPPOSITE, BELOW: Oscar Robertson displays his famous one-handed shooting form from the free throw line as a member of the Milwaukee Bucks. A deadly mid-range jump shooter, the Big O was also a fine marksman from the line, making good on 84 percent of his free throws. Always adept at drawing fouls, only Chamberlain, Malone, and Abdul-Jabbar stepped up to the charity stripe more often than Robertson; and only Moses Malone made more free throws than Oscar.

away jumper or use a pump fake and go straight up for a jump shot, perhaps drawing a foul in the process. Old foe Dick Barnett summed up Robertson's primary tactic: "If you give 'O' a twelve-foot [3.6m] shot, he'll work on you until he's got a ten-foot [3m] shot. Give him a ten and he wants an eight. Give him eight and he wants six. Give him six, he wants four, he wants two. Give him two, you know what he wants? That's right, baby, he wants a layup." On defense, noted Kareem Abdul-Jabbar, Oscar "was quick and smart and solid, as easily slap the ball away from his man as be the wall that would not crumble before a drive." Oscar Robertson was the perfect textbook player.

Robertson joined an anemic Cincinnati Royals club in the NBA. The Royals originally hailed from Rochester, where they were one of pro basketball's leading franchises in the early fifties. But things had dropped off since then and prospects for a turnaround in so small a city seemed bleak. So the Royals moved to Cincinnati, which was gripped by college basketball fever during Oscar's time at the University of Cincinnati. Many, of course, attributed the Royals' move to the fact that they were then assured territorial rights to the great Robertson. The Royals had finished 19–53 and 19–56 the two seasons before the Big O's arrival. With Oscar, the team improved to 33–46, but failed to make the playoffs. Remarkably, on a team with little else going for it, Robertson's statistics were superb: 10.1 rebounds, a league-leading 9.7 assists, and 30.5 points per game. Oscar was named Rookie of the Year.

Behind Oscar, the Royals began to metamorphose into a winning team in 1961–62, finishing 43–37. Robertson averaged a triple-double in his second year, getting 12.5 boards, 11.4 dishes, and 30.8 points per game—the only player ever to accomplish such a feat. The next year, the Royals made a run at the title, winning in the opening round of the playoffs. They faced the dynastic Celtics in the semifinals. Remarkably, Oscar and his supporting cast, which included center Wayne Embry and forward Jack Twyman, won Games One and Three at Boston Garden for a two-to-one lead. However, the Celtics stormed back before the Royals tied the series up with a homecourt victory in Game Six. It all came down to Game Seven; the Celtics, of course, were up to the task, defeating the Royals 142–131. However, when collegiate sensation Jerry Lucas joined the Royals for the 1963–64 season, it seemed that perhaps the Celtics had met their match. The Royals played brilliantly all season, compiling a 55–25 record. Oscar was named the NBA's MVP and he contributed his usual awesome numbers—31.4 points, 11 assists, and 9.9 rebounds. Unfortunately, the Royals were squashed by the Celtics in five games in the league semifinals.

Robertson was more than a fierce competitor—he was a perfectionist. When a teammate made a mistake, he usually heard about it from Oscar. Jerry Lucas observed that "Oscar would yell at you if you

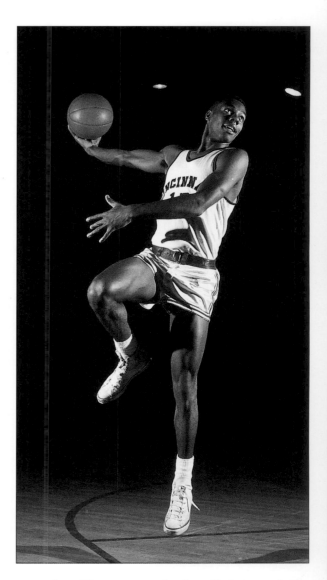

messed up. Then you saw that he yelled at everybody, so you learned not to take it personally." Robertson also complained regularly to referees and was one of the first "trash talkers" in the NBA. Even though at the time it was considered bad sportsmanship to taunt opponents, Oscar did it frequently. Robertson was so good that he was more or less immune to standards set for mere mortals.

Perhaps the reason Oscar lived by his own code of etiquette was that he was always his own boss. Robertson was so talented so early and so completely dominated the tempo of every game in which he played that his relation to the sport differed radically from those around him—he was playing on another level. Off the court, Robertson struck many people as aloof: never impolite to the media, he wasn't friendly either. He seemed to be a simple, quiet, mature man with just a few close friends—a far cry from his controlled, razor-sharp on-court persona.

If Robertson's inability to capture the NCAA championship was frustrating, his years with the Royals must have been absolutely galling. After the 1963–64 season, Oscar played in Cincinnati for six more years, during which the Royals slowly deteriorated. Embry and Twyman were aging by 1964, and the Royals failed to find replacements who provided the team with the same chemistry. Nevertheless, Robertson remained one of the league's premier performers throughout his ten years with the Royals.

Then, miraculously, in the twilight of his career, Robertson was traded to the Milwaukee Bucks, where he teamed up with a young Kareem Abdul-Jabbar. Oscar was elated to join Kareem, and Kareem thrilled at the prospect of playing with the Big O. Kareem marveled that if he gave Oscar "even a glimpse of space to work with, he would drive past, leading the defender into my shoulder, which would stop the man, and once past me either hit a layup or have the court awareness to hit the teammate whose defender had momentarily left him free while trying to stop Oscar....[He] was the epitome of the subtle, no-flash ballplayer." Life in Milwaukee was good. The Bucks compiled a 66–16 record in 1970–71 and trampled all opponents on their way to the NBA title. After thirteen years of frustration, Oscar was finally a champion again.

When Oscar retired after the Bucks lost a heart-breaking seven-game championship series to the Celtics in 1974, he was the NBA's second all-time scorer and the leader in assists. From Crispus Attucks to his long tenure in Cincinnati to his brief stint in Milwaukee, he left a legacy of unparalleled court leadership and earned his reputation as one of the greatest all-around basketball players of all time.

BOB Pettit

Robert Lee Pettit, Jr., was born in Baton Rouge, Louisiana, on December 12, 1932. Raised in a middle-class family, Pettit was a conscientious student and not initially a basketball fanatic. Tall and thin, but not very coordinated, he tried out for the basketball team his sophomore year because he wanted to earn a varsity letter and thought that with his height basketball was his best bet. Bob didn't make the cut, but resolved not to give up: "I taught myself to play, through trial and error. I learned to shoot one-handed because that was the way the ball went in most often. I had no idea how you were supposed to shoot. I made the team as a junior, and didn't become much of a player until my senior year. By then, I was six foot eight [203.2cm]...." And he was a terror. Pettit was an All-American as a senior. Avidly recruited, he ultimately decided to attend Louisiana State University in Baton Rouge.

Bob continued to tear up the South in college. He was the Southeastern Conference Player of the Year his last three years, averaging 27.4 points and 14.6 rebounds per game. There was just one problem: Bob played center in college, and even though the Milwaukee Hawks made him the second player drafted, serious doubts arose that a six-foot-nine-inch (205.7cm), 220-pound (99.8kg) low-post player could succeed in the NBA, especially since Pettit had yet to prove himself on the perimeter. Nevertheless, Hawks Coach Red Holtzman took one look at the skinny Pettit in his rookie training camp and declared him a forward.

Bob made the transition to forward successfully, averaging 20.4 points and 18.8 rebounds his rookie season. The Hawks moved to St. Louis in Pettit's second season and he really took off, leading the league in both scoring and rebounding, winning the MVP awards for both the 1955–56 season and the All-Star Game, and leading the Hawks to within one game of the NBA finals. The next year the Hawks won their first of five consecutive Western Division crowns and reached the final, where they lost a heartbreaking series to Bill Russell and the Celtics in seven games. The decisive contest was decided by 2 points in double overtime.

The Hawks had built an excellent team around Pettit in only a few years. Because they could have drafted Bill Russell, but were uncertain whether he was going to play in the NBA, the Hawks traded their high draft pick to Boston in exchange for a

The St. Louis Hawks' great star Bob Pettit tries for a basket in typical Pettit style in a game against the Cincinnati Royals in New York City on December 10, 1957. Pettit was one of the great scorers in NBA history: his career average of 26.4 points per game ranks fifth on the all-time list. Pettit also was the first NBA player to score 20,000 points. However, Pettit was an unorthodox scoring machine. Pettit had an accurate outside shot, but was a lousy dribbler and rarely drove to the basket. His greatest offensive assets were his skill at drawing fouls and his uncanny ability beneath the offensive glass.

The best way to describe Bob Pettit in terms of contemporary players would be as a Dennis Rodman who could shoot. Rodman, known as The Worm, starred for the champion Detroit Pistons in the late eighties and early nineties, and now, as a member of the San Antonio Spurs, is the NBA's leading rebounder. But though Rodman is a terror on the boards and a tenacious defender, he is a joke outside the paint—every defender in the league loves to see The Worm with the ball on the perimeter because he has the outside touch of a mason. Not so with Pettit: the wiry forward from Louisiana could bring down offensive rebounds with the best of his generation and he could also shoot the lights out. Over his eleven-year career, Pettit averaged not only a remarkable 16.2 rebounds but also 26.4 points per game as he led the St. Louis Hawks to five Western Division titles, four appearances in the finals, and one NBA championship. Unquestionably, Bob Pettit was one of the greatest stars in NBA history.

proven forward, Ed Macauley, and a bright prospect, Cliff Hagan, a six-foot-four-inch (193cm) college center who became a star forward for the Hawks. Veteran point guard Slater Martin, a textbook field general, ran the team (literally for two weeks, after Red Holtzman was fired and before backup guard Alex Hannum was promoted to coach), and either Charlie Share or Clyde Lovellette provided solid support at center.

The St. Louis Hawks reached the 1958 NBA finals and vowed they would exact their revenge against the Celtics. With the series tied at two games apiece, the Hawks won Game Five in Boston and returned to St. Louis with a golden opportunity to win their first title, on their home court. In perhaps the greatest clutch performance in NBA history, Pettit scored 50 points, including 19 of St. Louis' final 21 points, including a medium-range jumper with 15 seconds to play, as the Hawks defeated the Celtics 110–109. Bob Pettit blocked a remarkable 12 shots in the game and the Hawks brought St. Louis its only NBA championship.

Bob Pettit's formidable offensive repertoire featured three weapons: his jump shot, his uncanny ability to draw fouls, and, of course, his offensive rebounding skills. Pettit was a great jump shooter but his dribbling skills were marginal. Teammate Ed Macauley recalled: "He knew what he could do, and when he went out on the court, he did it....He really couldn't put the ball on the floor for more than one bounce, but he learned to be effective with that one bounce, to get past his man and go up for the jump shot." Pettit was so effective moving quickly to his left or right to set up his one-handed jump shot that once he was past his defender, he often hesitated before shooting in order to draw a foul. (In the late seventies and early eighties, Adrian Dantley was a master of drawing the foul by using a head fake to fool his defender into leaping to block a shot and then taking the shot where the defender had no choice but to land on him and send him to the foul line.) Bob Pettit scored almost a third of his career points at the foul line, hitting 76 percent from the charity stripe during his NBA tenure.

Pettit's incredible success as an offensive rebounder was the product of a perfected personal technique: "My offensive rebounding was not an accident. When my teammate shot the ball, I never watched the ball hit the rim. The first thing I did was look at the defender trying to block me out. By not watching the ball, it gave me a chance to make the first move and my first move was to block out my defender, then look up to see the ball hit the rim. I made it into a science and it reached the point where I didn't believe anyone could block me out." Another factor that aided Pettit under the boards were his strong, viselike hands. Pettit averaged more rebounds per game than any forward in NBA history, a remarkable 16.2 per game throughout his career. Pettit's job on the offensive boards also usually contributed 8 to 12 points to his scoring total.

St. Louis had its best regular season ever in 1958–59, finishing 49–23, and Pettit won a second scoring title and a second MVP Award. However, Elgin Baylor and the upstart Lakers downed the Hawks in the NBA semifinals. St. Louis returned to the finals each of the next two years but lost to the powerful Celtics. Pettit had his best year ever as a scorer in 1961–62 with a 31.1 average, but the Hawks fell out of contention. The Hawks finished second in the Western Division each of Pettit's final three years, but they failed to return to the finals.

Bob Pettit retired following the 1964–65 season to pursue a career in law, having played only eleven seasons in the NBA. Nonetheless, Pettit had become the first player in league history to score 20,000 points, and left pro basketball as its all-time leading scorer. Pettit's success stemmed from his tremendous dedication and drive to win. He was very economical on the court, always playing to his strengths. "He was never known to make a foolish move."

In a 1960 game against the Cincinnati Royals, St. Louis Hawk Bob Pettit definitively snatches a rebound from Hub Reed, who flails helplessly in the background as Clyde Lovellette looks on. Pettit had an exceptionally powerful grip. Large, strong hands like Pettit's are a great asset on a basketball court, where opponents always try to slap the ball loose—especially under the boards, where Pettit did his best work.

ELGIN Baylor

Elgin Baylor floats above a powerless Celtic defender during a 1963 game at Boston Garden. The key for Baylor's aerial game was not altitude, but body control. Many players can leap high and far, but few have ever had Baylor's in-flight composure. Elgin was so strong throughout his body that his ability to maneuver his arms and torso did not diminish significantly when his feet were off the ground.

If professional basketball in the Mikan era of 1946 to 1954 was archaic by today's standards, three innovations introduced into the NBA before 1960 spurred the evolution of pro ball toward today's high-flying spectacle: one, the 24-second clock sped up the game; two, Bill Russell's shot blocking forced a change in offensive strategy; and three, Elgin Baylor's aerial game showed that forwards and guards could also take to the sky. Elgin's on-court audacity stemmed from the streets of Washington, D.C., where the style of play was considerably more upbeat than it was in organized ball. But Elgin possessed more than just the "shakes, fakes, and jazzy feints" of black street ball; he could walk on air. Like Dr. J in the seventies and Michael Jordan in the eighties, Baylor had the ability to leap over competitors as well as tremendous control over his body and the ball as he did so. Still Baylor was more than just an innovator. He was a tremendous all-around player who led the Lakers to eight finals while averaging 27.4

points per game, the third-highest ever, throughout his storied NBA career.

• • •

Elgin Gay Baylor was born on September 16, 1934, in Washington, D.C. He was six feet two inches (187.9cm) tall as an adolescent, when a family friend introduced Elgin to basketball. Taking to the recently integrated playgrounds of the nation's capital, Baylor rapidly improved his game and made the Spingarn High junior varsity squad. However, when he failed to make the varsity as a sophomore, Elgin refused to rejoin the junior varsity. Not much of a student, Elgin dropped out of school, played ball in a recreational league, and worked as a checker in a furniture store. However, Baylor's basketball skills continued to improve. He returned to Spingarn, made the varsity squad, and by his senior year was Washington's biggest high school cage star, selected as an All-American.

Baylor's late rise to stardom and his academic troubles kept big-time college recruiters away. Baylor's only college option was to attend the tiny College of Idaho, a small liberal arts school, on a football scholarship, which was arranged for Elgin by a friend at Idaho who knew of Baylor's tremendous athletic gifts. Baylor accepted the offer, happy to escape the racism of the nation's capital and attend college. At Idaho, the athletic department recognized that Elgin's true talent was on the basketball court; he switched sports and proceeded to dominate his junior college league. However, Baylor's days at Idaho were numbered because of new restrictions on athletic scholarships. Fortunately, a Seattle businessman persuaded Baylor to transfer to Seattle University. Baylor had to sit out a year to abide by NCAA rules, but he was happy to remain in the Northwest, where racial tensions were minimal, and excited at the opportunity to play big-time college ball.

Before the arrival of Baylor, Seattle had no basketball tradition to speak of. Elgin established himself as the team's star during the 1956–57 season and electrified the local basketball community with his spectacular play. Chick Hearn of CBS Television saw Baylor play his first year at Seattle: "I had never seen a player like this—all these high-flying moves and how he used reverse English on the ball to make a layup from unbelievable angles. He would hang in the air for so long that you'd worry that he'd get hurt when he came down. He was the pioneer for the kind of athletic players we see today. A lot of the moves people say were invented by Michael Jordan or Julius Erving, I saw Elgin do first." Baylor knew he was an innovator, but his creativity served a higher purpose: winning. "I don't know why I played like I did," Baylor recalled. "I had never seen anyone else do my moves. It starts with talent, you have to be able to jump. But more than that, things I did were spontaneous. I had the ball, I reacted to the defense. The important thing to me was making the shot."

Baylor was a great all-around player; at six feet five inches (195.5cm) and 225 pounds (102.1kg), Elgin could do it all on the court—rebound, pass, defend, and, of course, score. At Seattle, Elgin averaged 19 rebounds and 31 points against opponents who were focused exclusively on stopping the high-flying phenom. Behind Baylor, Seattle made it to the NCAA Finals in 1958 before losing to perennial power Kentucky.

Elgin chose to skip his final year of eligibility when the Minneapolis Lakers, the team with the worst record in the NBA, selected him in the draft. Lakers owner Bob Short later acknowledged that if Baylor hadn't signed with Minneapolis, he would have sold the team. Baylor exploded into the NBA, averaging 15 rebounds and 24.9 points per game. The Lakers improved enough to make the playoffs and then caught fire, defeating Detroit and then stunning the defending champion St. Louis Hawks, four games to two. The Celtics swept the Lakers in the finals, but Elgin had left his mark on the NBA in only his rookie season. In his second NBA season, Baylor's production improved to 16.4 rebounds and 29.6 points per game, though the Hawks exacted their revenge on the Lakers in the semifinals.

Laker teammate Rodney "Hot Rod" Hundley frequently compares Baylor's strength to that of six-foot-nine-inch (205.7cm) power forward Karl Malone of today's Utah Jazz. But as Hundley notes, Baylor also had tremendous "body control in the air," which allowed him to "hang there and shoot these little flip shots." Sometimes Baylor seemed out of control as he headed toward the basket, but he could regain control after he jumped. One further element added to Baylor's effectiveness: a nervous tick, a "twitching of his face," that often confused defenders—it was Elgin's built-in head fake. Baylor asked doctors about the twitch, which usually occurred on the court, and they said it was nothing serious, attributable to nerves. Elgin decided not to worry about it.

The Lakers moved out to Los Angeles for the 1960–61 season and added a slick guard by the name of Jerry West. The team, however, was still very much Elgin's, and he tore through the league, averaging 34.8 points and a remarkable 19.8 rebounds. Early in the season, on November 15, 1960, Elgin poured in a record 71 points at New York, breaking his own NBA record of 64, which he had set on November 8, 1959, against Boston. (Joe Fulks had set the pre-Elgin record of 63 in 1949.) In the game against Boston, Auerbach put four men on Elgin to try to keep him from establishing a new mark;

LEFT: Baylor takes to the air against the Knicks. BELOW: Elgin drives the baseline, running his man into a Wilt Chamberlain pick, as Warrior center Nate Thurmond prepares to intercept Baylor. Chamberlain said about Baylor: "[He] loved to drive toward the basket, go up in the air, stay there until everyone else came down, then do a corkscrew and a double pirouette and drop the ball in the basket. He was fantastic at that, the best I ever saw."

ironically, one of the Celtics fouled Baylor, who set the record from the charity stripe. The Lakers, however, once again succumbed to the Hawks in the spring of 1961 in another dramatic seven-game semi-final series.

Elgin was doing a part-time stint in the armed forces and could appear in only 48 games during the 1961–62 regular season. Without Elgin the Lakers were good, but with him they were fantastic. In his 48 games, Baylor averaged 18.6 rebounds and a sensational 38.3 points per game. Baylor was stationed in Seattle, but as he remembered: "I would get a weekend pass that began on midnight Friday and I had to be back on midnight Sunday. I'd take the red-eye on Friday night to wherever the team was, play the weekend games, and then kill myself to get back by midnight Sunday." Finishing first in the NBA's Western Division, the Lakers, with Baylor back full time, defeated Detroit to set up a final with the Boston Celtics, who had emerged as champions in four of the previous five seasons.

Over the next eight years the Lakers would lose six times in the finals to the Celtics, including three series in which the Celtics won Game Seven by 2 points or in overtime. The Lakers' inability to conquer the Celtics was one of the greatest "curses" in sports history. But if only one easy shot had fallen in the spring of 1962, it may have all been different. The series was tied at two games apiece when Baylor exploded in Game Five, grabbing 22 rebounds and scoring an NBA playoff record 61 points against every defensive tactic Red Auerbach could dream up to try to slow him down. Even Bill Russell couldn't stop him. The Lakers took Game Five 126–121 and returned to L.A. with a chance to win the title, but the Celtics put on a clutch performance and won Game Six 119–105. Game Seven at Boston was tied at 100 with 18 seconds left and the Celtics had the ball. Boston, however, missed a shot and the Lakers grabbed the rebound and called time-out. L.A. had 5 seconds left to try to score and win the title. They designed a play for Hot Rod Hundley to penetrate and pass to Baylor or West if either was open, but neither was. So Hundley found Frank Selvy open only eight feet (2.4m) from the basket on the baseline. Selvy got the ball and elevated for a shot he almost always made, but it clanked off the rim. The Celtics outscored the Lakers 10–7 in overtime to win yet another NBA crown. If only Selvy's shot had fallen, the history of Baylor and the Lakers might have been radically different; instead they lived under the spell of the curse, performing magically all the while, over the next decade.

Elgin takes it to the hole for an easy 2 points against the Hawks. Elgin's great "hang time," his ability to make brilliant plays off the ground, helped him become not only a lethal scorer but also a great rebounder. Baylor averaged 27.4 points and 13.5 rebounds per game throughout his career. Before his devastating knee injury in April 1965, Baylor's career averages were 30.2 points and 15.4 rebounds per game.

In 1964–65 the Lakers were full of enthusiasm heading into the playoffs when Baylor suffered a severe knee injury in the first round of the playoffs on April 3. "I went up for a shot, and my knee exploded," recalled Elgin. "I could hear a crack and a pop and everything else." The doctors said Elgin's playing days were over. At first, walking was almost impossible; Elgin had snapped the main ligament in his knee and virtually split the kneecap in the process. But the pain subsided and Elgin was determined to prove the doctors wrong. Miraculously, Baylor showed up at training camp and won a spot on the team. Over the course of the season, Baylor's presence made the Lakers stronger, but it wasn't the same. He returned to full speed, but he could not do the things he once could. "Afterward," Jerry West noted, "to watch the slow, painful process of him getting better and improving and never really getting back to where he was, that was the thing that was difficult for the rest of us to accept. We wanted him back having all his greatness. He came back and played, and played incredibly well. But he wasn't the Elgin Baylor of old." When the Lakers reached the finals again in the spring of 1966, Elgin led the way, scoring 36 points in an overtime victory in Game One over the Celtics. Sadly, however, the Celtics crushed Elgin's comeback dream, winning again in seven games.

The Lakers lost in the finals to the Celtics in 1968, but they had new hopes next autumn when the legendary Wilt Chamberlain joined their ranks. Over the next two years, the Baylor-West-Chamberlain Lakers were awesome but lost two successive seven-game finals to the Celtics and Knicks. Baylor sat out almost the entire 1970–71 season as the Lakers rebuilt. But 1971–72 would finally be the Lakers' year. Baylor started with the team, but after appearing in nine games and averaging only 11.8 points, Elgin stepped down gracefully. Baylor left the Lakers after thirteen seasons as the league's third all-time scorer (23,149 points) and fifth greatest rebounder (11,463). His per-game scoring average of 27.4 remains the third highest ever, behind Wilt Chamberlain and Michael Jordan.

Elgin Baylor revolutionized the NBA with his phenomenal drives to the basket. Baylor had a great all-around game, but he will always be remembered for using lightning quick speed, astounding leaping ability, and tremendous in-air body control, for introducing the world to "hang time."

An airborne Elgin Baylor towers over Celtic Emmette Bryant as Baylor releases a jump shot during the 1969 NBA finals. Elgin played in seven finals for the Lakers (he missed the 1965 finals): six versus the Celtics and one against the Knicks. To Baylor's great dismay the Lakers lost all seven series, four of which went to seven games. The defeat in 1969 may have been the most painful, coming in the twilight of Elgin's career and ending with a 2-point loss at home in Game Seven. Nevertheless, Baylor always played brilliantly; he ranks third in both points and rebounds in the finals.

JERRY West

Two things stood out about Jerry West during his tenure in the NBA: he had an unparalleled jump shot, and he had an even better jump shot when the game was on the line. Laker teammate Rudy LaRusso recalled: "We'd get into a tie game with 15 seconds to go and we'd give the ball to Jerry, clear out the side of the floor. He'd take one dribble, then another, then go up with a jumper and we'd go home with a win." Nicknamed "Mr. Clutch," Jerry West averaged 27 points per game over his fourteen-year career and 29.1 during the playoffs. Only six feet two inches (187.9cm) and 185 pounds (83.9kg), West had unusually long arms, making him a tenacious defender and allowing him a surprisingly high release on his textbook jump shot. More significantly, West exuded confidence.

• • •

Jerry Alan West was born on May 28, 1938, in the small town of Cheylan, West Virginia, but grew up in an even more remote place called Cabin Creek, population twenty. Basketball was a popular diversion in Jerry's neck of the woods, and he began playing as a kid on local dirt courts and on his neighbor's backyard hoop. West was not overwhelmed with a passion for the sport, but he would spend many hours simply shooting by himself and, like youngsters the world over, concocting games with his imagination: "Sometimes, I used to shoot ten times just to make the last shot, which would, in my mind, win a game." But nothing much came of Jerry's efforts, and he aspired merely to make the high school team. A very skinny, gangly youth, Jerry played well enough on the junior varsity squad that he was moved up to varsity his first year, but promptly broke a bone in his foot. But West's initial success had sparked his interest, and he began to focus seriously on the game.

Jerry started for the East Bank High varsity team his junior year and averaged almost 30 points a game. The team, however, played only .500 ball. Still Jerry was disappointed by not earning many accolades for his performances. At first, he concluded that he must not be as good as the boys who made the all-state team but when he was selected to attend a statewide gathering of some of West Virginia's top students, he got to play in pickup games with many of the all-stars. Jerry West's teams never lost, and he entered his senior year confident that he was the top player in the state.

West's high school coach emphasized defense, and in his system Jerry became adept at stealing balls and using his great leaping ability to block shots. But Jerry himself was largely responsible for the development of his offensive skills, particularly his deadly jump shot. As a senior, Jerry tore up West Virginia basketball, taking little East Bank High to the state title. In the semifinals, East Bank played perennial powerhouse Mullens High. Shooting his signature line-drive jumper, Jerry poured in 43 points and pulled down 23 rebounds to lead East Bank to a 77–73 victory. Jerry collected 39 points as his team won the finals handily over Morgantown.

West, deciding to stay in-state for college, attended the University of West Virginia in Morgantown, where All-American Rodney "Hot

Rod" Hundley was helping to establish a winning tradition. While playing for the Mountaineers, West averaged 24.8 points per game over his career. In his junior year, 1958–59, Jerry led West Virginia all the way to the NCAA finals, in which they lost to California; but Jerry was named the tournament MVP. That summer he played on the gold medal–winning United States squad at the Pan-American Games. As a senior, West shared honors with Oscar Robertson as national collegiate Player of the Year, averaging 29 points and, though he was only a skinny six feet two inches (187.9cm), 17 rebounds per game. West and Robertson then cocaptained the gold medal U.S.A. team at the Olympics in Rome.

Heading into the pros, West still doubted whether he could be a star in the NBA. After all, Hundley had been a legend in his days in Morgantown, and although he started in the Lakers backcourt, he was certainly not a dominant player. West joined Hundley and the great Elgin Baylor on the Lakers when Los Angeles made West the second pick of the 1960 NBA draft, after only Oscar Robertson. West's fears were then seemingly confirmed when he failed to win a starting spot in the Lakers lineup. Ironically, the man who decided to keep West on the bench for virtually half of every game was his former college coach, Fred Schaus. West was at first disappointed and then furious because he felt he could do a better job than the men on the court. Schaus' rationale was that West had played forward in college and that too many young stars were hurried along. He felt that Jerry needed time to adjust to playing guard and to the new level of competition. Jerry averaged only 17 points per game his rookie year, but when he was given a chance to take center stage, *look out!*

In West's second year, the season Baylor played only 48 games because of army duty, Jerry started in the backcourt and the Lakers improved by 18 games over the previous season. Baylor averaged 38 points per game in his limited duty and West averaged 30.8; the Lakers were suddenly a team with two superstars, two dynamic scoring threats. The Lakers reached the finals that year and lost the first of the seven championship series that they would lose over the next nine years. Their foe in the first six of those series was the Boston Celtics.

Positively thrilled with his new Laker cohort, Elgin Baylor christened Jerry West "Zeke from Cabin Creek." But when teammates and the media noticed that West was comfortable taking key shots at the end of even the closest games, he became universally known as Mr. Clutch. West recalled, "I always thought that if we needed a basket, I could score. I didn't care who was guarding me or what the defense was, I could get the ball in the basket. As my career went on, it became easier and easier to score in clutch situations because my confidence grew. In fact, I would be irritated if someone else took a shot in those situations, because I knew that if I took it, we'd score."

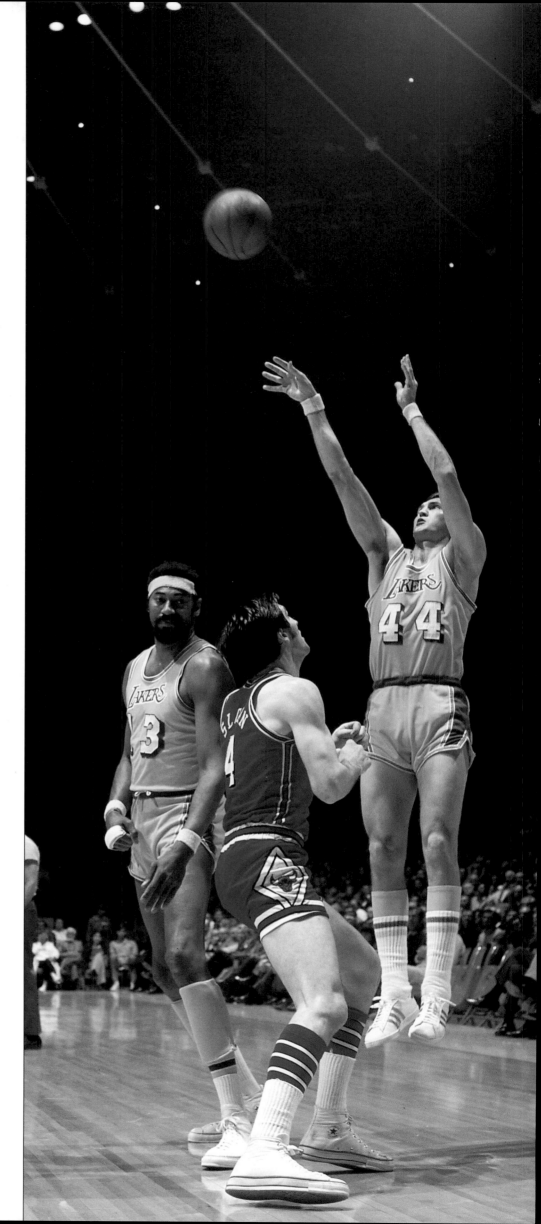

offense his long arms and great leaping ability allowed him to enjoy a much higher release point for his jumper than other guards his height did.

Over his fourteen-year career with the Lakers, West averaged 27 points per game, the fourth-highest in league history. In the 1969–70 season, West won the scoring title at the age of thirty-two with a 31.2 per game average. In 1971–72, as he and Wilt Chamberlain led the Lakers to a record 33-game winning streak, the best regular-season record in NBA history, and their first title in Los Angeles, West led the league in assists for the first time in his career. At thirty-four years old, Jerry's game was still growing.

West retired following the 1973–74 season, but by 1976 was back on the sidelines as the Lakers'

West simply had tremendous confidence in his jump shot. Before shooting his jumper, West would dribble the ball extra hard so that it rose up beyond his waist and he could begin to jump before the ball actually was in his hand; the maneuver took incredible coordination and was deadly. If the defender was up too far on West, he could use his lightning-quick moves to drive around him and either head to the basket or an open space, where he would dribble hard and then bang home a jumper. West worked extremely hard to improve his game throughout his career. Early on, the rap on him was that he could not go to his left, that he didn't have confidence as a dribbler in that direction. But West worked diligently to develop that skill and actually used his reputation to his advantage because defenders would focus on a move to the right, and he would get an opening to the left— a quick step to the left, a hard dribble, and *bang*.

By the time he was a pro, West had grown into his previously gangly body (weighing 185 pounds [83.9kg] in his maturity), but he still had extremely long arms for someone his height. Jerry used his long arms to tremendous advantage: on defense he was adept at stealing balls off the dribble, while on coach. Over three seasons, West compiled a 145–101 record and then moved on to be the Lakers' general manager, where he presided over the Lakers' glorious Showtime years. Ironically, West used his leadership and intelligence to lead the Lakers to nine appearances in the finals as a player, but captured only one title; as a general manager he has guided the Lakers to the same number of finals, but the team has won five championship banners.

As a player, Jerry West demanded nothing less than perfection from himself, and apparently he has since applied the same criteria to his work as general manager of the Lakers. Both on and off the court, Mr. Clutch has been a tremendous asset to the world of basketball.

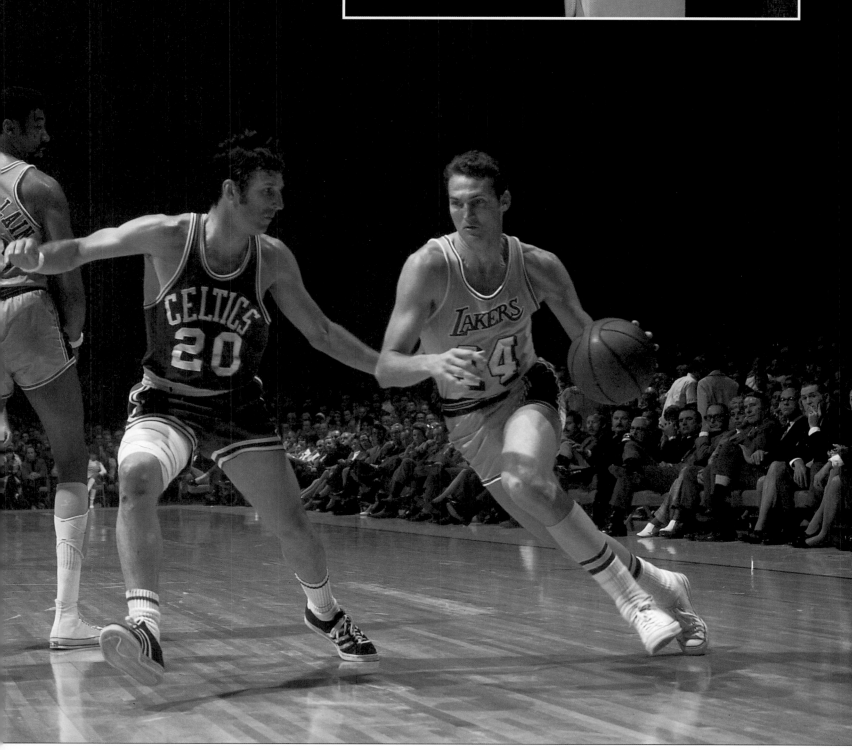

3

THE SEVENTIES: PARITY AND HARD TIMES

After the NBA's golden age in the sixties and before the league's boom years in the late eighties, the NBA struggled. The league's difficulties in the seventies were the result of an array of factors; but considering the eventual growth and prosperity of the league, perhaps the troubles of the seventies were, for all their complexity, merely growing pains. From the mid-sixties to the mid-seventies, the NBA expanded from a quaint, well-run, stable eight-team league to an unwieldy, ever-expanding, and rather unstable twenty-odd-team behemoth. This traumatic pace of growth was, in large part, a response to a rival league, the American Basketball Association. The ABA was much more unstable than the National Basketball Association. ABA franchises collapsed right and left throughout its colorful history, yet the quality of play in the upstart league managed to improve each year of its existence from 1967–68 through 1975–76. So the NBA responded by expanding rapidly as well. On one hand, as the sport was imported into new markets without any pro basketball tradition, arenas were often only half full. On the other hand, the NBA was exposed to such cities as Portland, Seattle, Phoenix, and Milwaukee, where the pro game became a big hit.

Basketball had continued to grow tremendously in popularity throughout the sixties, especially among young black men growing up in American inner cities. Thus, there was no dearth of players to fill the rosters of the NBA and the ABA. The style of basketball played on the streets of the American inner city contrasted sharply with more traditional, disciplined approaches. Before the liberating civil rights and black power movements of the sixties, young black players rarely displayed the spectacular, improvisa-

tional moves associated with black street ball in the professional ranks, but by the seventies that had all changed. The ABA, in particular, became the domain for the high-flying, fast-paced game of the inner city. Some analysts declared that the troubles afflicting the pro game were due to lingering racial tensions: they claimed that a sport dominated by black men would have a hard time drawing fans in a society in which the majority of the wealth is held by whites. Some fans, of course, were instantly converted by the sight of spectacular dunks; others were perhaps turned off by the increasing number of African American stars. The growing pains of the sport and society were reflected through the prism of professional basketball.

By the late eighties, of course, the younger franchises had found permanent homes, but in the seventies the new franchises struggled to find their feet. By the early seventies, the ABA had attained some stability and the successful franchises hoped for a merger with the NBA. The quality of play in the ABA was occasionally exceptional. Coaching legend Larry Brown (now with the powerhouse Indiana Pacers) called his 1974–75 Kentucky Colonels, which includ-

The old guard versus the new: the Lakers' venerable Wilt Chamberlain tries to reach a floating shot by Milwaukee's young Kareem Abdul-Jabbar while the Lakers' Jerry West tries to help out and the Bucks' Oscar Robertson looks on. For most of the seventies and early eighties, Jabbar reigned supreme among NBA big men. In contrast to the two dominant centers of the sixties, Russell and Chamberlain, Jabbar had no comparable foe to wage legendary battles against. Only Chamberlain, in the twilight of his career, and Bill Walton, in the rare instances when he was not injured, challenged Jabbar in his prime. Many feel that Jabbar's reputation suffered because he had no contemporary archrival to challenge him.

The starting five for the New York Knicks' first-ever championship team—Dick Barnett, Walt Frazier, Bill Bradley, Dave DeBusschere, and Willis Reed—celebrate their elimination of Lew Alcindor's Milwaukee Bucks on April 20, 1970. Over the following two weeks, New York City was riveted by the dramatic seven-game final versus Wilt Chamberlain, Jerry West, Elgin Baylor, and the rest of the Los Angeles Lakers. The teams split the first two games in New York and then each won an overtime game in Los Angeles. The Knicks won a tight Game Five at the Garden. Early in Game Six, Knicks team captain and league MVP Willis Reed, a powerful six-foot-ten-inch (208.2cm) center with a soft shot, injured his right thigh and had to leave the game; the Lakers evened the series in a blowout. The teams crossed the continent again as news spread of the severity of Reed's injury. However, nothing could keep Willis sidelined, and in one of the most inspirational moments in the history of basketball, the Knicks captain hobbled onto the floor to a standing ovation just before tip-off. Their spirits lifted by Reed's courage, the Knicks downed the Lakers 113–99 to bring New York its first NBA championship.

ed Artis Gilmore, Dan Issel, and guard Louis Dampier, the best team he ever coached. Other ABA stars included such NBA transfers as Rick Barry, Zelmo Beatty, Mel Daniels, the awesomely talented but erratic Spencer Haywood, the equally talented but even less consistent Marvin Barnes, power forward Maurice Lucas, long-range gunner Freddie Lewis, high-flying David Thompson, George McGinnis, and the young Moses Malone. But there was one player who single-handedly made the ABA a threat to the NBA: the incomparable Dr. J, Julius Erving. By the summer of 1976, NBA owners decided they needed to bring the game's greatest contemporary legend into their fold and acquiesced to a merger with the ABA that brought four more franchises into an already bloated league; there were now twenty-two teams. All of them still exist, though five relocated within the next few years.

There was a changing of the guard, or literally of the center, in the NBA in the autumn of 1969, as Bill Russell retired before the start of the 1969–70 season and Lew Alcindor, soon to be known as Kareem Abdul-Jabbar, joined the Milwaukee Bucks. Russell's exit signaled the end of the Celtic dynasty; no team would repeat as league champions for nearly two decades. The initial beneficiaries of Boston's decline were not the West-and-Chamberlain Lakers, but the well-balanced New York Knicks, who were as celebrated for their 1970 championship as the Celtics had been for all eleven of theirs. In 1971, Jabbar managed to bring a championship to Milwaukee in the franchise's third season—a remarkable feat, unparalleled since the days of George Mikan. Jabbar would remain the decade's dominant player, rivaled only by Bill Walton for a year and a half before injuries destroyed Walton's career. But the talent supporting Kareem was never adequate to carry one of his teams to another league title until the eighties. In 1972, the Lakers finally won a title, defeating the Knicks, but the Knicks returned the favor in the spring of 1973. A revitalized Boston Celtics team, built around old stalwarts like Don Nelson and John Havlicek and new-

comers like Dave Cowens and JoJo White, defeated Kareem and the Bucks in 1974 for the title and won over the young Phoenix Suns in 1976. In 1975, Rick Barry led the Golden State Warriors past Elvin Hayes, Wes Unseld, and the Washington Bullets. In 1977 Dr. J sparked the public's imagination, but Bill Walton led the well-balanced Portland Trail Blazers past the star-studded Philadelphia 76ers for the title. In both 1978 and 1979, the Bullets squared off against the Seattle Supersonics for the championship; Washington won the first round, but Seattle captured the rematch. Many of the championship series throughout the decade were followed closely across the nation. The Knicks were adored in New York and across the land, and the 1974 battle between the Celtics and Kareem drew high ratings. The crest of the league's popularity in the 1970s came with the entry of Dr. J into the league, and the 1977 playoffs were followed as closely as ever. But by the end of the decade, many of the most popular teams, such as the Celtics and Knicks, were struggling; attendance dropped, television ratings were in decline, and in many places throughout America the NBA was relegated to the back pages of the sports section. This trend would continue into the mid-eighties.

Still, the NBA was rife with great basketball players in the 1970s. Pistol Pete Maravich was a scoring machine for the expansion New Orleans Jazz, as was Bob MacAdoo for the Buffalo Braves. Center Bob Lanier and guard Dave Bing were a lethal combination for the Detroit Pistons. Jerry Sloan and Bob Love were the backbone of a solid Chicago Bulls team. Bob Dandridge provided Kareem assistance with scoring duties for the Bucks. Campy Russell helped make the Cleveland Cavaliers respectable. Guard Gus Johnson and center Jack Sikma sparked Seattle's years at the top. Paul Silas was pivotal for both the Celtic and Sonic champions. Wes Unseld was an unmovable force beneath the boards for the Washington Bullets. Paul Westphal and Alvan Adams led the Phoenix Suns. Center Dave Cowens of the Celtics captured a league MVP Award. Lloyd "World B." Free and Bobby Jones starred for the Sixers. Nate "Tiny" Archibald won a scoring title with the Kansas City Omaha Kings. And the Knicks of the early seventies, a group that personified teamwork, had a plethora of stars, including forwards Dave DeBusschere and Bill Bradley, center Willis Reed, guards Dick Barnett and Walt "Clyde" Frazier, and the irrepressible Earl "The Pearl" Monroe. The individual players who made the greatest impact on the NBA were the Celtics' Green Running Machine, John Havlicek; the Warriors' intense, yet smooth forward, Rick Barry; and the Bullets' all-around superstar, Elvin Hayes. No one stirred the public's interest in basketball like the inimitable Julius Erving, who had attained a mythical status in the ABA for his astonishing dunks and then brought his air show to the NBA in 1976. Yet the era's greatest player was, unquestionably, seven-foot-two-inch (218.4cm) Kareem Abdul-Jabbar.

THE WORLD CHAMPION NEW YORK KNICKERBOCKERS

In 1969 the upstart New York Jets stunned the Baltimore Colts in the Super Bowl and the New York Mets trounced the heavily favored Baltimore Orioles, bringing New York its first sports crowns in eight years. Seven months later, the New York Knicks won their first NBA title, overcoming the Los Angeles Lakers in seven dramatic games. All three champions became the toast of a sports-crazed Gotham City; however, whereas the Jets and Mets were upstarts, the Knicks had matured into a great team by the 1969–70 season. Knicks fans and the media scrutinized every moment of the playoffs, right up to the final, euphoric whistle. Along the way, the Knicks captured the imagination of New York City, and won its heart. Over the next few years, while the Jets and Mets became erratic, the Knicks remained brilliant and reigned as New York's team. Though renowned for its cynical fans and negative sports reporting, the Big Apple embraced the Knicks with an enthusiasm rarely found in the annals of American sports. The Knicks' 1970 championship proved so inspirational to writers that it spawned numerous books, far exceeding the volume published on the 1957–69 Celtics dynasty that captured eleven NBA titles. Overnight, the Knicks became the hottest ticket in town; celebrities flocked to Madison Square Garden to watch their heroes in action; most home games sold out; and television ratings soared. For the first time in league history, the NBA boasted a franchise as popular as any in the annals of American pro sports; and

since it was in the world's largest market, literally millions of fans rooted fervently for the Knicks.

Two factors fueled the Knicks' unprecedented popularity. First, New York City has a great basketball tradition, and, undoubtedly, had more hoop fans during the 1960s than any other city in the world. However, since the Knicks were perennial losers, the franchise was unable to exploit its massive fan base—that is, until the late sixties. Second, the Knicks squad that was built around center Willis Reed (a rookie in 1964–65) evolved by the 1969–70 season into one of the most skilled, fluid, and fundamentally sound teams ever assembled. Lacking a marquee superstar like Chamberlain, Russell, Jabbar, or even West, the Knicks compensated with total team basketball, a quality that basketball pundits lauded. While Reed and power forward Dave DeBusschere cleaned up on the boards, every Knick regular (the team always had depth) was an exceptional defender, passer, and shooter. Thus, the Knicks played exciting basketball, featuring multiple scoring threats and rapid ball movement, even while discouraging individual improvisation in favor of team play. New York fans embraced the team in 1968–69 when it went 54–28, then packed the Garden the whole next season as league MVP Willis Reed led the Knicks to 60 regular-season victories and their first NBA title. In the process, New Yorkers discovered that many of the Knicks were rife with character, including the high-scoring, flamboyant-dressing Walt "Clyde" Frazier and, of course, Princeton graduate, former Rhodes scholar, and future U.S. senator, Bill Bradley. More significantly, many commentators noted that, in an era of great social upheaval and widespread racial tension, the racially integrated Knicks were exemplary role models because they not only worked exceptionally well together, but they genuinely liked each other.

Since the Knicks emphasized team play, none of their stars produced statistics comparable to the NBA's all-time greatest players; furthermore, it seems unlikely that any of the group would have done better in a less disciplined environment. Certainly Willis Reed's considerable skills were allowed full expression on the Knicks; Reed was a six-foot-ten-inch (208.2 cm), wide-bodied center with a lethal baseline jumper. Perhaps guard Walt Frazier, the Knicks' other high-profile scorer, would have tallied higher totals in a different system (he consistently averaged over 20 points per game), but it's unlikely such a team would have been as successful; regardless, Frazier deserves his reputation as an NBA immortal. The third Knick who deserves special mention as an individual talent is Earl Monroe, who joined the Knicks during the 1971–72 season from Baltimore, where he had starred for the Bullets when they dethroned the Knicks in the previous season's Eastern Conference finals. Earl "The Pearl" Monroe was raised in Philadelphia, where he became a "playground" legend. Playing all summer long on outdoor courts, Monroe developed an astounding repertoire of herky-jerky spin moves that baffled defenders. Known as "Black Jesus" by Philly fans, Monroe entered the NBA in 1967–68 and averaged over 20 points per game each year before joining the Knicks. Upon arrival in New York he accepted a subordinate position to Frazier in Coach Red Holzman's offense. The Knicks adjusted well to Monroe's presence and they returned to the NBA finals in 1972, where they lost to the Lakers. When the two teams met again the next year, the Knicks garnered their second NBA championship in four years.

Earl "The Pearl" Monroe pulls up for a jump shot against the Lakers. Monroe was a brilliant offensive improviser. Avid Knicks fan Woody Allen wrote, "What makes Monroe different is the indescribable heat of genius that burns deep inside him. Some kind of diabolical intensity comes across his face when he has the ball...and yet he has enough wit in his style to bring off funny ideas when he wants to."

KAREEM Abdul-Jabbar

Power Memorial High's towering Lew Alcindor, only sixteen years old and nearly seven feet (213.3cm) tall, leaps to block a short jumper by an overmatched opponent. Big Lew was the greatest, most dominant player in the history of New York City high school basketball. Alcindor developed his basketball skills on the outdoor courts of the Big Apple, often competing against the game's greatest playground legends, and learned the tenets of disciplined teamwork at Power. An awesome combination of physical prowess, skill, and on-court intelligence, Alcindor led Power to three consecutive New York titles and back-to-back undefeated seasons.

The basketball career of Kareem Abdul-Jabbar was so long and full of accomplishment that it is nearly impossible to summarize his greatness. At seven feet two inches (218.4cm) and with the agile body of a sprinter, Jabbar was so awesome in high school, in college, and early in his pro career that critics held him and his teams to unrealistic standards—which they usually met. When the National Collegiate Athletic Association rule committee outlawed dunking to try to curtail his dominance, he developed a virtually unstoppable shot, the skyhook, that remained lethal twenty years later. He not only played but starred in the NBA for twenty seasons, shattered Wilt Chamberlain's all-time scoring record, won the league MVP Award a record six times, played in the NBA finals ten times (second to Bill Russell), and won the championship six times. In high school, his team won every championship available to it, and in college, his University of California at Los Angeles teams won an unprecedented three straight national titles.

Perhaps what was most impressive about Jabbar during his career, and what made his remarkable longevity possible, was that he did it all on his own terms. An immediately recognizable celebrity throughout his entire adult life, Kareem made up his mind early that he had to integrate his experience as a basketball superstar into his life in a manner that allowed him to pursue his spiritual and intellectual interests. Kareem always saw the big picture. He understood that he had to remain in excellent shape, establish a high level of performing excellence, and expend his passion when it was most important. Thus, Jabbar did not waste his time on the day-to-day controversies that fill up the sports pages; he simply remained focused, played excellently every day, and, by the end of each season, was on top.

• • •

Kareem Abdul-Jabbar was born Lew Alcindor in New York City on April 16, 1947. Lew was the biggest baby born in Harlem's Sydenham Hospital. His family emphasized discipline when Lew was young and kept him focused on his education. Mr. Alcindor was a well-educated and serious man. The Alcindor family came from the island of Trinidad, where Kareem would become a national hero.

Lew's father's passion was jazz. Mr. Alcindor, who was a trombone player, studied music at Juilliard on the GI Bill and jammed with jazz greats Art Blakey and Yusef Lateef. Kareem has been a huge jazz buff his whole life. He also inherited some of his father's countenance; Big Al had to concentrate to socialize and usually had a silent, menacing presence. Like his father, Kareem also became an avid reader and sports fan. Kareem's mom, by contrast, instilled in Kareem a sense of social ambition.

Shortly after Lew started attending school, the Alcindors moved from Harlem to Washington Heights, near the Cloisters. As an only child, Lew had his own room, and he took full advantage of it. He liked to venture out into the playgrounds and later the streets of New York, but always spent countless hours in his room reading and listening to music, an experience that, he later acknowledged, "went a long way towards shaping his 'reclusive personality'." An avid reader, he always excelled in school.

As Lew grew taller than his peers, basketball became a large part of his life. Though other kids made fun of him for being smart, he knew he could show them up on the court. Lew played at his junior high, St. Jude's, but his real basketball education came in the city playgrounds. Each summer he spent countless hours playing pickup games on the asphalt courts of New York City. By eighth grade, he was six feet five inches (195.5cm) tall, and could palm the ball, dunk, and dominate his peers. Recruited by every basketball powerhouse in the city, he chose Power Memorial High because it had a good reputation. He was also impressed by its coach, Jack Donahue.

At six feet nine inches (205.7cm) and growing, Lew made the varsity squad as a freshman. The team had a stellar year, losing only six games. The next summer Lew had hoped to stay in New York, but his mother and Coach Donahue conspired to send him to the coach's upstate basketball camp. There was nothing fun to do in Saugerties, New York, except play ball, so that's what Kareem did all summer. Previously, Kareem had not been too aggressive on the court, but as his coordination improved and he began to grow into his body, he started to control the space around him more thoroughly. When he returned to the courts of Harlem, he realized no one could stop him. He was becoming a seven-foot-tall (213.3cm) teenager with agility and tremendous leaping ability. Lew Alcindor was also about to become a high school legend.

In Lew's sophomore year, Power overwhelmed New York's high school basketball scene. Behind Alcindor, Power crushed every one in New York in 1962–63. At first, Kareem was pleased with the excitement the team generated at Power, which previously was not a major force in basketball, but then he realized the pressure of "shouldering a thousand people's self-esteem" could be daunting. Everyone said the group was a team, but Lew knew that he was the reason the team had ascended to the top and that everyone expected him to win. It was a burden Kareem would carry for the next twenty-five years.

Power again went undefeated during Lew's junior year, but Lew was offended when Coach Donahue used a racial epithet to try to motivate him. So after his junior year, young Alcindor attended only a few weeks of basketball camp and spent the rest of the summer in New York. It was the mid-sixties, the height of the civil rights movement, and Lew was in search of himself. He went to jazz clubs in the Village, wrote radical journalism on the Harlem riots for a youth newspaper, and played ball. He met Wilt Chamberlain that summer at the legendary Rucker Outdoor Tournament, and Wilt took young Lew under his wing. The two were both jazz buffs and, being giants, had some other things in common, too. In later years, Wilt and Kareem would grow apart, especially politically (Wilt became a Republican, Kareem a Socialist), and they always had contrasting personalities—Wilt was garrulous while Kareem was reserved—but the two men genuinely liked each other in 1964.

In his senior year, Lew and his Power High teammates finally lost a game, against DeMatha High in Maryland. The game was played before fourteen thousand fans at the University of Maryland field house and DeMatha upset Power by 3 points, breaking a string of 71 straight wins. Still, Power won the rest of its games to win the New York title, and was declared the best team in the nation for the second straight season. Lew was a consensus All-American for the third consecutive year and virtually every major college in the country tried to recruit him. Lew "wanted to play good, winning basketball at an insti-

tution that treated its athletes with an element of dignity, under a coach whom I could respect." Of course, Kareem was swayed by other things. When he visited UCLA, he "couldn't imagine why anyone would willingly live anywhere else," and there were "more pretty girls within arm's reach than I'd see all summer cruising the walkways of Central Park." Lew chose to play for John Wooden at UCLA.

Because freshmen were ineligible for varsity basketball in the sixties, Lew played only one big game his freshman year: the freshman recruits against the varsity squad. The UCLA team had won the NCAA title in 1964 and 1965, and had high expectations for the 1966 season (though they would not win the national title). However, no one on the varsity could handle the seven-foot-two-inch (218.4cm) Alcindor, and he scored 31 points in front of a packed house, as the freshmen crushed the varsity players by 15 points. In terms of basketball, Lew spent his freshman year preparing for his sophomore season, learning Wooden's system and working on his skills. Academically and socially, Lew's first year in California was a blast.

Alcindor was ready for all challengers his sophomore season. The Wooden system is very simple: "Run with the basketball, beat the defense down the

Seven-foot-two-inch (218.4cm) UCLA freshman Lew Alcindor slam-dunks the ball over USC's Ron Taylor, who seems either very impressed or very frightened, in the 1966 Bruin-Trojan freshman grudge match. Alcindor's Bruins won handily 108–74 to wrap up a perfect 21–0 season in which the team scored more than 100 points nineteen times. After Alcindor led the UCLA varsity to an undefeated, national championship season in his sophomore year, the NCAA outlawed dunking to try to curtail Lew's domination of the game. In response to this effort to handicap him, Lew developed his patented sky-hook, spending hours in the gym perfecting the virtually unstoppable shot.

court, play good defense yourself, and get the easiest shots you can get." Preparation, rather than rising to the occasion, was the key: "Let others try to raise to our level, we would be there to begin with." Indeed, UCLA swept through the 1966–67 season unblemished. Alcindor dominated everyone he faced from his first game, when he scored 56 points against crosstown rival University of Southern California, to the NCAA finals against upstart Dayton.

In the off-season, the NCAA banned the dunk shot in an effort to curtail Alcindor's dominance, so he began to work harder on his hook shot. In his junior year, Alcindor and UCLA won all their games until they encountered Elvin Hayes and the Houston Cougars in the so-called Game of the Century, played before fifty thousand fans at the Astrodome. UCLA had disposed of the Cougars in the previous year's

NCAA semifinals, but Houston was back, undefeated and ranked number two, on January 20, 1968. Lew, however, had been in the hospital all week after suffering a scratched cornea in a game against California. With Lew playing well below par, scoring only 15 points on 4-for-18 shooting, and Elvin contributing 39 points for the Cougars, UCLA lost its first game of the Alcindor era, 71–69. *Sports Illustrated* put a photo of Hayes, who bragged how he was superior to Lew, scoring over Lew on its cover. Lew didn't complain; instead, he put the magazine cover in his locker for inspiration and hoped for a rematch. The Bruins came back to sweep the remainder of their schedule and breezed through the NCAA regionals. Alcindor, then, got his wish as UCLA and Houston once again squared off in the national semifinals. Elvin scored all of 10 points and the Bruins demolished Houston, 101–69. UCLA then crushed North Carolina by 23 to win their second straight national title.

The Summer Olympics took place between Kareem's junior and senior years, but he chose not to participate, supporting an Olympic boycott by African American athletes intended to highlight racial injustice in the United States. Furthermore, if he played in the Olympics he would graduate late from UCLA. At the same time, Lew's intellectual and spiritual interests were taking him places beyond the realm of college campuses. Lew had always been impressed with the teachings of Malcolm X. When Lew realized he could no longer accept the tenets of Catholicism but still sought a spiritual life, he began investigating the Muslim religion that Malcolm embraced. He soon converted to Islam and changed his name to Kareem Abdul-Jabbar, though he would not assume this name publicly until his third NBA season. Kareem Abdul-Jabbar translates roughly as "generous and powerful servant" (of Allah).

Behind Alcindor, the Bruins once again swept to the national championship in 1968–69, losing only one game, to USC. In Lew's time at UCLA, the Bruins won three consecutive national titles and compiled an astounding 88–2 record, a record unrivaled in the annals of college basketball. Alcindor had perhaps the most complete game of any big man in history: he blocked shots, rebounded, ran the floor well, and had an exceptional low-post pivot game that featured a strong turnaround jumper and an unblockable hook shot. Secretly Alcindor was studying the martial arts. His teacher was none other than legendary film star Bruce Lee. Under Lee's guidance, Jabbar disciplined his concentration. This helped Kareem master his legendary skyhook. Because Kareem stood at seven feet two inches (218.4cm), it was difficult enough to block one of his shots, but he launched his skyhook a good foot and a half (45.7cm) directly over his head while he elevated off the ground. Hook shots are tremendously difficult to master because shooting a basketball involves coordinating three elements: the ball, the basket, and the shooter's eyes. For a conventional jump shot the ball is brought up directly in front of

RIGHT: Kareem posts up against Celtic Dave Cowens and awaits an inlet pass. A master in the low post by the time he reached the NBA, Kareem used his skyhook and spin moves to take extremely high-percentage shots and was also brilliant at passing the ball to an open teammate when he got double- or triple-teamed. Jabbar understood that it was essential to get his teammates involved in the offense in order to win.
BELOW: Kareem and Wilt look like two sumo wrestlers about to rumble as they face off for the first time in the NBA on November 21, 1970. Kareem has stepped away from his familiar position on the low post in order to face the basket, put the ball on the floor, and take Wilt one-on-one. Wilt seems to have other ideas. The Bucks' Oscar Robertson (Number 1) and Tom Dandridge (Number 10) offer Kareem other options, but Jabbar seems intent on challenging his legendary predecessor. While Jabbar almost never put the ball on the floor and drove to the basket during the second decade of his NBA career, it was in his repertoire when he was still a young Buck.

Kareem uses his tremendous wingspan to nab a rebound from Laker Gail Goodrich. Those who claim that Jabbar was weak on the boards for someone his height probably only saw him play late in his career. Kareem was a dominant rebounder in his prime. In his first decade in the NBA, Jabbar garnered 11,460 rebounds (which would be the fifteenth-highest career total), averaging 14.8 per game (sixth-best ever). He finished among the league's top five rebounders in each of his eight full seasons, winning the 1975–76 rebounding title with a 16.9 average. In contrast, Kareem only controlled 5,980 boards in his second NBA decade, for a 7.6 average. His career total of 17,440 rebounds is the third-highest in NBA history, behind Chamberlain and Russell.

the shooter's eyes, which makes it easier to gauge the trajectory necessary to reach the basket. With a hook shot, the ball never passes in front of the shooter's eyes, making the shooter gauge the trajectory necessary to sink the basket from a place he cannot see (above and behind his head). It takes tremendous discipline and concentration to master the shot. Bruce Lee's lessons helped Kareem perfect the skyhook, and the giant entered the NBA with the most lethal offensive weapon in the history of the sport.

After a complicated negotiation period in which the ABA's New York Nets tried to lure Alcindor away from the NBA, Lew signed a contract to play for the Milwaukee Bucks, an expansion team that finished its inaugural 1968–69 season with an abysmal 27–55 record. A devout Muslim in the Midwest, Alcindor didn't exactly blend into Milwaukee society, but the fans loved him and came in droves to see him play. It had to be a tough season for Lew. He lost far more games than he had in all of high school and college combined. Still, the single-season turnaround was the greatest in NBA history at that point as the Bucks improved to 56–26, the second-best mark in the NBA. Kareem grabbed 14.5 rebounds and scored 28.8 points per game, making him a consensus choice for Rookie of the Year. Bill Russell had retired after the previous season and Wilt Chamberlain missed all but six games that season because of an injury, so

Jabbar didn't face the two dominant centers of the previous generation. In the playoffs, the Bucks ousted the 76ers easily but were then excused by the Knicks in five games. The Knicks matched up well against the Bucks because New York center Willis Reed not only had a strong post-up game but also a good outside shot. Since man-to-man defense was required in the NBA, Kareem was unable to defend the middle against the Knicks as he could against other teams whose centers could not shoot from outside. The Bucks did not have a strong power forward to support Kareem in the middle and help on the defensive glass; the Knicks took advantage of this weakness.

The hype surrounding Alcindor was huge that first season. Hounded by the media in every city in which he played, he did not endear himself to the fourth estate with his brusque demeanor. Kareem also quickly recognized the sharp contrast between the pro and college experiences: "In the pros you may play as often as four times a week, and the preparation is less emotional than intellectual and physical. The best way to describe it is, overwhelming; you have to devote all your energy and time to your work. If you don't, you lose. It is your work; you are being paid to do this well. With more exertion and less emotion involved, you don't get the exhilaration that you can in college. The pros become a grind, a well-paying grind—you are being paid thousands of dollars a

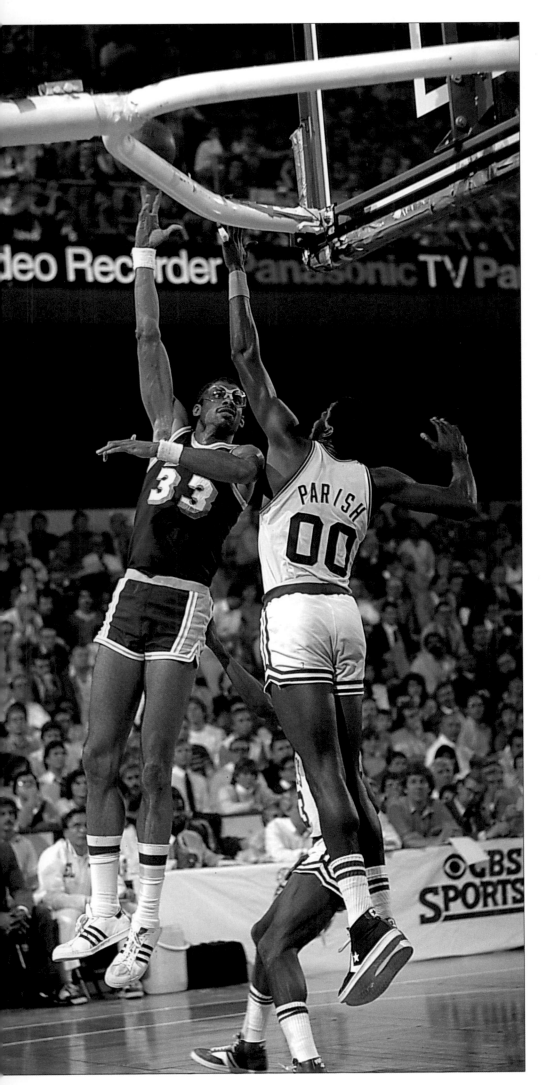

game—but a grind nevertheless. Winning is acceptable. Losing is costing somebody money. In the pros, I found, the game is very rarely fun."

In 1981, David Halberstam made these related observations about Jabbar: "He played with conservation of energy that befit a man in a league where there could be over a hundred games in a season and, worse, he played with conservation of emotion. That for the fans was the hardest thing to accept. He played hard but his style was cool. One could imagine him playing and listening to a Miles Davis cassette at the same time, playing to his own mood and tempo, not to the tempo of the crowd, in the process putting distance between himself and the fifteen or twenty thousand who had come to see him. It was as if he held back the part of him that should have said he cared. The crowd cared, its lives in other areas were sufficiently incomplete; this game, this minute, this basket, mattered; the crowd wanted him to care as well. He did not deny them his skills or even, in a curious way, his passion; rather he denied them passion revealed....He was...the perfect product of the NBA machinery: he understood the mechanics of the league, the demands of its schedule, and he understood how to keep his integrity while adjusting to the rhythm of the league." Thus, while journalists and fans had trouble accepting Kareem throughout his career, other NBA players recognized his greatness and "were in genuine awe of Kareem and what he did every night, and the burden which, as so great a player, he brought to every game."

The great Oscar Robertson joined the Bucks at the start of the 1970–71 season, and once again, the team improved dramatically. Milwaukee tore up the league, finishing with a 66–16 record, 14 games better than any other team in the league. Kareem led the league in scoring with a 31.7 average, collected 16 rebounds a game, and won the league's MVP Award. In the playoffs, the Bucks trampled the Warriors and Lakers in five games each and then swept the Bullets in the finals. In only his second year in the NBA, Kareem had lifted an expansion team to the championship, certainly one of the most astounding feats in league history.

The next season, Kareem won both the scoring title with a career-high 34.8 average, and the MVP

Jabbar releases his signature shot over Celtic center Robert Parish in the 1984 finals. Kareem's skyhook was the single most lethal offensive weapon in the history of basketball. Opposing centers had no hope of disrupting the shot, which was released about ten feet (3m) off the ground, on the other side of Kareem's body, and with a slight arc. Usually Kareem could catch an inlet pass, turn, and shoot the skyhook before the arrival of a double-team. When a second defender did reach Kareem in time to prevent the skyhook (by cutting off Kareem's mobility to his right), it was usually a trap designed to free up a teammate for an easy basket. So for twenty years, opponents mostly gazed up at the graceful skyhook and hoped Kareem was off target. He rarely was. Within fifteen feet (4.5m), Kareem buried skyhooks like clockwork. The league's most prolific scorer was also among the most efficient: his .559 career field goal percentage ranks ninth all-time.

Award again. The Bucks finished with the exact record, 62–15, against every team in the league excluding the Lakers as they had the previous year—except the Lakers. In 1970–71 they had beaten the Lakers four times and lost to them once, while in 1971–72 they were 1–4 against the Lakers and Wilt Chamberlain. From 1970 to 1973, the Kareem-Wilt matchups supplanted the Chamberlain-Russell battles of the previous generation. For the most part, the newcomer had the upper hand. Wilt, though powerful beneath the boards, didn't have the quickness to follow Jabbar away from the basket—and no one, not even Wilt, could stuff the skyhook. By 1973 Kareem was having his way with Wilt, and the veteran clearly resented it, accusing Jabbar of trying to show him up. This perceived affront disturbed Wilt particularly because he had been so kind to Kareem back in 1964. But Jabbar stated that if he tried any harder against Wilt it was because Wilt was a great center, and if he did not put out the extra effort, Wilt would have had his way with him. Anyway, Jabbar had to do everything in his power to help the Bucks against the Lakers. Los Angeles really came together as a team in 1972, producing the best regular-season record in history and a record 33-game winning streak (which the Bucks finally ended). In the playoffs, the Lakers faced the defending champion Bucks in the Western Conference finals. However, Oscar Robertson had gotten injured in the previous series, leaving the Bucks undermanned. The Lakers took the series in six games, despite Kareem's individual brilliance.

The next few years were very difficult for Kareem. His Muslim mentor's whole family was murdered by members of a rival religious sect in a house that Kareem owned. Jabbar, for whose life the authorities feared, had to skip the 1973 All-Star Game. A few years later his mentor snapped as a result of the tragedy and the lack of justice that had followed, and he and eleven gunmen took over three buildings on Embassy Row in Washington and held hostages. The event made headlines around the world. When the standoff ended, more people were dead and the religious community into which Kareem had invested so much of himself was in shambles. Still, he found solace in his faith and his basketball game.

Throughout the seventies Jabbar was the NBA's greatest star. However, Kareem's supporting cast in Milwaukee was getting thinner, not stronger. As one of the league's elite teams the Bucks never had good draft picks, and as a young franchise it consisted, except for Kareem, of a mishmash of journeymen and veterans. Still, in 1974 the Bucks made it back to the NBA finals, only to lose to the Boston Celtics in seven games, again despite Jabbar's brilliance. But Oscar Robertson retired after that year, and when Kareem missed six weeks because of injuries, the Bucks failed to make the 1975 playoffs. With his contract expiring, Kareem asked the Bucks to trade him, hoping to return to New York. However, a deal with the Knicks fell through and Kareem ended up being traded to the Los Angeles Lakers, who sent virtually

all their promising young talent to Milwaukee in order to get the rights to Kareem. Consequently, Jabbar had to carry the whole load his first season in L.A. And, though he won his fourth MVP Award and his first rebounding title, the Lakers missed the playoffs. The next season the Lakers started to assemble a decent supporting cast and climbed atop the league with the best regular-season record. However, injuries to two starters depleted the squad for the playoffs, opening the way for Bill Walton and the Portland Trail Blazers to eliminate L.A. in the Western Conference finals. The next year, Kareem's frustration exploded onto the court and he and his teammates were involved in many brawls, one of which left Kareem injured for a month. The club's reputation was considered such a blight to the league that the NBA offices put pressure on L.A. management to dismantle the team. Thus, the strong nucleus from the previous season dissipated and L.A. floundered in the playoffs again. In 1978–79, the Lakers again constructed a decent but flawed team; Kareem was the only player left from the Laker team that had finished with the league's best record only two seasons earlier. In the playoffs, L.A. was overcome by the power-house, and eventual champion, Seattle Supersonics.

Magic Johnson joined the Lakers for the 1979–80 season along with two strong power forwards, Jim Chones and Spencer Haywood, to give Kareem support down low. It was still Kareem's team, but the added support alleviated much of the pressure on him. He collected his record sixth MVP Award, averaged almost 11 rebounds and 25 points per game, and led the Lakers to the NBA title. Behind Magic and Kareem, the Lakers would capture four more NBA championships in the 1980s.

By the late eighties, the media's animosity toward Kareem and the public's suspicion of him had worn off and he was fully embraced as a true marvel. On April 5, 1984, Kareem surpassed Chamberlain's all-time NBA scoring mark. Before he retired, Kareem went on to compile almost 7,000 more points, giving him a remarkable total of 38,387. In his final three years, Kareem's talents diminished, especially during his final season, but he remained an offensive threat. His ability to draw the double-team and make sharp passes, always one of his greatest skills, meant that he remained an integral part of a championship dynasty. It was no coincidence that the Lakers failed to reach the finals for the first time in four seasons the year after he retired.

Larry Bird summarized the feeling about Kareem in the NBA: "I have all the respect in the world for what Kareem was able to do. Playing twenty years in this league is almost beyond comprehension....In '85 he was shooting [the skyhook] from the corner like it was a layup. It didn't matter how old he was, when you needed a basket, you'd want Kareem shooting that skyhook." From fourteen-year-old Lew Alcindor to forty-two-year-old Kareem Abdul-Jabbar, the scope and superb quality of his career reached a plateau that will never be matched.

JULIUS Erving

The ABA's greatest legend and arguably the most spectacular basketball player ever, Julius Erving, alias Dr. J, sails towards the basket during the 1976 ABA championship series between his New York Nets and the Denver Nuggets. Defensive stalwart Bobby Jones, a future teammate of Erving's, hangs suspended alongside the Doctor in a valiant effort to turn back the legend. Like Elgin Baylor before him and the young Michael Jordan after him, Dr. J often took to the air when driving to the basket and made the necessary adjustments in midflight to beat the defense. Erving in particular had such great body control and ability to manuever the ball when floating toward the basket that he would deceive defenders with midair fakes, forcing opponents to commit to defending phantom shots, in order to clear a path for a real shot. In his prime, Dr. J frequently offered two, three, or more such fakes during just one of his gravity-defying forays to the hoop.

In the mid-seventies, Julius Erving, known as Dr. J, was a living legend. Playing in the ABA, Dr. J's games were rarely televised. Many fans learned of his spectacular, mesmerizing feats only by word of mouth. Everyone who saw him in person—fans, announcers, other players—were in awe of him. He attained a mythical stature. The public's desire to see him play was so great that NBA owners felt tremendous pressure to accept a merger with the ABA in order to bring Dr. J into the league.

No player in basketball history, including Michael Jordan, affected an audience like Dr. J. His moves, the spectacular body control he exhibited in midair, and the power and grace of his dunks electrified crowds. At home or on the road, fans went wild with delight upon seeing the Doctor operate. A spectacular dunk by Erving often changed the entire tempo of a game because of the fans' exuberance. Knowing this, Dr. J made even uncontested dunks spectacular. On a breakaway, the crowd would rise in anticipation and then explode with joy over Julius' spectacular improvisation. Even more impressive was when Julius beat the man guarding him and drove the lane against another couple of defenders. The Doctor would take to the air—somehow maneuvering in midflight around and between his foes—and, at the last second, reach out and jam the ball home with authority. Erving was beyond spectacular: he frequently did things that did not seem possible. Watching him was a transformative experience. The mystique and thrill he brought to the sport changed basketball forever.

• • •

Julius Winfield Erving II was born in Roosevelt, New York, on February 22, 1950. Julius grew up in this working-class suburb of New York City on Long Island, where he learned to play basketball in the playgrounds. He earned his nickname, the Doctor, which would evolve into Dr. J, while at Roosevelt High. Erving explained: "A friend of mine kept telling me he was going to be a professor, so I told him I was going to be a doctor. We just started calling each other that, professor and doctor. And later on, in the Rucker League in Harlem, when people started calling me Black Moses and Houdini, I told them if they wanted to call me anything, call me 'doctor'." Erving starred in the Rucker League and in high school, but he was not widely recruited and, thus, chose to attend the University of Massachusetts, which did not yet have a strong roundball tradition.

Consequently, Julius did not get much attention nationally. He was, however, a dominant force, becoming the seventh player in college history to average 20 points and 20 rebounds per game over the course of his career. Occasionally, a New Englander would comment that Erving was the greatest talent in college at the time, but few people listened because Erving was a man among boys in the Yankee Conference. In his junior year, he led UMass to the postseason NIT, then declared himself ready for the pros. As a nongraduating collegian, his best bet for a contract was in the renegade ABA. After some backroom negotiations, Julius Erving signed a contract with the Virginia Squires of the ABA.

When Erving showed up at the Squires' tryout camp, no one really knew what to expect. But once he was on the court, Erving absolutely dominated the scrimmage, running past everyone for dunks. The coaches took him out, fearing that he would be undercut in midair. General Manager Johnny Kerr recalled: "Julius was on the floor for a few minutes in that tryout camp and then a shot banged against the back of the rim and went straight up. It was one of those rebounds where it seems that all five players were jumping for it. Out of the middle of the pack came Julius...up...up...up. He cupped the rebound with one hand and then slammed it through the rim, all in one motion. The gym went silent. All the players just stopped for a few seconds. This was a tryout camp and I had just watched one of the best plays I had ever seen in my life. That's when I told coach Al Bianchi to get Julius off the court."

Erving combined considerable size (six feet seven inches [200.6cm], 200 pounds [90.8kg]), unbelievable jumping ability, and in-air agility with another amazing resource: his hands. Squires Coach Bianchi measured Erving's hands and found that they were twelve inches (30.4cm) from the base of the palm to the fingertips; when he spread his hand, it was eleven inches (27.9cm) from the pinky to the thumb. Throughout the course of Erving's career, players would marvel at his hands. For instance, Bobby Gross, who had to guard Erving during the 1977 NBA finals, said: "The Doctor's hands. They were huge and yet surprisingly delicate, with extremely long fingers." It was odd, Gross suspected, for a player to be so fascinated with another player's hands, but Julius Erving had beautiful hands. "They allowed him to hold the ball lightly and yet still control it, to do tricks with the ball, to drive past the bas-

ket and then at the last minute to score by putting all sorts of different spins and reverse spins on the ball in ways denied mere mortals with mortal hands."

Virginia's small forward, George Carter, had been an ABA all-star the year before, but he was traded by the end of training camp to open a place for Erving. The Squires' first exhibition game was against the Kentucky Colonels and seven-foot-two-inch (218.4cm) Artis Gilmore, a great shot blocker. On a break, Julius flew right over Artis and dunked on him. When the Doctor drove the baseline, Gilmore moved over for a block, but Erving floated right past him, under the basket, and made a reverse layup. Every time out, Julius amazed. Said Johnny Kerr, "A young Julius Erving was like Thomas Edison. He was inventing something new every night." The Squires had found a diamond in the rough.

In Julius' rookie year, 1971–72, he amazed the fans of the ABA with countless spectacular moves and led the Squires to a second-place finish in the Eastern Division. Erving, now known as Dr. J, led the team in scoring with a 27.3 average, fifth in the league, and in rebounding with 15.7, third in the ABA. In the playoffs, the Doctor really took off, averaging 20 rebounds, 32 points, and 17 assists per game. The Squires swept Florida in four straight games and then lost to the New York Nets and Rick Barry in seven games. During the Nets series fans flocked to the games to see the Doctor. In his second season Julius led the ABA in scoring with a 31.9 average, though the Squires weakened to .500 and were eliminated by the powerful Colonels in the first round of the playoffs. In the off-season Erving was traded to the ABA's New York Nets.

The Nets were 34–50 in 1972–73; in 1973–74, they finished in first place at 55–29 and won the ABA championship. The difference was Dr. J; he averaged 27.4 points (tops in the ABA), 10.7 rebounds, and 5.1 assists per game, and shot 52 per-cent. He won the league and playoff MVP Awards. The Nets struggled early to find the right chemistry and then became a terror. In the playoffs, they swept to the title, winning 12 of 14 games. And with his inexhaustible repertoire of exhilarating and unstop-pable moves, displayed in the world's media center, Dr. J became a legend. The Nets looked to repeat in the spring of 1975 after a marvelous regular season, but in one of basketball's greatest upsets they were ousted by the Spirits of St. Louis in the first round.

Perhaps the seminal event in ABA history was the first-ever slam-dunk contest held at halftime of the 1976 league All-Star Game in Denver. Five all-stars were selected to compete, but it came down to Denver's own high-flyin' David Thompson and the Doctor. The other all-stars could spend intermission in the locker room, but they all stayed to watch. From the left side Erving did his "iron cross dunk," where he jumped by the basket, spread his arms like he was flying, and dunked behind him "without ever looking at the rim." Thompson retaliated with an in-air 360-degree reverse slam. With each dunk the crowd went

wild with appreciation. For his standstill dunk Erving slammed home two balls, one in each hand, in one jump. Thompson, however, outdid both the Doctor and himself, producing a reverse dunk from the standstill position. Then Dr. J brought down the house as he approached the basket from the right side grabbed the rim with his right hand, swung under the basket, and dunked with his left hand. Thompson actually missed his next dunk, so if Erving made his final dunk, the contest was his. Erving went to the foul line, turned around, and start-ed walking toward the other direction. The crowd began to cheer, anticipating that the Doctor was going to try to dunk from the free throw line with a running start. As he paced off, the roar increased from the audience. Then as he turned and faced the basket from about three-quarters court, silence fell over the auditorium. Denver's general manager, Carl Scheer, related the event: "Julius stared at the basket for a moment. Then he took off with his long, majes-tic strides. The arena was so quiet you could hear his every step as his shoes touched the floor. I can still see that long galloping stride as if he were an ante-lope, so graceful he was. Then he was off, in the air, and he brought the ball back from behind himself somewhere as if he were a helicopter. He rammed it through the rim, and only when the ball hit the floor did the crowd react. People just went crazy."

The Nets rebounded in 1975–76 behind Dr. J, who once again led the league in scoring with a 29.3 average and won his third-straight league MVP. The Nets faced the Denver Nuggets in the finals. The Nuggets had not only Thompson and Dan Issel, but also Bobby Jones, considered the ABA's best defensive forward. Against Jones, Erving averaged 37.6 points and 14.2 rebounds per game and shot 60 percent as the Nets won the series in six games.

After the season, the ABA merged with the NBA. The Indiana Pacers, the San Antonio Spurs, the Nuggets, and the Nets joined the NBA. Before the next season, the financially troubled Nets sold Erving to the Philadelphia 76ers. Public interest in the NBA reached record levels during the 1976–77 season, primarily because of the mythical Dr. J.

The Sixers instantly became the NBA's high profile team with such stars as George McGinnis, Lloyd Free, and the Doctor. Plagued by infighting (which the ever-graceful Doctor stayed out of), the 76ers won their division and advanced to the NBA finals, in which they faced a well-balanced, disciplined Portland Trail Blazers team anchored by Bill Walton. Though Erving was adored by fans and foes alike, the media and other basketball people cast the Sixers as the bad guys against the protagonist Blazers. It was deemed a matchup between unruly street ball and practitioners of textbook basketball. Dr. J was spectacular in the finals, but the rest of his teammates failed to provide him with much support, and the Blazers upset the favored Sixers in six games.

Over the next few years the 76ers tried to find the proper chemistry to complement the Doctor. Gone were McGinnis and Free; in were team players like Bobby Jones, guard Maurice Cheeks, and ex–Trail Blazer Lionel Hollins. Dr. J was clearly one of the league's prime talents, but he was never a great outside shooter, so the Sixers relied heavily on the threat of sharpshooting guards whom Erving could pass to when defenses collapsed on him during his drives to the basket. In 1980, the Sixers made it back to the finals, but lost to the Lakers. In 1981, Erving had his best year in the NBA, scoring 24.6 points per game to go with 8 rebounds and 4.5 assists. The Sixers tied for the best record in the NBA and the Doctor was named league MVP. But after leading the series three games to one, the Sixers fell to the Celtics in the Eastern Conference finals. In 1982, the 76ers once again reached the finals, only to lose to Los Angeles.

Help, however, was on its way in the form of awesome "power center" Moses Malone. Up until 1982–83, Dr. J's NBA career was rife with success, but defined by failure. His had been the most ballyhooed arrival in league history, yet every spring the high-flying, well-paid Sixers failed to capture the crown. With Moses, the Sixers were a different team. They tore through the league and the playoffs. In the finals, they dismissed the Lakers in four straight games. The Doctor finally earned his NBA ring.

During the next four years, the Sixers remained strong but never seriously challenged for the title. Julius Erving retired in 1987 as an elder statesman; over his career he proved himself to be an utmost gentleman and one of the most eloquent figures in American sports. The grace with which he departed from the NBA was in contrast to the awesome force

with which he exploded into the world of professional basketball. Of Dr. J in his prime, David Halberstam wrote: "Erving dunked with such power, force, grace and originality—each move seemed invented at the very moment he made it—that it was not simply a matter of scoring two points. His moves electrified not just his teammates, but the crowd as well." And he raised basketball to a new level.

JOHN Havlicek

John Havlicek tries to move past Jerry West while Bill Russell watches nearby. No player ever fit the Celtic mold as perfectly as John Havlicek. Thoroughly versatile, Havlicek could play guard or forward and had very good, though not great, shooting, passing, rebounding, and dribbling skills. He played tenacious defense, continually disrupting the other team's rhythm. Havlicek never stopped hustling and always played smart.

In 1969–70, the year after Bill Russell's retirement, the Boston Celtics dropped to sixth place in the Eastern Conference and failed to make the play-offs. Having won eleven NBA titles in Russell's thirteen years, the Celtics were in need of rebuilding. Celtic fans anticipated a long dry spell. Miraculously, Boston rebounded to win the Eastern Division only two years later with a mix of new faces and old veterans. Foremost among the holdovers from the dynasty was forward-guard John Havlicek. When the Celtics won the championship in 1974 and again in 1976, Havlicek was the heart and soul of the team. An integral part of the sixties dynasty, the man they called the Green Running Machine bridged the gap between two great Celtics teams.

• • •

John Havlicek was born in the small town of Martins Ferry, Ohio, on April 8, 1940. While growing up, John was a tremendous athlete, excelling at baseball, football, swimming, and basketball. In high school, John earned a letter in all four sports, but was most gifted in football. Though his team was mediocre, John was named all-state quarterback. Legendary Ohio State Coach Woody Hayes offered Havlicek a scholarship to play football at Ohio State, but John decided that his future was in roundball.

Havlicek met Ohio hoop stars Larry Siegfried and Jerry Lucas at some postseason high school all-star games, and the three decided to attend Ohio State and play for the basketball team. Having been offered

a football scholarship, John was able to win a basketball scholarship, to the dismay of Coach Hayes. Together, Siegfried, Havlicek, and Lucas formed the backbone of Ohio State's greatest basketball team. The Buckeyes compiled a 78–6 record during the time the three were on the varsity, winning consecutive Big Ten titles, reaching the Final Four each year, and winning the national championship their junior year, 1960.

However, of the three, Lucas was the big name. Havlicek was a solid six-foot-five-inch (195.5cm) forward who could score (he averaged 14.6 points and 8.6 rebounds per game during his college career) and play tenacious defense, but he was not considered a future star. So when the Cleveland Browns drafted Havlicek in the seventh round of the NFL draft, he decided to give football another shot. Placed at wide receiver, Havlicek played in one exhibition game, and was cut. Celtics Coach Red Auerbach later commented that "the biggest mistake the Cleveland Browns ever made was when they let him go, because they were trying him for end when in my opinion he would have been the greatest—the greatest—defensive back in the history of pro football." Regardless, John's days on the gridiron were over and he signed with the Celtics.

Havlicek's disciplined, hardworking style fit in perfectly with the Celtic machine. Most Celtic rookies rarely played, but Red Auerbach used Havlicek at guard. John's feisty defense was invaluable and he contributed offensively, especially during fast breaks, when his speed came in handy. He averaged more than 14 points per game in his rookie season and earned a larger role as the season progressed.

In Havlicek's second season, 1962–63, he took over the role of the Celtics' sixth man. Auerbach had previously used Frank Ramsey in this capacity. The idea of the sixth man was that he would enter the game midway through the first and third quarters and provide a lift to the Celtics when the starters for both teams were starting to tire. Like Ramsey, Havlicek became as integral a part of the Celtics team as any player (except, of course, Russell). Havlicek evolved into a scoring machine as the sixth man. On the wings during the fast break or from the outside in a set offense, Havlicek fulfilled the role of the sixth man by providing an instant offensive spark. John played as many minutes as the starters and led the team in scoring with almost 20 points per game.

In the 1964–65 season, Havlicek once again sparkled in his role and made a play in the playoffs that will forever be renowned in Celtic lore. The Celtics ran away with first place in the Eastern Conference with their best record yet, 62–18. But in the conference finals they faced a powerful Philadelphia team with Wilt Chamberlain, who had joined the 76ers at midseason. The teams split the first six games of the series, each winning its home games. In the decisive seventh game, Boston led 110–109 with 5 seconds remaining and had the ball out-of-bounds, under its own basket. Bill Russell tried to pass the ball in but hit one of the support wires that held up the basket, which, by rule, was a turnover. The Sixers had the ball and a chance to end the Celtic string of championships at six. Boston called time-out. When the players took the court, the Sixers had Hal Greer take the ball out-of-bounds. The Sixers' plan was to inbound the ball to Chet Walker and have Johnny Kerr set a pick for Walker, to free him for the final shot. Chamberlain would be a decoy because of his troubles at the foul line. As Greer tried to inbound the ball, Havlicek stayed close to Walker. Greer had 5 seconds to get the ball in, so Havlicek was counting "one thousand one, one thousand two, one thousand three...." When Havlicek reached "one thousand four," he looked back at Greer and saw he was going to lob a pass to Walker above the top of the key. Sixers' coach Dolph Schayes recalled that

During the Celtics' renaissance in the mid-seventies, only Havlicek and Don Nelson remained from the sixties dynasty. Havlicek's roots in the dynasty proved valuable as the Celtics rebuilt. Havlicek helped his former teammate, Coach Tom Heinsohn, teach the Celtic playbook to new comers. More significantly, Hondo was a living, playing, running, hustling, clutch-shooting example of what it took to be a true champion, i.e., a true Boston Celtic. Of course, this former teammate of Bob Cousy's made other contributions as well: Havlicek led the champion Celtics in scoring in 1973–74.

"Walker and Havlicek went for the pass like an end and a defensive back." With his look back, Havlicek knew Greer's pass was a little short and he leaped up and tipped it to Celtic Sam Jones. Boston announcer Johnny Most immortalized the proceedings with his famous call: "Havlicek stole the ball! Havlicek stole the ball!" Russell came up to John, then hugged and thanked him. The Celtics, of course, went on to win another title.

A selfless and tireless player, Havlicek fit in perfectly with the dynastic Celtics. John was not the star of his team in college, but he was a great team player; the Celtics were a great team unit. Late in his career, when he was already a legend, Havlicek stated: "I am not, and never have been, a one-on-one player. The Celtics were the perfect team for me." The man Havlicek replaced as the Celtics' sixth man, Frank Ramsey, summed up John's early days: "He could run all day, he loved to play defense, and he had a conservative personality that fit in well with the team." "My game," John said, "has always been to go as hard as I can, as long as I can." The Celtics' running offense and team concept were ideal for Havlicek, and Havlicek was ideal for the Celtics.

After Auerbach passed on the coaching reigns to Bill Russell and forward Tom Heinsohn retired, Havlicek moved into the starting lineup. As a starter, Havlicek led the Celtics in scoring for the next eight years and also became their leading assist man. The Celtics won two titles with Russell as player-coach and then the great center retired. Suddenly, Havlicek

was the team's leading star and a link to their glory years. However, the Celtics plummeted out of contention in 1969–70. In 1970–71, the team began to improve behind John's scoring; he finished second in the league to Kareem Abdul-Jabbar with a 28.9 average, at the time the highest in Celtic history. A rookie center named Dave Cowens showed great promise that year. The next year, the Celtics finished 56–26, first in their division, though the Knicks bounced them from the playoffs; John averaged 27.5 per game. In 1972–73, the Celtics finished with the best record in the history of the storied franchise at 68–14. The team had Cowens at center, veteran Don Nelson (who played alongside Russell for four seasons) and Havlicek at forward, Don Chaney and JoJo White at guard, and power forward Paul Silas coming off the bench as the sixth man. Unfortunately, the Knicks once again ended the Celtics' season in the playoffs.

By the spring of 1974, the team had matured and advanced in the playoffs to face the Milwaukee Bucks and the great Kareem Abdul-Jabbar in the finals. The series was a classic. The Celtics led three games to two and had a chance to close out the series at home. However, the Bucks hung tough and Kareem was hot. Game Six was tied at the end of regulation. Then Havlicek and Jabbar took over, each making one clutch shot after another. The score was still tied after the first overtime. In the second overtime, the Bucks went ahead by 1 point with 30 seconds left to play. The Celtics brought the ball downcourt and Cowens set a pick for Havlicek, who got the ball in the corner. With the seven-foot-two-inch (218.4cm) Jabbar jumping out at him, Havlicek had to alter the shot, sending a towering rainbow toward the basket; he hit nothing but net. The Celtics led with only seconds left, but Kareem would match Havlicek on the other end and force a Game Seven. Havlicek had scored 9 of the Celtics' 11 points in overtime and once again shown the nation that he was a true superstar. When the Celtics rebounded to triumph in Game Seven at Milwaukee, John was named the playoff MVP. Havlicek and Company had restored the Celtic tradition. In 1976, Boston captured another NBA crown with a victory over Phoenix in the finals. It was the Celtics' thirteenth title, and it was number eight for the Green Running Machine.

In the early seventies, Havlicek was more than the Celtics' star and an inspirational figure from the dynasty. He assisted Coach Tom Heinsohn in making sure new players learned the Celtic system, from the heralded fast break to set plays in the half court offense. As Havlicek's career came to a close, he was received as a hero at arenas across the land. He also retired as the NBA's third leading scorer, behind only Wilt Chamberlain and Oscar Robertson. Sadly, the Celtics declined rapidly after 1976 and failed to make the playoffs in 1978, John's final year.

John Havlicek was a consummate Celtic: skilled, aggressive, and, foremost, a great team player. Red Auerbach said it best: "Havlicek is an example of what the Celtics are all about."

RICK Barry

At six feet seven inches (200.6cm) and 220 pounds (99.8kg), forward Rick Barry could do it all on the court: shoot, drive, pass, rebound, and—better than almost anyone in the history of the NBA—bury free throws. At age twenty-three, he led the NBA in scoring with a higher single-season point total than anyone ever except Wilt Chamberlain and Michael Jordan, and Barry's team, the Warriors, reached the league finals. At thirty-one, Barry once again averaged more than 30 points per game and the Warriors won the NBA crown. Sadly, during the seven years in between these great accomplishments, Barry was, in his own words, "a basketball gypsy," jumping from team to team in the ABA during the prime of his career. Barry did wonders for the upstart league and for future free agents, but he damaged his own career irreparably. Nevertheless, Rick's accomplishments during the short time that he was in the NBA established his place among basketball's all-time greats.

● ● ●

Richard Francis Dennis Barry III was born on March 28, 1944, in Elizabeth, New Jersey. Rick's dad was his first basketball coach, at Saints Peter and Paul Grammar School, where he schooled his pupils in the fundamentals of the game; he was hardest on Rick. But the lessons Rick had received from birth paid off, and he became a high school basketball star.

Rick had thirty-five to forty college scholarship offers, but he decided on the University of Miami because he was impressed with Coach Bruce Hale's sincerity. By the time Rick joined the varsity as a sophomore, he was a sleek six-foot-seven-inch (200.6cm) 190-pounder (86.2kg) with a smooth outside shot and tenacity on the boards; he could also drive the lane. Hale convinced Barry that he had pro potential and that he should not stop working to improve his game. In his junior year, Rick averaged 16 rebounds and 32 points per game, and the Hurricanes went to the NIT. As a senior, Rick was even better, with his averages improving to 18 rebounds and a nation-high 37 points per game. The team, meanwhile, posted a 22–4 mark, but was excluded from postseason play because of a minor recruiting violation. A consensus All-American his senior year, Rick was a player of unrelenting drive and a perfectionist—a consummate competitor.

The San Francisco Warriors drafted Barry in the first round. The team showed promise in 1965–66; Rick averaged 25 points and 10 rebounds as a rookie,

but center Nate Thurmond got injured late in the season and the Warriors missed the playoffs by a game.

The next season the Warriors dismissed legendary coach Alex Hannum and hired former Celtics great Bill Sharman. Barry was unhappy about the move and disliked playing for Sharman. However, the Warriors matured as a team that year and won the NBA Western Division. Barry became the team's top star, scoring 35.6 points per game to lead the league (thus snapping Wilt Chamberlain's string of seven consecutive scoring titles). Barry's explanation of his phenomenal scoring ability show both his modesty and the tremendous expectations he had for himself: "My philosophy of scoring is simple. I think it's easy to be a scorer if you have good talent and are willing to work at it. Without doing anything else but hustling on fast breaks I'll get at least 10 easy points a game. If I drive ten times, I'll get 10 more points. On fast breaks and drives, I'll get fouled and go to the line ten times and make 8 or 9 of them. The ball is going to pop to you by sheer chance a few times, so you'll make 1 or 2 garbage baskets if you're alert. Now I have 30 points and haven't taken an outside shot....If I score 3 or 4 baskets and 2 or 3 free throws a quarter I've got my 35 points a game....What I ask

Rick Barry takes a breather during his first stint with the Warriors. Had Barry remained with the Warriors after leading them to the NBA finals in 1967, instead of jumping to the upstart ABA for five "lost" years, and played roughly as well as he did before and after his hiatus, Rick Barry might rank in the top echelon of all-time NBA greats. A Warriors team with a nucleus of Rick Barry and seven-foot (213.3) defensive great Nate Thurmond, both in their prime, would probably have altered the outcome of a few seasons between 1968 and 1972. In Barry's first year back, the Warriors eliminated Jabbar's Bucks from the 1973 postseason.

Rick Barry concentrates on the basket as he prepares to shoot one of his patented underhand free throws, for the San Francisco Warriors. This unorthodox technique produced exquisite results: Rick made 90 percent of his free throws in the NBA and 88 percent in the ABA. Barry's foul shooting was a potent offensive weapon; not only was Rick skilled at drawing fouls when he drove to the basket, but he also could recognize when a defender was playing him softly (for fear of sending him to the charity stripe), take advantage of the situation, and score.

of myself is well within reason." He makes it sound like anyone could do it. Of course, Barry's point totals were always helped by his amazing free throw shooting. Using an archaic underhand motion, Barry had the highest career free throw percentage in NBA history, 90 percent (though after eight seasons in the NBA, Mark Price of the Cleveland Cavaliers has a 90.6 percent lifetime average).

The Warriors opened the 1967 playoffs by sweeping the Lakers of Elgin Baylor and Jerry West. They then defeated the powerful St. Louis Hawks with Lenny Wilkens, Zelmo Beatty, and Lou Hudson in six games. In only his second season in the NBA, Barry was the league scoring champ and had led his team to the finals. There the Warriors faced Wilt and Company: the Philadelphia 76ers. The Sixers' coach was Alex Hannum, who Barry still believed should be running the Warriors. Hannum had guided his talented lot of Sixers to the best regular-season record in history and past the dynastic Celtics in the playoffs. The series was closer than expected; the Sixers won in six hard-fought games. Barry averaged 41 points per game and felt that the Warriors should have won the championship—after all, they had lost Game One in overtime and the decisive contest by the slimmest of margins. Nonetheless, the future looked bright for the San Francisco Warriors: they were the league's up-and-coming team. Then Rick up and left.

After his triumphant 1966–67 season, Barry decided to leave the Warriors and the NBA altogether to join the Oakland Oaks of the American Basketball

Association in their first year of operation. Barry felt he was underappreciated by the Warriors, and had not enjoyed playing for Bill Sharman. He was promised not only more money by the Oaks, but also part ownership of the franchise. Oaks owner Pat Boone, the singer, also brought in Rick's college coach, Bruce Hale, to guide the Oaks. Hale also happened to be Rick's father-in-law. The Oaks—indeed, the whole of the ABA—thrilled at the prospect of luring away the NBA's brightest young star. Rick's departure from the Warriors sparked a flurry of lawsuits that forced him to miss the 1967–68 season.

Rick finally played for the Oakland Oaks in the fall of 1968. With Barry averaging 34 points a game, the Oaks tore up the league. But Rick was injured at midseason and sat out the remainder of the season. Ironically, the Oaks won the ABA title without Rick, behind the play of Doug Moe and Larry Brown.

The next three years of Rick's career were spent in the upstart league; off-days were spent playing a legal chess game. The Oaks picked up and relocated to the Washington, D.C., area for the 1969–70 season. Barry, claiming he was promised that the franchise would remain in the Bay Area, tried to return to the Warriors, but the Caps won in the courtroom and retained his rights. Barry, ever the consummate professional, drove across the country and reported to the Caps' training camp. Rick was traded to the New York Nets for the 1970–71 season and remained there until he was finally able to return to the Warriors in the autumn of 1972. Barry led the Nets to the ABA finals in 1972, where they lost to the ABA's top club, the Indiana Pacers. Rick won the 1968–69 ABA scoring title, becoming the only player ever to win the NCAA, NBA, and ABA scoring titles. The ABA improved greatly during Rick's time in the league, in part because of his presence, but his time there was unfortunate in terms of his own career.

Returning to the Warriors, who, ironically, now played in Oakland and were known as the Golden State Warriors, the twenty-eight-year-old Barry reestablished himself as an NBA star. Golden State had depth, but they were no match for Chamberlain's Lakers or Jabbar's Bucks. Then, in 1974–75, there was a power vacuum in the West as Wilt had retired and Kareem was injured. Behind a resurgent Barry, who averaged 30.6 points per game, second-best in the league, the Warriors filled the void. Going only 48–34 in the regular season, Golden State came together during the playoffs. Coach Al Attles rotated almost all the players on the squad, except Rick, who played practically all the time. Displaying exceptional teamwork, the Warriors steamrolled the Seattle Supersonics and then squeaked by the Chicago Bulls in seven games to reach the finals. Once there, Barry took over and the Warriors stunned Elvin Hayes, Wes Unseld, and the rest of the favored Washington Bullets in four straight games to become NBA champions. Barry was named MVP for the playoffs.

Rick played another five years in the NBA, but the 1975 title was the pinnacle of his career. Of course, it is impossible to look at the 1967 Warriors and then the 1975 Warriors without wondering what might have been, had Rick not left for the ABA. But regardless of whether he was playing for the NBA title or before a sparse crowd in some remote ABA arena, Rick Barry was a player of uncommon skills and even rarer intensity: "I can honestly say there's never been a game I've played that I was totally happy with," Barry recalled. "I knew that it was impossible to play a perfect game, yet being the perfectionist that I am I always strived to play it....I was watching a Celtics-Lakers game and noticed the look on Magic Johnson's face during the last few minutes. He was so intense. He had something to prove. That's the way I was when I played."

Just like his father, Rick taught his sons well. His three sons were collegiate stars, who went on to play professional basketball in the NBA. In all likelihood, however, the Barry clan will be remembered for Rick III. And Rick III will be best remembered for leading the Warriors to the 1975 title, for averaging 35.6 points per game in 1967, for his strange but deadly free throw style, for his ill-conceived wanderings in the ABA, for his smooth game, and for his incredibly fierce intensity.

RIGHT: Surrounded by three Virginia Squire defenders, New York Net Rick Barry prepares to shoot as he flies through the lane during a 1972 ABA playoff game. He made the shot. BELOW: Golden State's Rick Barry lets fly a long-range bomb during the 1975 NBA finals. Playoff MVP Barry averaged 29.5 points per game in the Warriors four-game sweep of the Bullets. Rick has the highest career scoring average, 36.30, in NBA finals history. Michael Jordan is second at 36.29. The 1974–75 Warriors were the last NBA champions to lead the league in scoring during the regular season.

ELVIN Hayes

RIGHT: All eyes are on Elvin. University of Houston Cougar star Elvin Hayes hangs above a crowd of players near the UCLA basket after flipping up a soft shot from directly beneath the hoop during the legendary Game of the Century, played on January 20, 1968. Besides the central conflict between two undefeated teams, the game featured the individual rivalry between Houston's All-American senior Elvin Hayes and UCLA's All-World center Lew Alcindor. Following UCLA's sound defeat of Houston in the 1967 national semifinal, Hayes had criticized Alcindor's game. Heading into the rematch, Hayes continued to reproach Alcindor in the media. Big Lew did not indulge Elvin with a rebuttal; it was not Alcindor's style. Suffering from a scratched cornea, Lew scored 15 points on 4-for-18 shooting. In contrast, Elvin scored 39 points, including the 2 game-winning free throws. The crowd roared "E! E! E! E!" as the final buzzer sounded. OPPOSITE: Washington Bullet Elvin Hayes elevates for one of his classic short-range jump shots against the Buffalo Braves. Elvin was extremely quick, and exploited this asset in his jump shooting. When Elvin took a jumper, he would fully elevate, square up to the basket, focus on his target, and release a soft, accurate shot. The point of release for his jumper was very high off the ground; he released his bread-and-butter shot at the apex of a powerful leap, with his long arms extended well above his head. His quick take-off and the altitude of his release made it very difficult for defenders—even great shot blockers—to disrupt his jump shot.

For most basketball fans, the name Elvin Hayes evokes images of the so-called Game of the Century played at Houston's Astrodome between Hayes' Houston Cougars and Lew Alcindor's dynastic UCLA Bruins. Thus, Hayes is remembered primarily as a young, sleek, jump-shooting center. In fact, the Big E was such a legendary college star that high school seniors are often touted as the next Elvin Hayes. This phrase is rarely used to describe NBA rookies, however. This discrepancy stems from the fact that Elvin was a high-profile college star who stood out spectacularly from the crowd, while as a pro he was just consistently great for sixteen years.

•••

Elvin Ernest Hayes was born in little Rayville, Louisiana, on November 17, 1945. Elvin grew up in extreme poverty in rural Louisiana. He became a regional celebrity when he single-handedly led Rayville's Eula D. Britton High to the state champi-

onship in his senior year. Britton High won all 54 games it played that year and Elvin Hayes, the school's star six-foot-ten-inch (208.2cm) center, averaged an impressive 35 points a game.

Elvin decided to attend college at the University of Houston, where he would play for coach Guy Lewis. Hayes and classmate Don Chaney became the first two black players on the Houston team. In college, Elvin was a scoring machine, averaging more than 25 points per game each of his three years on the varsity. The Cougars advanced to the 1967 NCAA Final Four in Elvin's junior year and faced Lew Alcindor and the undefeated UCLA Bruins in the semifinals. Although Hayes was accustomed to being the big star, his fame was dwarfed by that of Alcindor. The Bruins handled the Cougars easily; out of envy, Hayes said he was unimpressed with Alcindor.

Great things were expected for the Cougars in the next season. Hayes and Chaney, who would later star for the 1974 NBA champion Celtics, were both seniors. Coach Lewis, recognizing that there would be great public interest when UCLA played at Houston in January, had the game moved from the small campus gym to the cavernous Astrodome. When the two teams met, both were undefeated and ranked one and two. The Astrodome was packed with 52,693 people, the largest crowd ever to see a basketball game at that point, and the game was broadcast around the country. It remains the most famous regular-season college basketball game in history. UCLA came in with a 47-game winning streak, but with a handicap. A week earlier, Alcindor had suffered a scratched cornea during a game and had spent the interim in the hospital. He declared himself ready to play, though his vision was still blurry. Elvin was still talking trash to the media, and true to his word, he played a brilliant game. In the first half, Hayes poured in 29 points, while Alcindor was clearly way off his game, but the Cougars still led by only 3 points. With the game tied at 69 and less than a minute left to play, Hayes was fouled. He stepped up to the line and, to the frenzied applause of the huge partisan crowd, buried both free throws. UCLA then turned the ball over and the Cougars held on to win. Elvin was carried off the court. Now the Big E was a household name, too.

The Cougars carried their number one ranking back to the Final Four and another semifinal matchup with UCLA. At the tip-off, Elvin leaned over to Alcindor and said: "We're gonna beat you. We're gonna beat you bad!" This time he was wrong. Behind a healthy Alcindor, the Bruins devoured the Cougars, 101–69. Elvin was held to 10 points (29 less than the previous meeting) and his glorious college career ended ignominiously.

Elvin was the first player chosen in the 1968 NBA draft. He was selected by the San Diego Rockets, an expansion team that had just finished its inaugural season with a horrendous 15–67 record. Hayes didn't disappoint, leading the NBA in scoring with a 28.4 average and pulling down 17.1 rebounds per game. With Elvin at the helm, the Rockets improved 22 games over their first year and made the playoffs, in which the Atlanta Hawks eliminated them in six tough games. Amazingly, Elvin did not win Rookie of the Year; that honor, as well as league MVP, went to Elvin's future teammate Wes Unseld.

Elvin's offensive repertoire was impressive. He had a deadly jump shot, lethal from as far as twenty five feet (7.6cm). He also could put the ball on the floor, though this was not his preferred tactic. And he was a demon on the offensive and defensive glass. In all branches of the game, Elvin displayed an unwavering drive to win. Though the Rockets had a terrible 1969–70 season, losing ten games more than the previous year and failing to reach the playoffs, Elvin won the NBA's rebounding title. The Rockets improved slightly the next year, but again failed to make the playoffs. The club then moved to Houston, where Elvin was still a folk hero, but the team had another off-season and traded him to the Bullets.

were defeated in four straight games, decided by a cumulative total of 14 points. The next two years the Bullets failed to win their division by one game each time and were eliminated both years in the conference semifinals.

The Bullets played barely over .500 ball in the 1977–78 season, but came together for the playoffs. They defeated Atlanta in the first round of the playoffs and then moved past George Gervin and the San Antonio Spurs. They squared off against Julius Erving, George McGinnis, and the high-flying Philadelphia 76ers in the conference finals. With Bill Walton of the champion Trail Blazers injured, the Sixers, the league's highest profile team in this era, were favored to win the championship. But the Bullets, on a roll, upset the Sixers in six games. During the series, Bullets coach Dick Motta used the phrase "It ain't over till the fat lady sings" to inspire his troops to never give up. The Washington Bullets, as they were now known, faced the Seattle Supersonics in the finals. It was a hard-fought series that came down to Game Seven in Seattle; when the dust had settled, the Bullets had won 105–99. It was Elvin's first championship since high school.

The Bullets reached the finals again the next year, and with the home-court advantage, they tried to become the first team in a decade to repeat as NBA champions. They faced Seattle again, but the well-balanced Sonics of Jack Sikma, "Downtown" Fred Brown, Gus Williams, and Dennis Johnson got their revenge, defeating the Bullets in five games.

The Bullets fell off drastically the next two years losing in the first round of the postseason in 1980 and failing to qualify for the playoffs in 1981. So the Bullets traded the Big E back to Houston, where he successfully teamed up with Moses Malone for a year before Moses split to Philadelphia (though the Rockets lost in the first round of the 1982 playoffs to the Sonics). Elvin closed out his career on horrendous Rockets teams, which at least earned the club a bevy of high draft picks that turned into Ralph Sampson, Hakeem Olajuwon, and, eventually, the championship Houston club of the early 1990s.

When Elvin Hayes retired after the 1983–84 season, he had played in more games and for more minutes than anyone in NBA history (records now held by Kareem Abdul-Jabbar). Hayes never played in fewer than 80 games in any of his 16 seasons, a record that may never be broken. Elvin scored 27,360 points in his NBA career, which is still fourth on the all-time list, averaging 21 points per game. Hayes also stands fourth on the all-time rebounding list with 16,279. In his prime, Hayes was recognized as one of the top players in the NBA by the media, the fans, and his peers. However, in the era of Dr. J, Elvin didn't make his mark flying above the rim, but by battling in the paint and lofting soft, short jumpers. Elvin had let the world know, when he was in college, that he deserved the spotlight; as a pro he remained there by doing the hard work that was necessary to win in the NBA.

Hayes pulls down a rebound during the fifth game of the 1979 NBA finals between the Bullets and the Sonics. Elvin was one of the NBA's all-time greatest rebounders, utilizing his quickness to complement his strength, height, and leaping ability. Hayes used finesse and muscle to win position in the area beneath the glass, which he called the "butcher shop." "That's what it's like when people are trying to get a rebound. Every time a shot is taken there are going to be hips and elbows and chests and heads flying around, slamming and bumping. It's a rough proposition, one of the roughest you will find anywhere in sports."

With the wide-bodied Wes Unseld at center, Hayes moved to power forward. The two formed perhaps the greatest rebounding tandem in NBA history, becoming the centerpiece of one of the league's most successful franchises in the seventies. The Bullets, still playing in Baltimore, won the Central Division in 1972–73, but were ousted from the playoffs by the Knicks. In 1973–74, as Unseld struggled through an injury-plagued season, Elvin picked up the slack and once again led the league in rebounding, averaging more than 18 per game. The Knicks, however, knocked out the Bullets again.

The next year Unseld was healthy (and led the league in rebounding) and the Bullets won 60 games. The team had balanced scoring, with Elvin leading the way with 23 points per game. In the playoffs, the Big E and Company snuck by Bob McAdoo and the Buffalo Braves in the first round of the playoffs and then overcame the defending champion Celtics to reach the finals. The Bullets were heavy favorites against Rick Barry and the Golden State Warriors, but

The Saga of Bill Walton

Bill Walton is the only player in NBA history whose impact on the league was so profound when he was healthy that he merits mention as one of the game's all-time greats even though his career was severely truncated by injury. Basically, Walton was damaged goods. During his tremendous growth spurts during adolescence, his lower legs and feet could not keep up with the rest of his body, and this caused structural damage that proved debilitating throughout his career. However, for one and a half years, Walton's play as the center of the Portland Trail Blazers transformed a good team into a great team that won an NBA championship. The only other players who made such an impact on a team are recognized as the league's all-time greats. Walton lifted his team to a championship in the only truly complete season he ever played, suggesting that if he had played a full career he might be considered one of the very best ever. As it is, his injuries made him a liability to his team as much as his considerable skills made him an asset.

Bill Walton was born on November 5, 1952, and grew up in La Mesa, California, where he attended Helix High School. Walton grew to six feet eleven inches (210.8cm), and behind his towering leadership, Helix won 49 straight games. Legendary UCLA Coach John Wooden was so impressed with reports about Walton that he broke his own rule and recruited Bill in person. Walton attended UCLA and was the consummate Wooden player; unselfish, disciplined, and defense-minded. Remarkably, the Bruins went undefeated each of Walton's first two years on their way to consecutive national titles. When he played against Memphis State in the 1973 NCAA championship final, Walton scored a record 44 points in an unbelievable 21-for-22 shooting performance. In Walton's senior year, Notre Dame snapped the Bruins' record 88-game winning streak, and North Carolina State ended UCLA's string of seven straight NCAA crowns with an overtime victory in the national semifinals.

Expectations for Walton were sky-high as he entered the NBA with the Portland Trail Blazers. However, chronic aches and pains kept Bill inactive for large stretches of his first two seasons, and the Blazers failed to make the playoffs. Walton was healthier in his third season, playing in 65 games, in which he averaged 18.6 points and approximately 14 rebounds per game, displayed his brilliant passing, and anchored the Blazer defense. With Walton healthy for the playoffs, the Blazers caught fire, dismissing Chicago and Denver before trouncing the Los Angeles Lakers and Kareem Abdul-Jabbar. The 1977 NBA finals featured a matchup between the disciplined, team-oriented Trail Blazers and the high-flying, high-profile Philadelphia 76ers led by the legendary Dr. J, Julius Erving. Despite Erving's individual brilliance, Walton and the Blazers took the series in six games. Throughout the series Walton played flawlessly, dominating the boards, playing exceptional interior defense, passing brilliantly, and even scoring—it seemed like the second coming of Bill Russell. The next year Walton and the Blazers were even more spectacular, racing to a 48–10 record and earning comparisons to the greatest teams in NBA history. Then Walton removed himself from the lineup, complaining of unbearable pain in his feet. His value to the team was instantly apparent as the Blazers plummeted, going 10–14 the rest of the season and losing to Seattle in the first-round playoff series. Over the next seven seasons, Walton made numerous comeback attempts but could not overcome his chronic injuries. Then, miraculously, Walton returned to form, contributing a full season as the Boston Celtics' sixth man in 1985–86. Playing with his signature enthusiasm and vigor, Walton's contribution made the 1986 NBA champions one of the greatest teams in NBA history. But Walton's injuries flared up again the next year and he retired shortly thereafter. In retrospect, Bill Walton, who had one of the greatest college careers in basketball history, displayed similar mastery as the leader of the Portland Trail Blazers from 1976 through early 1978. Had injuries not devastated his career, he most certainly would have earned a place among the NBA's all-time greatest players.

Bill Walton was a celebrated defensive center, a great rebounder and passer, and a high-percentage shooter. In short, he was a consummate team player. He was not renowned for putting the ball on the floor, yet if a situation called for taking his defender off the dribble, Walton was up to the task. Here he drives toward the baseline against another great finesse center of the 1970s, Boston Celtic Dave Cowens.

Chapter

THE LARRY AND MAGIC SHOW

At the beginning of the eighties, a consensus emerged in the media that the NBA was in the doldrums. College basketball had once again surged ahead of the pro game in popularity, and a chorus of critics declared that the NBA game was too slow and that its players were paid too much money and did too many drugs. Just as these problems were surfacing, however, two players appeared who would, in time, lift the faltering league to new heights.

These two superstars were none other than Larry Bird and Earvin "Magic" Johnson. It's a telling sign that the two "giants" of this era were only six feet nine inches (205.7 cm)—the same height as Bill Russell— and were not dominating centers but a guard and a small forward. The game in the eighties became faster; the trend was away from a controlled half court game to one that emphasized improvisation and used the whole court. Both Bird and Johnson specialized in spectacular passing.

Of course, many factors contributed to the NBA's renaissance in the late eighties, which is not to say that Larry and Magic weren't instrumental, but that it was more complex than the arrival of two saviors. In fact, the first few years of the Larry and Magic era were perhaps the low point of the league's slump. CBS broadcast weeknight games of the 1981 finals between Bird's Celtics and Malone's Rockets on tape delay rather than fill up their prime-time schedule with NBA basketball. For the first half of the decade, few teams other than the Lakers, Celtics, and 76ers received any national attention. Some franchises, like Portland, Seattle, and Milwaukee, continued to have strong local followings, but most struggled and some were in deep trouble. Half-full arenas were not just common, they were the norm.

Then things began to turn around. David Stern replaced Larry O'Brien as commissioner in 1984, and implemented a new marketing strategy that emphasized the NBA as a league of star performers like Magic and Bird. This campaign built well upon the league's strengths from the first half of the decade. By the mid-eighties, the Lakers and Celtics were so far superior to the other teams in the league that they

Larry Bird's gaze is fixed upon the basket; the ball rests in his right hand; and his body hangs in mid-jump-shot form. While Magic Johnson tries in vain to cover the uncanny shooter, the Boston Garden crowd follows the movements of their mythic hero, who came from the heartland to thrill and astound them. In an instant, the most critical moment in any jump shot will transpire: the release. Bird will throw his arm and wrist forward in a fluid motion; his shoes will begin their return trip to the parquet floor; and the ball will leave his hand with a lazy backspin and a high arc on its way from three-point land toward the basket. Johnson will turn around and watch the flight of the ball along with the Garden faithful, while Larry will already "know," without actually watching the ball, whether his shot will pass through the basket.

After playing against each other for the national championship in their final college game and then entering the NBA at the same time, Larry and Magic became inextricably linked in the public's imagination. The two midwesterners played a decade-long game of one-upmanship, each man tracking the other from opposite sides of the continent.

Magic wrote, "I had always imagined that the two of us would retire together—at the exact same moment. It's the seventh game of the finals, the Lakers against the Celtics. There's one minute left in the game, and the score is tied. And then, suddenly, it's time to leave. Larry and I just shake hands, walk off the court, and disappear.

"But even that wouldn't be the end of it. When we were old, we'd sit down together every summer and play checkers. And I'd whip his ass."

Moses Malone, playing for the Washington Bullets, goes up for a short shot against Lakers Kareem Abdul-Jabbar and Kurt Rambis during the 1986–87 season. Malone was the last dominant center before Bird and Johnson took over the league, winning three MVPs, in 1979, 1982, and 1983. Kareem won a record six MVP Awards, the last in 1980. Bird and Johnson then initiated a unique era in NBA history, one in which centers did not dominate the league. From 1984 through 1993, no center was named MVP; from 1960 to 1983, the league MVP was a center every year except 1964 (when Oscar Robertson won the title) and 1981 (when it went to Julius Erving). Recently, centers have once again asserted their dominance, garnering the MVP Awards for 1994 (Hakeem Olajuwon) and 1995 (David Robinson).

had a transcontinental rivalry that had everyone in the nation choosing sides. The teams met in the finals three out of four years—and the series were epic. The downside to this excitement was that few people knew anything about the other teams in the league.

This public indifference began to change around mid-decade, when a new generation of stars entered the league. The early 1980s were a golden age for college basketball, and the NCAA tournament was followed fervently across the country every March. Such highly charismatic players as Patrick Ewing, Ralph Sampson, and the crew from Houston's Phi Slamma Jamma were virtual superstars before they entered the pro ranks. The public followed these players into the NBA. Suddenly teams like Houston, Detroit, and Chicago had exciting young superstars. Stern's vision of a star-studded NBA was coming true, and arenas started to fill up. Casual fans turned out to see not only the Celtics and the Lakers but also Michael, Isiah, Dominique, and the Twin Towers.

A few other factors contributed to the turnaround. The NBA had expanded dramatically in the seventies, and there were teams in cities with no particular passion for basketball. That changed, probably for good, once a team got turned around, for instance by the arrival of a college superstar or the development of a winning tradition like the Utah Jazz's. The NBA also benefited from the widespread popularity of hip-hop music in the late eighties. African Americans have made up a large and increasing majority of players in the NBA over the past two decades. The young black men who play in the NBA

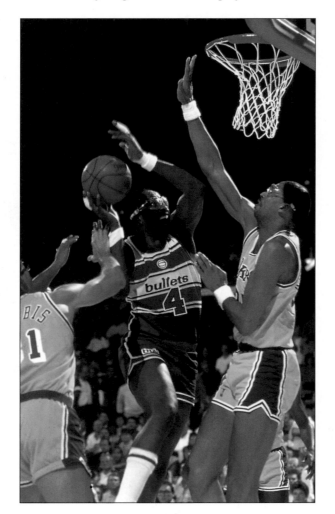

are responsive to trends in black culture, and the rhythm of the game often reflects those trends. Rap music or, more generally, hip-hop became tremendously popular in the late eighties—not only among black youth, but among white youth as well, thereby infiltrating mainstream media culture. Basketball shoes became part of the hip-hop dress code. And basketball was the only sport that jibed—or rather jived—with the late eighties zeitgeist. Stern's marketing people, picking up on hip-hop's allegiance with basketball, used it as the primary motif in spectacular televised commercials promoting the NBA.

By the late eighties, the Celtics were an aging team, and the Detroit Pistons began to challenge their supremacy in the East. The nation watched as the heroic Celtics, who had produced so many memories, battled the bad boys of Detroit. The games were riveting, and the Pistons were becoming household names. The NBA was back—and about to take off like never before.

The battles for championships in the eighties were restricted to only five teams, and Larry Bird or Magic Johnson played in the finals each year of the decade. The Lakers represented the Western Conference each year except 1981 and 1986, when the Houston Rockets had the privilege of losing to the Celtics. The Sixers reached the finals three times, winning in 1983, while the Pistons played the Lakers in 1988 and 1989, capturing the crown the second time. Boston played for the jewel five times, raising banners to the Garden rafters in 1981, 1984, and 1986. L.A. took the title in all the other years: 1980, 1982, 1985, 1987, and 1988.

A plethora of stars populated the NBA throughout the eighties. San Antonio's George Gervin started the decade as the league's most prolific scorer. A few years later, Bernard King thrilled New York Knicks fans with his awesome scoring abilities. Yet it was Denver Nuggets' forward Alex English who scored more points than any NBA player throughout the decade. Mark Aguirre and Rolando Blackmon turned the expansion Dallas Mavericks into a winner for a few seasons. Marques Johnson and Sidney Moncrief kept the Milwaukee Bucks on top of the Central Division for most of the decade (six straight first-place finishes). Atlanta Hawk Dominique Wilkins earned the nickname The Human Highlight Film. Andrew Toney sparkled from the perimeter for the 76ers. Adrian Dantley mastered scoring from the low post for the Jazz and Pistons. And flashy point guard Isiah Thomas led a cast of Pistons to the championship at the end of the decade.

In his prime, Moses Malone was one of the fiercest forces ever to bang bodies beneath the glass. He took the Houston Rockets all the way to the finals in 1981 almost single-handedly and turned the great Sixers team of the early eighties into a champion. But the two greatest stars of the eighties were a six-foot-nine-inch (205.7cm) point guard appropriately known as Magic and a shy young man from backwoods Indiana, Larry Bird.

LARRY Bird

One word and one phrase always seem to come up when the subject is Larry Bird. The word is "instinct." The phrase is "makes the players around him better." In fact, a summary of Larry Bird's basketball legacy would go something like this: Bird used his uncanny instinct for the game of basketball to make the players around him into the best team possible. Though he was slow of foot and had little jumping ability, Bird was a lethal weapon on the courts of the NBA during the 1980s. Possessing a deadly outside shot, a knack for pulling down rebounds, and a sublime court sense that suggested he knew exactly where all the players were going to be a few moments in the future, Bird simply did things that won games. Whether it was a no-look pass that brought down the house, a steal in the last seconds of the game, or a clutch three-point bomb, Larry always seemed to make the big play. How did he get that way? Nobody ever worked longer or harder on his game than Larry Bird; thus he refined that "something extra" he possessed that separated him from all the rest—that "something" that said he knew how to beat you, but you didn't know how to beat him. Basketball was in his soul.

• • •

Larry Joe Bird was born on Pearl Harbor Day, December 7, 1956, in West Baden Springs, Indiana. Larry grew up in the town adjoining West Baden, French Lick, in the poor rural southwest corner of Indiana. Larry's parents, Joe and Georgia, grew up in the area and met when they were working together at a shoe factory in nearby Paoli. Larry was the fourth of six children. His father always held a job, but never earned much money, and the same was true of Georgia Bird. The family's finances were further complicated by Joe Bird's heavy drinking.

For Larry, however, life as a child in French Lick was all right. He didn't know much about the rest of the world and spent his days playing sports with his brothers. They played whichever game was "in season": baseball in summer, football in autumn, basketball in winter. Joe Bird always encouraged his sons to play hard and become better. Both parents taught their children to look out for one another, and they did. And though times were tight, there was always food on the table.

Then one day when Larry was thirteen, he fell in love—with basketball. He was at his aunt's house in Hobart, Indiana, when he joined in a pickup game. He had played some roundball in junior high, but

baseball had been his main game. But on that summer afternoon something clicked: "I took my first shot in the game and it went in. I took my second shot and that went in, too. Even though I was playing against bigger kids that day, it seemed as if everything I lofted went in. The kids on my team started slapping me on the back and telling me what a great player I was...and I just loved it." From then on, Bird was hooked on hoops. He returned to French Lick and practiced continually.

Larry went out for the Springs Valley High School basketball team that winter and made the B team. Coach Jim Jones, who schooled the players in the fundamentals, became Larry's mentor. As Jones showed him all the maneuvers of fundamental basket-

Indiana State's sensational Larry Bird demonstrates his flawless jump shot. In his seasons in Terrre Haute, Bird led the previously unheralded Sycamores to 81 victories, only 13 losses, and an appearance in the 1979 NCAA championship game. Larry's exploits mesmerized basketball-crazed Indiana; the state's only comparable native son, Oscar Robertson, played his college ball across the state line in Cincinnati, Ohio.

The Celtics had a winning record for sixty-one consecutive months beginning in the autumn of 1979, when Larry joined a team that had won only 29 games the previous season. The record-setting streak ended in 1989, when Bird was sidelined. Bird's impact on his team was so great that Celtics President Red Auerbach, the man who coached Bill Russell in eight championship seasons, said, "If I had to start a team, the one guy in all of history I would take would be Larry Bird." Bird's tremendous versatility is reflected in his career statistics. In thirteen seasons Bird scored 21,791 points, for an average of 24.3 per game. He also averaged 10 rebounds, 6.3 assists, and 1.73 steals per game. He shot 50 percent from the field and 88.6 percent from the free throw line, the fifth-best in league history. Most significantly, the Celtics won over 70 percent of the games that Bird played in, giving him the highest winning percentage of any player in NBA history.

ball, Bird caught on instantly. Jones also insisted that Bird learn to use his left hand as well as his right. Still, Larry played little his freshman year and broke his ankle early in his sophomore season. While he had the broken ankle, he still practiced free throws and passing, which he discovered he loved. When he returned from the injury, he was making passes never before seen in southwest Indiana. Every high school varsity team plays in the year-end state tournament, and to his surprise, Bird was selected as a reserve for the Springs Valley Black Hawks. To everyone's surprise, Springs Valley made the sectionals, and once there, Bird got a chance to play. He hit his first shot. Then he began rebounding, scoring, and passing all over the place. With his team down by a point and seconds left, Bird got fouled and went to the line for two shots. He produced two swishes and pandemonium. Bird was a hero, though Springs Valley lost its next game.

Larry grew five inches (12.7cm) before the next season to reach six feet six inches (198.1cm). The Black Hawks went 19–2 that year and Larry was the star, but Springs Valley was upset in the tournament. By his senior year Larry was six feet nine inches (205.7cm) and the top player in his region, averaging 30.6 points and 20.7 rebounds per game. The team went 18–3, but failed to move beyond the sectional finals. During Larry's senior year, all the top college basketball programs in the region—Indiana, Purdue, Louisville, and Kentucky—recruited him. In the end, everyone he knew wanted him to play for Bobby Knight at Indiana, so he chose the Hoosiers.

Larry lasted only twenty-four days in Bloomington before he hitchhiked back to French Lick; he never even played in an official basketball practice. The huge, sprawling Indiana campus, full of sophisticated students, proved too intimidating for the sensitive Bird. Away from the hills of southwest Indiana, young Larry had a tremendous inferiority complex unless he was playing basketball.

Back in French Lick, people felt betrayed by their local hero, but they soon forgave him. Larry needed to earn money, so he drove a garbage truck for the French Lick Public Works Department. But he didn't stop playing ball. He joined the local AAU team and practiced constantly. For the most part, Larry enjoyed his days working in French Lick.

Tragedy, however, struck the Birds during this period. Joe and Georgia Bird had divorced four years earlier because of Joe's drinking. Unable to make his child-support payments and losing his self-esteem, Joe decided he was tired of living. Like most of the people of southwest Indiana, Joe Bird was very direct; he explained to Larry that he planned to take his own life. The local police had come to arrest him for failing to pay child support, and he had asked for one more day, which was granted. He didn't have the money, and Larry knew his father was too proud to go to jail. Still in love with Georgia, no doubt heartbroken, Joe phoned his ex-wife and shot himself to death, allowing her to hear the blast. It took Georgia

Bird, who was devastated by the suicide, years to overcome her grief. Larry has missed his father ever since. (Larry himself got married shortly thereafter. Though the marriage was a disaster, the couple produced a beautiful baby girl, Corrie.)

Indiana State's new coach, Bob King, persuaded Larry Bird to attend college and play for the Sycamores. Living with his wife at the time, Larry was able to make the adjustment to life away from French Lick in comparatively cosmopolitan Terre Haute. Bird had to sit out his freshman year (ISU went 13–12) because of his twenty-four days as an Indiana Hoosier. The next year, 1976–77, Larry Bird finally played college basketball. What a debut! Bird averaged 32.8 points and 13.3 rebounds per game, and shot 54 percent from the floor. The Sycamores went 25–2 and would have qualified for the NCAA tourney, but because it was their first season in the Missouri Valley Conference, they were ineligible for the league title. Ranked sixteenth in the nation, ISU was shunned by the NCAA, but invited to the NIT. The team lost to Houston in the first round by 1 point when Bird missed a last-second shot (he thought he was fouled).

In the summer of 1977, Denny Crum selected Bird to play on the U.S. team at the World University Games in Sofia, Bulgaria. The team swept the basketball tournament and Larry was named the MVP. But Larry didn't become a celebrity until the autumn of 1977, when *Sports Illustrated* put him and two ISU cheerleaders on the cover of their college hoops preview issue. Bird was declared college basketball's secret weapon. The Sycamores won their first 13 games and rose to number four in the polls. Bird was becoming a household word, showing up on the sports highlights on the ten o'clock news around the country. Indiana State University, however, lost its next five games and failed to win the Missouri Valley Conference. They finished a disappointing 22–8, went to the NIT, and lost in the second round when Bird missed another last-second shot (he again thought he was fouled).

Larry had every intention of returning to ISU for his senior year, but he was technically eligible for the NBA draft because, at the time, the rule was that a player could be drafted after the class with which he entered college had graduated. Since Larry went to Indiana in the fall of 1974, his class had just graduated. Before 1976, no one would have dared to draft Bird because if an eligible junior chose to return to college, the team's rights to the player were negated. (Elgin Baylor was selected as a junior eligible by the Lakers in 1958; if he had played again for Seattle University, the Lakers would have lost their rights to Baylor, but Elgin decided to go pro. The rules were different for territorial picks, which is why the Warriors held the rights to Chamberlain after drafting him when he finished high school.) But under the collective bargaining agreement made in 1976, if a team selected an eligible junior, he could return to college and still sign with the team that had drafted him at any

Larry is defended by his alter ego in Game Three of the 1984 finals. For Magic, competing with Bird was the greatest on-court challenge he faced: "During my career in the NBA, I've gone up against hundreds, maybe even thousands of players. Many were good. A few were very good. A tiny handful even deserved to be called great. But there was nobody greater than Larry Bird. Michael Jordan can do incredible things, including moves I've never seen before. There's nobody like him. But Larry was the only player I ever feared. I felt confident that the Lakers could beat any team in the league, and we usually did. But when we played the Celtics, no lead was safe as long as Bird was on the court."

time until the next draft. As it turned out, the rule was changed shortly thereafter and Larry Bird was the only eligible junior to be signed to a team under these circumstances.

Had Bird declared himself ready to turn pro following his junior year, he probably would have been the first pick. But teams at the top of the draft wanted instant help. Also, since he could reenter next year's draft, he was a tricky proposition not only because he could nullify the draft pick, but also because he would have incredible bargaining leverage. A chess match ensued. The Indiana Pacers had the third pick, and there was much speculation that they would spend it on their favorite son, but they had just lost Dan Roundfield, an important player, to free agency and needed instant help. They drafted center Rick Robey. The Portland Trail Blazers had the first and seventh picks in the draft. They selected Mychal Thompson first, and everyone in the basketball community knew the Blazers were going to take Bird if he was available as the seventh pick. But Boston had the sixth and eighth picks, and had the leisure to choose Bird with their first pick. When Boston chose

Bird, longtime NBA fans knew that crafty Red Auerbach had done it again—against all odds he had acquired a franchise player.

When Bird, who was playing golf during the NBA draft, was told that he was selected by the Celtics, he was thoroughly confused. He had no intention of leaving school. He wanted to graduate (he eventually did) and was enjoying college; he was also looking forward to his final season with the Sycamores. He didn't understand how he had been drafted until he watched the television news.

Back in Terre Haute, Bob King was forced to retire for health reasons, and in the power struggle that followed, Bird's choice for coach won out. The 1978–79 Indiana State Sycamores were Larry Bird's team. And Larry Bird was better than ever: "I had a pretty good year [as a junior], but I knew I needed more range on my shot, I needed to be able to take the ball low and make moves with both hands and I needed to control the ball a little better on the fast break." Larry practiced hard, and come senior year he had a complete arsenal of weapons. The Sycamores went undefeated during the regular season and won their conference tournament. In one game Bradley triple-teamed Bird all night long; although they held him to 4 points, his teammates had banner games and ISU won in a blowout. Larry broke his left thumb in the conference championship game, but nothing would have kept Larry out of the national championship tournament. The Sycamores defeated Virginia Tech and Oklahoma easily, then faced Arkansas and Sidney Moncrief in the final of the Midwest Regional. The game was a hard-fought battle from start to finish and ISU survived by just 2 points. The Sycamores were 31–0 and headed to the Final Four in Salt Lake City.

In the national semifinals, ISU squeaked past DePaul and Mark Aguirre by 2 points, and prepared to face Michigan State and college basketball's other superstar, Earvin "Magic" Johnson. The media buildup to the final was incredible: Magic versus Bird. More people watched the the 1979 NCAA final on television than any previous college basketball game. Michigan State had too many weapons and too many athletes for the Sycamores. Michigan State and Magic won by 11. When the final buzzer sounded, Magic joined his teammates cutting down the net, but he remembers turning around and seeing "Larry Bird...sitting there with his face buried in a towel. He was obviously crying, and my heart went out to him...As I turned back to join the celebration, I knew in my gut that this wasn't the end of the story. Somewhere, somehow, Larry Bird and I would be seeing each other again." Larry's dream season ended in disappointment, but it had been a great ride. Bird had single-handedly transformed a school with no basketball tradition into a championship contender; very few players (and even fewer noncenters) have ever done that.

Larry knew little about the Celtics before he was drafted by them. While basketball was king in

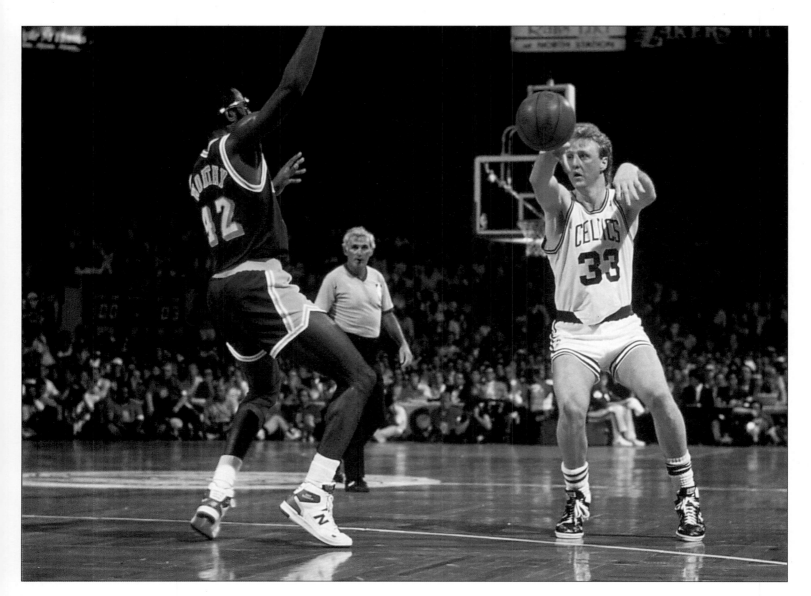

Indiana, pro ball, compared with high school and college hoops, was hardly followed. Nevertheless, Bird was impressed that he was drafted by the NBA's greatest franchise. Having matured tremendously in his time at Indiana State, he was also excited about going to the "big city." However, Larry broke his right index finger in a softball game back in French Lick that summer and it wasn't set properly (the finger would look mangled throughout his entire pro career). Unable to play sports that summer, he spent his time reading up on Boston and the Celtics. One thing he learned was that the Celtics were suffering through the darkest days in their history.

After the Celtics had won its thirteenth title in 1976, the team began a rapid decline. Gone were John Havlicek, Paul Silas, Don Nelson, and JoJo White. The Celtics were 32–50 in 1977–78 and dropped to 29–53 the next year, finishing in last place for the first time since 1949–50. Bird's teammates would include veteran center Dave Cowens, power forward Cedric "Cornbread" Maxwell, and playmaking guard Nate "Tiny" Archibald. Bill Fitch was going to be the new coach. Red Auerbach was going to be Red Auerbach. And Larry Bird was the highest-paid rookie in NBA history. Boston wondered whether Larry would live up to his price tag.

Bird impressed everyone during training camp. During exhibition season, Julius Erving had this to

say: "You can feel the intensity he has, the moves. He can create his own offense." On opening night, Boston Garden was abuzz; the Celtics defeated the Rockets, though Bird was less than spectacular because of persistent foul trouble. The next game was in Cleveland and Bird put on a show. He scored 28 points, but more impressively, when the Cavaliers began to press to try to get back in the game, Bird shredded their defense with his passes. Soon it was evident that the Boston Celtics were a force once again as they challenged the 76ers for the division lead throughout the season.

Praise for Bird began to pour in during his rookie season. "I would never have retired if I had known there was a chance to play with someone like him," John Havlicek said. Coach Fitch called Bird "Kodak" because he seemed able to photograph the court mentally. Players were in awe of his huge hands, his eyesight, his shooting, his rebounding, his positioning, and, especially, his passing. He was frequently called the best passing forward in the history of the game.

Bird was still French Lick Larry and he was uncomfortable with his fame. The Celtics made sure that the press honored Bird's wish to be left absolutely alone once he left the arena. He remained awkward when dealing with fans and commented only on basketball to the press. The more attention he received in the media, especially on television, the

Larry the Legend sends a pass into the open space—where he knows his teammate will meet the ball—past Laker James Worthy. Bird's abilities to anticipate the movements of his teammates and keep tabs on the pulse of the game were among his greatest assets. The Celtic offense always moved through Larry—uncommon for a forward—because his knack for seeing what others were unable to see consistently broke down opposing defenses, creating opportunities for his teammates.

more he worried that his teammates would see him as different from them. He was most comfortable with his teammates, immersed in a basketball world. And once the season was over, he was going straight back to French Lick.

The Celtics won the division in Bird's rookie year. Boston's 61 wins equaled the Celtics total from the previous two seasons. Bird averaged more than 21 points, 10 rebounds, and 4 assists per game. The Celtics swept the Rockets in the playoffs, but were then handled by Philadelphia in five games. Bird was named Rookie of the Year, and the Celtics were back.

Dave Cowens retired after the season, but the Celtics had the rights to the first pick in the draft the next year because of a trade they had made before the past season with the Detroit Pistons, who then finished with the league's worst record. They traded that pick to Golden State for center Robert Parish and the Warriors' first-round pick, which was the third overall. The Warriors drafted Joe Barry Carroll first; the Utah Jazz selected Darrell Griffith second; and the Celtics grabbed up Kevin McHale third. Auerbach's wheeling and dealing again paid off spectacularly. Parish, McHale, and Bird would become known as the "Big Three," perhaps the greatest frontcourt in the history of the NBA.

The Celtics and the Sixers battled all season in 1980–81. The two teams finished with identical records in the regular season, 62–20, but Boston was declared the division champ because of a better division record. The two teams advanced to the conference finals, and when the Sixers won three of the first four games, it looked just like the previous season. In Game Five, the 76ers actually had a 6-point lead and possession of the ball with a minute and a half left in the game, when usually sure-handed Bobby Jones made 4 consecutive errors that revived the Celtics. Archibald and supersub M.L. Carr scored the key points as the Celtics won by 2. Back in Philadelphia, Kevin McHale blocked a shot with 14 seconds left and the Celtics ahead by a point, evening the series. Both teams knew that the winner would face an over-matched Houston Rockets team in the finals and almost certainly become the new champions. The Sixers once again had control of the game with a 7-point lead late in the game. But Larry Bird stepped up and made 3 key steals and scored the final 2 points of the game on a bank shot. The Celtics won 91–90. Although Houston and Moses Malone actually gave Boston a scare in the finals by winning Game Two in the Garden, the Celtics returned the favor in Game Three with a resounding 23-point road victory. The boys in green proceeded to wrap up their fourteenth title in six games, and Larry Joe Bird won his first-ever championship.

The Sixers got their revenge in the 1982 playoffs, upsetting the defending champions in Game Seven of the conference finals in Boston Garden. In the 1982–83 season, the Sixers added Moses Malone and, for a year, were unstoppable, bringing Philadelphia its first NBA crown since 1967. However, the Celtics of McHale, Parish, and Bird were on the rise, while the Sixers' nucleus was aging. In 1983–84, the Celtics captured the first of four consecutive Eastern Conference crowns and finally squared off against the L.A. Lakers, starring Magic Johnson and Kareem Abdul-Jabbar. By 1984, the Celtics had some new faces. Veteran Dennis Johnson had replaced Tiny Archibald at point guard, and young sharpshooter Danny Ainge moved into the rotation. More than ever the Celtics were Larry Bird's team. Parish and McHale were demons under the boards, but Bird provided the team with an ethereal ingredient that made the team more than just great. Magic Johnson summarized this by saying, "Whenever we play Boston, it's always in the back of my mind that no matter what the game situation is, Larry Bird can come back and beat us."

In the 1983–84 finals, the Lakers dominated the first four games, but two went to overtime and the Celtics won both. Then Boston won Games Five and Seven at the Garden; Larry had defeated Magic. The Lakers overcame an even greater historical obstacle the next season when Kareem led Los Angeles over Boston in six games in the finals, preventing Boston from repeating. That snapped the Lakers' jinx against the Celtics, which had extended through eight finals. The 1985–86 squad was the greatest Celtics team of the decade. Legendary center Bill Walton joined the team; McHale, Ainge, and Bird were all in their prime; and during the course of the entire season the Shamrocks lost only one game at home, a record. They topped the Houston Rockets of Ralph Sampson and Hakeem Olajuwon, who had upset the Lakers in the West, in a six-game final.

Larry Bird won the league MVP three years running from 1983–84 to 1985–86. In his prime Bird did everything on the court: score from outside and inside, bury three-pointers, drive the lane, steal the ball, block shots, rebound, lead the break, make circus passes, and even, on occasion, dunk. He also had a propensity for last-second heroics. After 1986, Father Time began to catch up with the Celtics. They lost the 1987 finals to the Lakers, and in 1988 were dethroned in the East by the Pistons. After Bird had major surgery on both his ankles during the 1988–89 season, his days at the top of the sport were numbered. He played through extreme back pain in the early nineties, playing his last NBA game during the 1991–92 season, and closed out his career as a member of the Dream Team at the Olympics in Barcelona.

Throughout his career, analysts marveled at Bird's dominance in an era of high-flying pyrotechnics. Bird, they said, flew the highest of anyone without leaving the ground. Watching Bird in his prime was not like watching a clinic, as the cliché goes, because he did things that were uncoachable. He somehow had a different relationship than every one else to the geometry of the court, to the mind-set of the people on the court. His brilliance primarily resided not in his skills, although they were considerable, but in his capacity to anticipate and guide the flow of the game.

The Lakers vs. the Celtics Revisited: Magic vs. Bird

Heading into the 1995–96 season, the Celtics had the best regular season winning percentage, .628, having collected 2,389 victories against 1,416 defeats; the Lakers had the third-best percentage, .606, matching 2,239 wins with 1,456 losses; and the long-defunct Chicago Stags were second at .612. The Celtics have won more regular-season NBA games than any other franchise; once again, the Lakers are second (though they've played two fewer seasons, 1946–48, in the "NBA" than the Celtics). Back on our subject, the Celtics lead the Lakers 142–102 in head-to-head regular-season meetings. The Lakers, however, lead the Celtics and the league in playoff games played, won, and lost. The Lakers' postseason record is 303–203; the Celtics are 272–189 in the second season. The Lakers have qualified for the postseason a record forty-three times, while the Celtics are second with forty-one; 1994 was the first year in which both storied franchises failed to make the playoffs. On a brighter note, the Celtics lead all franchises in the most important statistic, NBA championships, with sixteen; naturally, the Lakers are second with eleven; and the Bulls, 76ers, and Warriors are tied for third with three each. The Lakers and Celtics' combined total of twenty-seven titles represents the majority of the NBA championship squads. The Lakers have appeared in twenty-four NBA finals, exactly half of the total; the Celtics have reached the finals nineteen times. The Lakers and Celtics squared off ten times in the finals, with the Celtics winning the first eight and the Lakers gaining a measure of revenge by taking the last two. The Celtics won 36 games against the Lakers in the NBA finals and lost 25. The two clubs have never met in any other round of the playoffs.

When Larry Bird and Magic Johnson joined the Celtics and Lakers, respectively, at the start of the 1979–80 NBA season, they swung the balance of power in the NBA back to its traditional poles (or coasts). Long-dormant hostilities stirred. Throughout the decade the Celtics and Lakers dominated the NBA just like old times. The two teams accounted for eight of the decade's ten championships. Fans across the country debated which team was better.

It wasn't until 1984 that the NBA's two hallowed franchises renewed their legendary and previously lopsided rivalry after a fifteen-year hiatus. In one of the most hotly contested finals ever (literally, as the Boston Garden was like a sauna for Game Five), the Celtics picked up right where they had left off in 1969, squeaking by the Lakers in seven nip-and-tuck games. By the mid-1980s both teams were reaching maturity. The Lakers exorcised the ghosts that had haunted their franchise for so long in the 1985 finals by topping the Celtics in six games. The Lakers then failed to reach the finals in 1986. Perhaps it was for the better, because the 1985–86 season belonged to the Boston Celtics. Bird and Company compiled the best regular-season record of the decade, losing only one game at home all year and squashing the Rockets for their third title of the decade to pull even with their hated rivals from leisure land. The 1986 Celtics were a simple team: they had a brilliant starting five led by all-world Larry, who won his third straight MVP in 1986; a backcourt of wily veteran Dennis Johnson and feisty Danny Ainge; and a lethal low-post tandem of Robert Parish and Kevin McHale. Relieving McHale and Parish was the legendary Bill Walton, who returned from the dead to make a great team even greater. Walton played with joyous, bouncy enthusiasm all year long; the next year he was back down to ten appearances, compounding the sense that the 1985–86 Celtics were so good they were surreal. By the 1987 finals the Celtics were exhausted, having narrowly advanced past the Detroit Pistons in the conference finals. By way of contrast, the Lakers were thoroughly revitalized. Following their 1986 debacle, Coach Pat Riley decided it was time for a changing of the guard, a passing of the baton from Kareem to Magic. Kareem would still be key to the half court offense and the interior defense, but the team would be remade in the image of Magic's game. Showtime! The 1987 final was not a classic like 1984 or 1985—the Lakers won handily in six games.

By 1988, the Celtic reign atop the Eastern Conference was over, but the Lakers returned to the finals and edged out the Pistons to become the first team to repeat as NBA champions since Bill Russell and the 1969 Celtics. The Lakers had managed to replenish their talent pool throughout the decade, while the Celtics, in stark contrast to the Russell dynasty, failed to generate an influx of young talent. At their peak in 1986 the Celtics were certainly as good as any of the Lakers teams of the decade (1986–87 was probably the best Lakers squad), but over the long haul the Lakers won out because of their flexible long-term strategy (of course, the Celtics were snakebit by the death of top prospect Len Bias). The 1988 title gave the Lakers five championships for the decade, clinching their status as team of the eighties.

So who was the player of the decade, Larry or Magic? The conventional wisdom is that Bird was the more complete player when he entered the league, but that Magic's game improved more than Larry's. Certainly Magic's outside shot improved tremendously over the years, and there's no analagous sphere of growth in Bird's game. Johnson was still at the top of his game when he retired. At his peak, Bird was an awesome weapon, a threat from anywhere in a half court offense, making up for his lack of speed with his great court sense. Was Magic, who always seemed in control of every element on the court, ever as great as Bird at his peak? He was certainly close, and gave the Lakers three years of superstar play after Bird's effectiveness was in decline. Perhaps it is safest to say that Magic and Bird were the players of the decade.

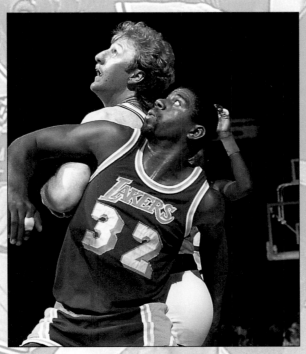

Following the path of the ball during the 1984 NBA finals, Larry and Magic battle for position beneath the boards. The two seminal figures in the NBA throughout the eighties became friends after the 1984 finals, when they shot two commercial spots together.

EARVIN Johnson

Johnson

BELOW RIGHT: Michigan State Spartan Earvin "Magic" Johnson dunks the ball against Kentucky while his teammate Greg Kelser (Number 32) bears witness. Jerry West first saw Magic play during Johnson's freshman season at Michigan State: "I thought I'd seen it all when it came to basketball—and then I saw Magic Johnson. Here was this six-foot-nine-inch kid [205.7cm] with a big man's body playing point guard. He was the floor leader, calling all the plays and moving everybody around like an orchestra conductor. He was handling the ball like a six-footer [182.8cm], like it was an extension of his hand. He was absolutely in complete command. And he was making the kind of moves I'd never seen from a player his size. He was dribbling the length of the floor, looking one way and passing another. He was hitting every open man, making all the right decisions." OPPOSITE: Magic prepares to toss up a shot as he floats towards the bucket. Celtic Kevin McHale tries to reach out and block the shot as teammates Darren Daye and Dennis Johnson and Laker Michael Cooper await the results. Always more interested in keeping his teammates involved in the offense than in accumulating points himself, Magic was very efficient when he did decide to shoot. Magic hit 52 percent from the field and 85 percent from the free throw line throughout a career in which he averaged just short of 20 points per game.

Either the hand was quicker than the eye or something otherworldly transpired when Magic Johnson led a fast break. Imagine you're a player on the wing, racing down the right side of the court. Kareem has already cleared the boards and fed Magic with an outlet pass, and he's pushing the ball past half court at full speed. Worthy's on the left flank, but three defenders are racing back. You are ahead of the pack and cut toward the basket, but two defenders have closed down the passing lane—you know this because you can barely see Johnson through them. Then, somehow, you swear you don't know how, the ball is flying past the two defenders and right into your hands. Without breaking stride, you catch the ball and elevate at full speed to slam the ball home. Showtime! Magic!

Throughout his career Earvin "Magic" Johnson continually made passes that stunned opponents, astonished fans, and, invariably, worked like a charm. Perhaps Magic succeeded because he had the gump-

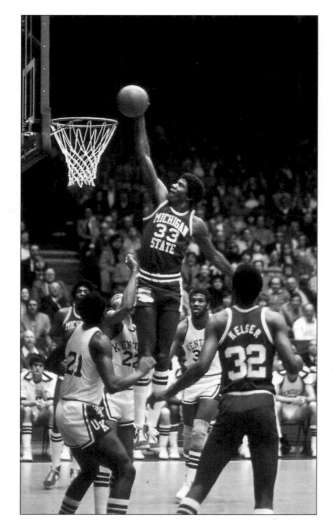

tion to attempt passes no one else would have thought possible, or perhaps opponents fell back on their heels because they recognized that Magic was capable of so many things. Whatever the reason, from high school through his professional career, the Magic Man turned his teammates into winners: he created more opportunities more spectacularly than any player in basketball history.

• • •

Earvin Johnson, Jr.'s unique American odyssey began on August 14, 1959, in Lansing, Michigan. Earvin was the fourth of seven children born to a hard-working father and devoutly religious and loving mother. Magic opened his autobiography by saying: "I grew up in the kind of black family that people today worry is disappearing. Even though there were nine of us, we had what we needed—two great parents, food on the table, and time for the whole family to be together." Lansing was a comfortable place to grow up. About the only conflict in Earvin Johnson's early life came when his mom joined the Seventh Day Adventists, a Christian church that celebrates the Sabbath on Saturdays. That meant Earvin could no longer play Saturday games in the peewee basketball league.

Earvin Sr. was a huge basketball fan and Magic grew up loving the game. Every Sunday during the season Earvin Sr. and Earvin Jr. would sit down in front of the television and watch the *NBA Game of the Week*. His father was an attentive fan and taught young Earvin the nuances of the game. Earvin Sr.'s favorite player was Wilt Chamberlain, but Magic's was Detroit hero Dave Bing. Magic would play fantasy games between the two when he was alone on the court, developing inside moves when he was Wilt, and getting ample practice on his jumper and ballhandling when he put himself in the role of Bing. Before he was ten years old, Magic was developing an all-around game.

Young Earvin's hours of practice paid off when he not only made his junior high school team, but became its star. In one game, Earvin poured in 48 points, an amazing accomplishment since he sat out the fourth quarter and quarters were only 6 minutes long. Magic was always tall for his age, but it was during junior high that he sprouted from six feet (182.3cm) to six feet five inches (195.5cm). In the neighborhood, everyone was getting excited about the young basketball phenom and couldn't wait until he attended nearby Sexton High, a perennial high school powerhouse.

However, it was the seventies and the era of "forced busing." So young Earvin was sent from nearly all-black West Lansing all the way to nearly all-white South Lansing and Everett High, a school with no basketball tradition whatsoever. It was only the second year of busing and there was considerable tension at Everett about the imported students. In retrospect, Magic considered his experience at Everett to be one of the best things that ever happened to him, forcing him to broaden his perspective on life and society, learn firsthand to accept and befriend white people, and to confront racism in American society. At his first practices with the varsity basketball team, many white players would not pass him the ball. So Earvin would grab a defensive rebound and go coast to coast and score, refusing himself to pass the ball. A fight almost broke out, but Coach George Fox pulled Earvin aside and told him that he would talk to the white players. The problem was soon resolved, and the white players began to accept the black freshman star.

Coach Fox turned out to have a tremendous influence on Johnson's career. Fox recognized Magic's tremendous ballhandling and passing skills and went against all tradition by putting a tall, talented player in the backcourt. Earvin responded spectacularly: he loved being the general on the court. Coach Fox's maneuver kept the ball in the hands of the best young player in Lansing.

After a game in Magic's freshman year against Jackson High in which he had 36 points, 18 rebounds, and 16 assists, a reporter came up to Earvin and said that since Dr. J and Big E were already taken, how about the nickname "Magic"? Once Earvin established that the game against Jackson was no fluke, the name stuck. Earvin's mother never liked the moniker because of her religion (Lakers Coach Pat Riley would later express the thought that the name implied that Earvin did not practice, which was never the case), but before the end of his freshman year in high school, the legend of Magic had begun. Everywhere Johnson played, opposing fans would hang banners saying something like, "There will be no Magic tonight." Earvin loved the challenge and accepted the nickname.

Everett went all the way to the state quarterfinals in Magic's first year. By his junior year, Magic had led the Vikings to an undefeated season and the Michigan state championship. Every college recruiter in the country seemed to descend on Lansing during Magic's senior year. Earlier it seemed that Earvin was spending too much time on the courts and not enough studying, but he attended summer school after freshman year, gained discipline, and was a strong student the rest of his time at Everett. Magic found many of the schools recruiting him to be alluring, but his sense of loyalty to his hometown won out, and he chose Michigan State in East Lansing.

The Big Ten, however, was loaded with talent in the late seventies, and Michigan State had virtually no basketball tradition. Remarkably, Magic turned things around instantly. Because Magic grew up in Lansing and was the city's biggest hoop star, he had played countless pickup games with the Michigan State upperclassmen. Thus, he knew their game and they knew his, and the team jelled instantly. At six feet eight and a half inches (204.4cm), Magic remained at guard and stunned the Big Ten with his brilliant passing and court leadership. He worked especially well with Spartan forward Greg Kelser and guard Jay Vincent. The three

led Michigan State into the NCAA tournament, where the team advanced to the quarterfinals, to face number-one-ranked Kentucky. The Spartans led at halftime but played the second half trying to protect the lead, and the strategy backfired. Kentucky came back to win and swept to the national championship.

Magic became a national celebrity next autumn when Sports Illustrated put him on the cover of their college basketball preview issue. The magazine described how Johnson was unlike any player who had come before, not only because he had sensational passing skills and was a six-foot-nine-inch (205.7cm) guard, but primarily because he played competitive ball with a unique charisma and joy. Over the next few months, the nation's fans would learn firsthand what the article was talking about.

The Spartans started the season with a winning streak and soared to the number one ranking in the wire service polls. Then, however, the Spartans went into a slump, losing four of their first eight games in the Big Ten. With the season in jeopardy, a team meeting was called and the Spartans decided to go with a running game to accent Magic's skills in the open court. They won the next ten games and headed into the national tournament on a roll. The Spartans breezed into the Final Four, where they crushed the Cinderella team of the tourney, Penn from the Ivy League, by 34 points. Meanwhile, Indiana State squeaked past DePaul, and the final matchup was set: Michigan State and Magic, with his magnetic enthusiasm, versus the upstart Indiana State team with Bird, a truly sublime forward. The media hype for the contest was sensational. As it turned out, more people watched the 1979 NCAA final than any college basketball game in history up to that point. Magic made innumerable sensational passes and the Michigan State defense frustrated Bird. The Spartans cruised to an 11-point victory. Magic had lifted lowly Michigan State, his hometown team, to the national championship in his second year.

After his sophomore season, Magic had to decide whether he would remain in college. With Greg Kelser graduating, Earvin felt the Spartans would not be the team they were the year before and he felt he was ready to go on to the next level, the NBA. Still, many felt Magic's game wasn't complete enough and counseled him to remain in Lansing to round out his game. Magic let his decision ride on a coin toss. Johnson assumed he would be the first player chosen in the draft, since Bird's rights were already held by the Boston Celtics. The draft lottery did not exist yet and the team that chose first was determined by a coin flip between the two teams with the worst records in their respective conferences. In 1979, the two teams were the Chicago Bulls and the New Orleans Jazz, but the rights to the Jazz's pick were held by the Los Angeles Lakers. Magic decided that if the Bulls won the coin toss he would remain in Lansing, but if the Lakers won he would turn pro since he felt the opportunity to play alongside Kareem Abdul-Jabbar was something he could not

pass up. Of course, the Lakers won the toss and selected Magic as the first pick of the draft. Earvin was a Laker at the tender age of twenty.

Even though Magic became a renowned celebrity following the national title, his unwavering exuberance surprised the NBA. At training camp, Earvin went diving for loose balls and playing every scrimmage like a title game. Laker guard Norm Nixon quipped, "Earvin's running around like a young buck," and Johnson was forever known as Buck by his Laker teammates. After Jabbar sunk a last-second shot to defeat the Clippers in Magic's first regular season game, Earvin jumped into Kareem's arms to celebrate as if he had just clinched a title. Veterans rolled their eyes. Kareem reminded him there were 81 more games left in the regular season. Everyone told Magic to conserve his energy—the NBA season was a long haul—and to adapt to the laid-back style of the NBA. Thankfully, he never did. In fact, the NBA would come to adopt Earvin's enthusiasm and intensity, and it was one of the best things that ever happened to the league.

With Magic aboard, the 1979–80 Lakers were a great team. They were not yet playing the fast-paced Showtime style they would be famous for in the mid-eighties; Kareem was very much the centerpiece. Magic contributed points, assists, and rebounds to a unit that featured Kareem in the middle, Norm Nixon as the other guard, Jamaal Wilkes at small forward, and Jim Chones and Spencer Haywood splitting time at power forward. Swingman and defensive specialist Michael Cooper also played important minutes. The team finished with the best record in the Western Conference and advanced to the finals, where they faced off against Dr. J and the high-flying Philadelphia 76ers. The Lakers won the title in six games as Magic poured in a season-high 42 points in the final contest while playing center in place of the injured Jabbar. On the strength of his Game Six performance, Johnson was named playoff MVP. Even more significantly, Magic Johnson became the first player since Bill Russell to lead his team to the college and professional championships in back-to-back years. Magic's fairy-tale career not only continued, it seemed to get even more unbelievable each year.

Magic's string of glory ended in his second year with the Lakers. In November, young Earvin tore some cartilage in his left knee and played only 37 games in the regular season. In the playoffs, the Lakers faced the Rockets in a best-of-three mini-series. Injuries to the Lakers' front line meant that Rockets center Moses Malone, who was league MVP three times between 1979 and 1983, dominated the boards. Still, the Lakers had a chance to win the series in the decisive game. Down by a point with 15 seconds left, Coach Paul Westhead called for a play in which Magic fed the ball to Kareem. But the Rockets were waiting for this, so Magic drove the lane and put up a shot over Malone. It was an air ball. Magic had gone from hero to goat in one season, and faced adversity for the first time in ages.

Magic Johnson revolutionized the game of basketball. Before Magic, point guards were exclusively six feet five inches (195.5cm) or shorter. Magic was six feet nine inches (205.7cm) and had the body of a low-post player, but he also had the ballhandling skills of a point guard, passed like few players before him, and saw the whole court as well as any player ever. As author Nelson George put it, "Magic Johnson destroyed all stereotypical notions of how size dictated position." Big players who came of age in the 1980s emulated Magic Johnson, mastering ballhandling and passing skills. By the early 1990s, six-foot-eight-inch (203.2cm) Jalen Rose and the "next Magic Johnson," six-foot-seven-inch (200.6cm) Anfernee Hardaway were starting NBA point guards. But size and skill alone were not what made Magic one of the greatest player of all time—the essential ingredient was the fierce competitiveness that motivated him to control the pace of every game, at all times.

By all accounts, he did not respond well to it. At the beginning of the 1981–82 season, Johnson was bickering with the Lakers. Johnson objected to the Lakers' new style, which emphasized Jabbar and his lethal skyhook over a fast-break running offense. The team started slowly, and Magic and Coach Paul Westhead clashed. Magic blasted Westhead in the press and demanded to be traded. Within two days, Westhead was fired. Magic was vilified throughout the NBA as a spoiled brat; even the fans in the Forum booed him after Westhead's dismissal. Magic got depressed, but slowly things returned to normal.

In fact, they got very good. The Lakers' new coach was their former assistant coach, Pat Riley. Magic also had his best year yet, coming within 37 assists and 29 rebounds of averaging a triple-double for the entire season. The Lakers rolled into the playoffs, sweeping their Western Conference opponents, and met Dr. J and the Sixers once again in the fnals. This time the Lakers captured Game One in Philadelphia and never relinquished command of the series, winning all their home games by 10 or more points. The Lakers were champs once again, and Magic's storybook career was back on track.

Moses Malone joined the already powerful 76ers in 1982–83, and they crushed the injury-weakened Lakers in the finals. The Sixers, however, were an old group and faded after that year. In contrast, the Lakers kept replenishing their forces with new talent. In 1983–84, rookie James Worthy joined their ranks and guard Norm Nixon was traded for the younger Byron Scott. The Lakers once again reached the finals, where they faced the Boston Celtics and Larry Bird. Though the Lakers dominated the series early,

the Celtics held on by capturing Games Two and Four in overtime and then used their momentum to roll to a seven-game victory.

The same two teams would meet in the finals two of the next three years, creating a legendary rivalry, one that had roots not only in the Celtic-Laker rivalry of the sixties but also in the 1979 NCAA championship finals. In 1984, when David Stern replaced Larry O'Brien as commissioner, the NBA was struggling on many fronts. The league would undergo many transformations over the next few years, but none more significant than Stern's decision to advertise the NBA as a league of stars. The primary figures who were featured were, of course, Magic Johnson and Larry Bird. While many franchises in the league continued to struggle throughout this period, the whole nation tuned in to the finals. The Celtics and Lakers of this era were like two nationwide teams, and sports fans of every variety followed the rivalry with partisan passion. Of course, the teams were equally matched. The Lakers rebounded with a six-game victory over the Celtics in 1985. The Celtics devastated the league in 1986 and triumphed in the finals over the Rockets, who had upset the Lakers in the Western finals to the dismay of fans across the nation. The Lakers rebounded to conquer the aging Celtics in 1987.

Before the 1986–87 season, Coach Pat Riley decided to transform the offense so as to emphasize Magic's talents and start to fade out Kareem's dominance. The Lakers' captain was turning forty that season. The transition worked smoothly, and Johnson finally had the opportunity to display the full range of his talents. The Laker offense, known as Showtime, had reached its maturity. For the first time in his career, Magic averaged more than 20 points (23.9) per game, and he led the league in assists for the fourth time in his career. Every night Magic produced some eye-popping no-look pass or other spectacular fast-break play for the highlight reels. The Lakers also finished with their best record of the eighties and had home-court advantage throughout the playoffs for the first time in Magic's career. After conquering the Celtics in a six-game final, Coach Riley "promised" that the Lakers would be the first NBA team to repeat as champions since the Celtics of Bill Russell.

The Lakers once again swept through the regular season with the NBA's best record in 1987–88, but the playoffs were another matter. After sweeping San Antonio in the first round, the Utah Jazz and the Dallas Mavericks extended the Lakers to seven games. In the finals, the Lakers met the fast-improving Detroit Pistons, led by Earvin's longtime friend Isiah Thomas. With the nation tuned in to see if the legendary Lakers could repeat, the Pistons almost stole the show. The Lakers won Game Six by a point on last-second free throws by Kareem and withstood a frantic comeback by the Pistons in Game Seven to claim their fifth title in Magic's eight seasons. After the finals the press acknowledged the Lakers as the team of the decade and among the greatest of all time.

Magic dribbles against a tenacious defender, Michael Jordan. In the late 1980s, some promoters proposed a one-on-one Jordan-versus-Johnson showdown, to be played after the end of the NBA season and aired on pay-per-view TV, with some of the proceeds to go toward charity. Magic and Michael loved the idea; the league and the NBA Players Association, however, were less than thrilled. Ironically, Michael and Magic considered retiring temporarily in order to play the match and not breach any contracts; they quickly realized that this would further infuriate the NBA. When the game was still a possibility, Jordan was listed as an eight-to-five favorite. While Magic acknowledges that he couldn't replicate or even stop some of Michael's moves, he always declares, "I would have won."

Magic won the NBA's MVP Award the next two seasons and was heralded as the game's best all-around player alongside Michael Jordan. By the late eighties, the Lakers were probably the most beloved celebrities in a city that was full of stars. Since Kareem cherished his privacy, Magic was the celebrity's celebrity. And Magic, with his huge smile and sincere kindness, played the role perfectly. However, the Pistons swept the Lakers in the 1989 finals after Magic pulled his hamstring in Game Two. Then, the Phoenix Suns upset L.A. in the second round of the 1990 playoffs. In 1991, however, the Lakers advanced to the finals to meet Jordan and the Bulls. It was another matchup made in heaven for the NBA and NBC, which broadcast the NBA finals. However, the Lakers didn't have enough firepower to stay with Michael's Bulls and went down to defeat.

Going into the next season, the Lakers had cause for optimism. They felt that they had successfully rebuilt after the disappointment of 1990. Then, suddenly, everything changed. On November 7, 1991, Magic Johnson announced to the world that he had contracted HIV, the virus that causes AIDS, and that he was, at least temporarily, retiring from basketball. The world was stunned. Magic was one of the world's most famous people and a great athlete at the height of his powers. Suddenly, he was a tragic and controversial figure. Friends, family, and fans were stunned as Magic explained that he had been extremely promiscuous, sleeping with countless women throughout his career. He also announced that he would campaign to raise consciousness about the deadly virus and how to prevent contracting it. And he was grateful to announce that neither his wife nor his child, which she was carrying at the time, had contracted the disease.

Since the autumn of 1991 Magic has continued his association with basketball. The NBA allowed him to play in the 1991–92 All-Star Game when fans elected him to the team. He played a sensational game, drilling 3 three-pointers and scoring 25 points, and was named the game's MVP for the second time in his career. Then Magic was a part of the 1992 U.S. Olympic Team, winning a gold medal in Barcelona. Following his triumph as a part of the Dream Team, during which fans from across the globe showered their support and affection on him, Magic decided that he wanted to come back with the Lakers. Unfortunately, many players in the NBA expressed fears about being infected by Magic if he were to bleed while on the court, and Johnson decided that the superstition about the transmission of HIV was still too strong for him to come back to the NBA and not be treated like a pariah.

Since that time Magic has remained a visible figure in NBA circles, and even coached the Lakers for a brief period at the end of the 1993–94 season. Perhaps even more significantly, Magic has remained a crusader to raise consciousness about AIDS. He remains in good health and good spirits, as do his wife and young child; he also maintains his faith that HIV can be defeated.

Magic Takes Centerstage: Game Six, the 1980 NBA Finals

The 1980 NBA final was an epic struggle between the Los Angeles Lakers, led by league MVP Kareem Abdul-Jabbar and rookie sensation Earvin "Magic" Johnson, and the Philadelphia 76ers, led by Julius Erving. Since Erving had arrived in Philadelphia in 1976–77, the Sixers were the NBA's perennial overdogs, but they hadn't even reached the finals since 1977 and they were hungry for the championship. Likewise, Jabbar hadn't played for the title since he had been the leader of the Milwaukee Bucks in 1974, and he hadn't won one since 1971—so he too was famished. Magic, in contrast, was leading a charmed life: it was his first year in the NBA and he was playing for the championship; the previous year he had led Michigan State to the NCAA title as a sophomore. When the Lakers won the rights to the first pick in the draft, Magic decided to enter the pro ranks. He enjoyed a good rookie season, averaging 18 points, 7 assists, and 7 rebounds per game. The Lakers stormed by Phoenix and then-recent nemesis Seattle in five games each. The Lakers were still very much Kareem's team, but the newspaper stories that appeared before the start of the series attributed the posi-tive changes in the Lakers, and in Kareem himself, to Magic's enthusiastic presence.

The Lakers won Game One at home, but Philly took Game Two. Los Angeles captured Game Three, and the 76ers evened things up in Game Four. The series headed west again all knotted up. Game Five was close in the third quarter, when Jabbar made a layup, but he came down wrong on his ankle and heard a pop, which was followed by intense pain in his left leg. Jabbar hobbled to the bench as the Forum crowd grew quiet. Kareem had virtually carried the Lakers in the series. The game continued. The team doctor thought there was a fracture, but he wrapped Kareem's leg tight and the team captain limped out on the floor. The pain was intense, but Kareem found a way to limit his movement and still be effective. He added 14 points in the fourth quarter for a game-high 40 and the Lakers won by 5. Game Six was in Philadelphia and Jabbar was unable to make the trip. The injury was diagnosed as a severe sprain; Kareem was determined to play if there was a Game Seven, which would be back at the Forum.

Few people gave the Lakers much of a chance in Game Six without Kareem and in Philadelphia. On the plane to Philly, Lakers Coach Paul Westhead asked Magic how he felt about starting at center. Magic loved the idea, responding with "I'd love to, I played some center in high school" (which was only three years earlier). Westhead figured that with Magic's height and strength, he could hold his own near the basket. Laker power forward Jim Chones would match up against the Sixers' massive Darryl Dawkins, while Magic was paired with six-foot-eleven-inch (210.8cm) Caldwell Jones. All of Philadelphia was ready for a cakewalk, but Magic had other ideas. Earvin jumped center to start the game against Jones; the taller man controlled the tap, but the Lakers raced to a 7–0 lead. The Sixers roared back and led by 8 in the second quarter. But Magic was on fire from outside, and since Jones was uncomfortable away from the basket, he kept giving Earvin the shot and Earvin kept making it. At halftime the game was knotted at 60. The tie was a psychological edge for the Lakers and they knew the Sixers were confused about how to match up against the smaller Laker lineup; the Sixers were used to Kareem anchoring the half court offense in the low post. Without Kareem, the Lakers were whipping the ball around, drawing their big men away from the basket, and switching positions frequently. The Sixers failed to solve their problems at halftime and the Lakers took control of the game by running off 14 straight points to start the second half. The Sixers narrowed the lead to 10 at the end of the quarter and made a series of runs at the Lakers in the fourth quarter. Three times Julius Erving sparked Sixers rallies in which they closed the margin to 2; but each time, with Magic at the helm, the Lakers would step on the gas and run away from them. The Lakers won, pulling away 123–107. Magic didn't do it all himself—Jamaal Wilkes was equally deadly from outside and he poured in his highest point total since high school, 37—but it was Magic's night. He played center "in Lew of Alcindor," scoring 42 points on 14-for-23 shooting and a perfect 14-for-14 from the charity stripe, grabbing 15 rebounds, and adding 7 assists and 3 steals. Magic said he was brimming with confidence before the game, and it showed throughout the contest; he seemed on top of everything on the court. After the game Sixer guard Lionel Hollins shook his head and said, "Magic. He is his name."

Having spun free of the Sixers' low-post defense, Magic releases a short jumper while Julius Erving looks on helplessly during Game Six of the 1980 NBA finals. On this one night, May 16, 1980, Magic confirmed what many already suspected: the sensational young point guard had the size, strength, and skill to play—and excel at—any position in the NBA.

MOSES Malone

Offensive rebounds are one of the keys to winning a basketball game. A team that can control the offensive glass will usually prevail. In the history of basketball only Wilt Chamberlain rivaled Moses Malone as a force beneath the offensive glass. Bill Russell and Dennis Rodman also collected numerous offensive boards, but they lacked the skill of the Big Dipper and Mo at putting the ball right back up and in the hole. Moses was especially adept at rebounding and scoring while getting fouled. And, unlike Chamberlain, Malone was an expert foul shooter. In his heyday, from 1978 through 1985, Moses made three-point plays a habit.

Perhaps because of his unflashy personality and his blue-collar style of play, or because he was stranded on otherwise pathetic Rockets teams and then traded to a perennial overdog (which he nonetheless led to the title), fans and historians often exclude Moses from their lists of all-time greats. The oversight is glaring. Moses won as many MVP Awards (three) as Magic, Michael, or Bird, trailing only Chamberlain (four), Russell (five), and Jabbar (six) in this category. He also won more rebounding titles (six) than anyone in NBA history except Chamberlain (eleven). He was also the greatest player in history under the offensive glass.

• • •

Moses Eugene Malone was born on March 23, 1955, in Petersburg, Virginia. His father left the family when Moses was only eighteen months old. Consequently, Moses was raised by his mother, Mary, who worked as a nurse's aide and later as a meat packer in a supermarket. Moses spent much of his youth learning to play basketball on Petersburg's playgrounds. The game meant more to Moses than it did to the rest of his peers: when the games were over he remained on the asphalt courts and practiced alone, often well into the evening, under the meager glow of the street lamps.

As Moses grew taller and stronger, he began to concentrate on his inside game, particularly offensive rebounding. At one summer camp, Coach Dick Vitale noticed Moses practicing rebounding and putbacks by himself in the gym during lunch hours. When Vitale asked him why he was so focused on that part of his game, Moses explained matter-of-factly (as he always did, if he deigned to answer at all): "When you get an offensive rebound, you're right there to shoot it back up." By high school, the countless hours of practice had paid off: he scored 32 points in his varsity debut

Houston Rocket Moses Malone grabs a rebound against the Lakers' Kareem Abdul-Jabbar during the fourth quarter of the third and decisive game of a playoff miniseries on April 5, 1981. The Rockets, who finished 40–42 during the regular season, stunned the defending champion Lakers 89–86. A one-man wrecking crew, Malone led Houston all the way to the finals, where they lost to the Celtics in six games.

at Petersburg High. Soon he was recognized as the greatest high school player in the history of Virginia. Moses led Petersburg High to 50 straight victories and back-to-back state titles. As a senior he averaged 36 points, 26 rebounds, and 12 blocks per game. The agile six-foot-ten-inch (208.2cm), 210-pound (95.3kg) Malone was named a High School All-American in both his junior and senior years. He also became the most heavily recruited player in the history of basketball, being pursued by three hundred colleges.

Malone received the highest ratings possible in all the summer camps after his junior year. Thus, an army of recruiters descended upon Petersburg in the autumn, winter, and spring of 1973–74, Moses' senior year. Included among these was Bernie Bickerstaff, who was scouting for the Utah Stars of the ABA. Since Spencer Haywood had left college after his

Playing for the 76ers, Malone puts up a shot from close range against Celtic center Robert Parish. Larry Bird observes the action from beneath the basket while Julius Erving watches from a safer distance. In his prime, Moses was a master at tossing up point-blank shots against the league's big men, grabbing the rebound if he missed, going back up for the putback, and grabbing the rebound again if he missed...until he either scored a field goal, was fouled, or both. Not that Malone missed that often: he consistently shot around 50 percent from the field. With his ability to grab the rebound off a miss or get to the free throw line (he made more free throws than anyone in NBA history), where he shot 77 percent over his career, Malone was one of the most efficient offensive machines in basketball history. Note the method to his madness: with Bird in position to grab an off-side rebound, Moses puts up a soft shot that will either go in the basket or will bounce out on Moses' side of the rim.

sophomore year to turn pro in 1970, professional scouts had begun to watch underclassmen and high schoolers more closely. The NBA had a pretty strict code stating that a player had to wait until his college class had graduated before he could play in the league. The ABA had no such code. Also, the courts had ruled that the NCAA could not keep underclassmen or anyone from pursuing professional money.

When Bickerstaff reached Petersburg, Malone was leaning toward attending college at New Mexico, Clemson, or Maryland. However, observers felt that whatever school Moses attended would end up on probation for having solicited him illegally. One college had purchased him a new car; he frequently received money in the mail. Moses himself demanded two hundred dollars to visit any school. Star collegiate players visited Moses at home, a clear violation of NCAA rules. New Mexico and Maryland ran up huge bills in local Petersburg hotels. Moses, who had never been a strong student, suddenly began receiving straight A's, so he could qualify as eligible for his first college season.

Slowly, Bickerstaff began to win Moses and Mary Malone's confidence. Critics accused Utah and the ABA of immorality, but to Moses they were the only nonhypocrites in the bunch. Many thought that Moses, who rarely spoke, was dumb, but Bickerstaff recognized that the huge young man was not only very proud, but also extremely discerning. Bickerstaff understood that Malone's poverty worked in his favor. Unlike the colleges, Bickerstaff could promise Malone real money in large amounts. Once Moses began to seriously consider turning pro, he better perceived the hypocrisy of the college recruiters who spoke often of the sanctity of education but clearly didn't give a damn about Moses learning anything but basketball, which made them money. On April 17, 1974, the Utah Stars drafted Malone in the third round, and shortly thereafter he signed to become the first player to turn pro directly out of high school. In doing so, Moses also took care of those who truly loved him; three of the contract's first five clauses concerned direct payments to Mary Malone.

Thus, Moses was a legend before his first official game away from Petersburg High. He was six feet eleven inches (210.8cm) but still had the thin, lanky body of a late adolescent. While Boston Globe columnist Bob Ryan was attending one of the exhibition games before Moses' first year in the ABA, Larry Brown, now coach of the Indiana Pacers, came up to him and said, "Moses Malone is the greatest offensive rebounder I have ever seen in my life." Ryan was incredulous, but over time Brown was proved right.

In high school, Moses had displayed an amazing overall game, including dribbling, passing, and some outside shooting. But in the pro ranks Malone was restricted to rebounding and foul shooting for his first years. Oddly, late in his career his exceptional rebounding ability was often attributed to his tanklike body, but as a rookie, long before his body filled out,

Moses was grabbing many rebounds. In fact, Malone's uncanny rebounding ability was never the product of sheer muscle, but rather an ability to read shots, position himself accordingly, and then use his quickness to grab the ball. The key to his quickness was his exceptionally agile footwork. Often Moses would position himself near the baseline and then move back into the court as a shot went up. Then, he would grab the rebound and go up for a putback, often getting fouled and still making the shot in the process.

As a nineteen- and twenty-year-old rookie with the Utah Stars, Malone averaged almost 19 points and more than 14 rebounds per game. The Stars barely made the playoffs and were eliminated in the first round, but not before Moses grabbed 38 boards in one game, 23 on the offensive end. The next year Moses fractured his foot in training camp, and the Stars franchise folded before he returned. He was thus sold to the Spirits of St. Louis, where he teamed up with a plethora of future NBA stars like Maurice Lucas, Caldwell Jones, M.L. Carr, and wayward superstar Marvin Barnes. However, the overloaded Spirits had no team unity and failed to make the playoffs. When the ABA merged with the NBA in the following off-season, the Spirits folded and their players were placed in a dispersal draft. Moses was selected by the Portland Trail Blazers. But Portland already had superstar Bill Walton and had little interest in paying Malone's huge contract; they had drafted him to use as trade bait. Thus Moses was shipped to Buffalo, which also had little use for Malone's elaborate contract, and after two games, he was shipped to Houston to join the Rockets.

Thus, Moses joined a competent but aging Houston team that included forward Rudy Tomjanovich and flashy guard Calvin Murphy. With Moses crashing the boards, the Rockets improved nine games over the previous season and captured the Central Division. Moses was third in the league in rebounding with 13.1 per game. The Rockets advanced to the conference finals, where they were eliminated by the high-flying 76ers. The next year, however, was a disaster as the Rockets suffered a torrent of injuries and plummeted to last place. Moses missed 23 games, but his productivity increased to 15 rebounds and 19.4 points per game.

In 1978–79, Moses Malone fully matured as a basketball player. Behind Malone, the Rockets improved 19 games and once again made the playoffs. The league has kept official statistics on offensive rebounding since only the 1973–74 season, but before Malone came into the league the record was held by Paul Silas with 365 offensive rebounds in a season. In his first year in the NBA, Moses shattered that mark, garnering 437 offensive boards. In 1978–79, he broke *that* record by collecting an amazing 587 rebounds off the offensive glass. The record still stands. In fact, Dennis Rodman is the only player besides Moses to collect over 500 offensive rebounds in a season. Rodman did it once (523 in 1991–92); Malone did it three times. In 1978–79, Malone led

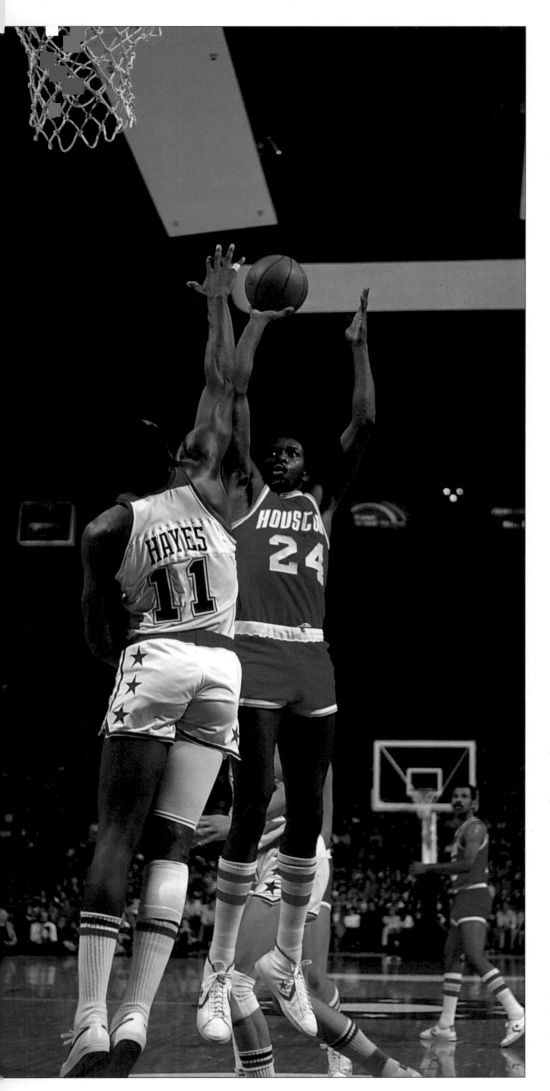

the league in overall rebounding by almost 5 rebounds per game over the nearest competition with a 17.6 average. He also finished fourth in scoring with 24.8 points. Not surprisingly, Moses was voted the NBA's Most Valuable Player.

The next season the Rockets and Malone fell off their game somewhat, though they advanced past the Spurs in the playoffs before losing to Larry Bird and Boston. In 1980–81, the Rockets shifted into the Western Conference and struggled in the regular season. The two first-round picks traded to Buffalo for Moses had taken their toll, and except for the young Malone, the Rockets were an aging cast. The Rockets never found a stable rotation of players all season, but Moses caught fire in the playoffs. In the opening round, they stunned the defending champion Lakers in Game One of a miniseries. L.A. bounced back to even the series at Houston and was confident heading back to the Forum for the decisive game. No such luck said Moses, and Houston pulled off a stunning upset, 89–86. Next, Houston bounced the heavily favored San Antonio Spurs and the Kansas City Kings, another Cinderella team, in the conference finals. Moses had won the NBA MVP two years before, but leading a team of has-beens and nobodies to the NBA finals served notice that Moses was truly among the league's elite players, if not, as some claimed, the best basketball player in the world. However, Moses was no match for a deep Celtics team that included Bird and three strong inside players, Cedric Maxwell, Kevin McHale, and seven-foot (213.3cm) Robert Parish. Still, the Rockets gave the Celtics a scare by winning Game Two at Boston Garden before losing in six games.

Moses once again won the league MVP in 1981–82 as he led the NBA in rebounding for the second straight season and averaged a career-high 31.1 points per game (second in the league). Seattle, however, knocked the Rockets out of the playoffs in round one. With Moses' contract nearing its expiration, the Rockets knew they had to trade their superstar. So in the off-season, Moses was dealt to the powerful Philadelphia 76ers. With Dr. J, Bobby Jones, and Andrew Toney, the 76ers had a great nucleus that had just lost in the NBA finals. Moses was expected to finally put them over the top and end six years of frustration (that had begun when Dr. J had arrived) in which the Sixers had won more games than any team in the league but lost in three finals.

The 1982–83 76ers are considered one of the greatest teams in NBA history. From the outset of the season, it was evident that Moses jelled perfectly with Dr. J and the rest of the Sixers. A man of few words, Moses led by example with his blue-collar work ethic. Bobby Jones summarized Malone's effect on the club: "His was silent leadership. He always had confidence and so you always had confidence because he was so dominant at his position. Even if things weren't going right for you, you always knew, 'Well, we can depend on Moses.' Because every night he's gonna grab the rebounds. Every night he's gonna put it back in and get to the free throw line. That was reassuring." Moses won another MVP Award, and the Sixers stormed through the league in the regular season, compiling a 65–17 record, the best mark in a decade. When asked how the Sixers would fare in the playoffs, Moses responded with the usual Malonian monosyllables "Fo, Fo, Fo," meaning that the Sixers were going to sweep all three of their opponents. They came close, losing one game to Milwaukee (a virtually meaningless Game Four) in the conference finals; they swept defending champion Los Angeles in the finals. It was the most impressive playoff performance in NBA history.

During his championship season Malone impressed upon America that he was truly one of the game's all-time greats. As usual, Malone controlled the glass and was a great free throw shooter, but he also exhibited a nice outside touch on occasion (though he rarely ventured outside, since he couldn't collect offensive rebounds there), proved he could run the court (even dribbling and passing on breaks, rarities that always made the highlight reel), and proved he was a defensive force in the lane by blocking shots.

Malone also shed the stereotype of the unintelligent man, which had followed him since he had chosen to skip college and was further exacerbated by his curt responses to questions. By ruling with an iron hand over the whole NBA for a season, Malone was regularly in the public spotlight, in which he proved to be a highly insightful man, attuned to society's misgivings, and, by example, an advocate of intense personal pride. In fact, his mature on-court game was a reflection of the man: hardworking, no nonsense, an unflinching tower of power. In an extended interview in Playboy magazine, Malone even came out of his shell and proved to be eloquent beyond all expectations and knowledgeable about every facet of the game. At the age of twenty-eight, Moses ruled the basketball world.

Unfortunately for Malone, the Sixers' reign atop the NBA lasted only one year. Moses missed 11 games in 1983–84, and the team finished 13 games worse than they had the previous season and were unceremoniously dispatched by the New Jersey Nets in the first round of the playoffs. The club bounced back the next season, but were bumped off by the Celtics in the conference finals in five games. Moses won an unprecedented fifth consecutive rebounding title in 1984–85, but by that time it was clear that the Sixers team he had joined was aging fast. Charles Barkley became a star in his second year with the 76ers in 1985–86, and he petitioned the club to keep Moses. However, Philadelphia management thought Barkley could supplant Malone, and in the off-season Moses was dealt to Washington in a trade that proved disastrous for the 76ers.

In Washington, Malone led the Bullets to back-to-back playoff appearances, but was unable to rally a weak supporting cast to greater accomplishment. His days as an elite star in the league were over. He still averaged 11 rebounds and more than 20 points a

game and collected as many offensive boards as any player, but he was no longer a one-man wrecking crew. Recognizing that they had to rebuild, the Bullets shipped Moses to Atlanta, where the Hawks, led by Dominique Wilkins, hoped Moses could lift an always competitive team to a championship. Moses responded with a strong season and the Hawks won 52 games, but were upset in the first round of the playoffs. Moses was clearly in the twilight of his brilliant career. He played one more year for the Hawks before moving on to a weak Milwaukee team and a final year as a starter, in which he finished fourth in the league in offensive rebounding. The next year he played in only 11 games. Most fans assumed it was the end of his career, but high-quality backup centers are few in the NBA, so Moses signed with the 76ers for 1993–94, and then with the Spurs for the 1994–95 season (to back up superstar center David Robinson). With the best regular-season record in the league, the Spurs had a serious shot at a title, but were dispatched by Hakeem Olajuwon and the Rockets in the Western Conference finals.

In his twenty-one professional seasons, Moses has climbed up the all-time lists in many statistical categories. He ranks third in scoring in the NBA, behind only Jabbar and Chamberlain. He is fifth in rebounding, behind Chamberlain, Russell, Jabbar, and Elvin Hayes. In the combined ABA-NBA stats, he is third in rebounding, though fourth in scoring (Erving passes him in third place). He ranks third in games played, behind Jabbar and Robert Parish. On both the ABA-NBA and NBA lists he ranks first in free throws made and second in free throws attempted. And, of course, Moses Malone ranks first all-time in offensive rebounds.

Chapter 5

MICHAEL AND THE DREAM TEAM

By the mid-1980s the entire nation was caught up in the Lakers-Celtics rivalry. That was the visible upside to the NBA. After 1983, the Sixers declined into an afterthought and few fans knew much about the NBA beyond the two superteams. That was the downside. College superstar Ralph Sampson was exiled to Houston, which was a downer, but the Patrick Ewing lottery was won by the New York Knicks, a big plus for the league. When Hakeem Olajuwon joined Sampson in Houston to form a vaunted "Twin Towers" attack and the Rockets upset the Lakers to reach the finals against the mighty Celtics in 1986, the Rockets' audacity did little for the nation's fans, who mainly sulked about the interruption of the Boston–Los Angeles duel. But perhaps the problem was that the Rockets were upstarts who really had little chance against the Celtics, who won in six games. However, in Detroit a championship ensemble was slowly being pieced together, gaining momentum each year, and in Chicago a man named Michael Jordan was establishing himself as a legend of spectacular dimension with an unrivaled desire to win. In 1986–87, the Pistons came within one terrible mental lapse of defeating the Celtics (when Isiah Thomas threw the ball away to Larry Bird in the closing seconds of the pivotal Game Five of the Eastern Conference finals, allowing the Celtics to win by 1 point) and Jordan won his first league scoring title. The league was no longer bipolar.

The Pistons and Jordan's Bulls continued to improve during the next season. The Pistons knocked off Boston and then challenged the Lakers in a seven-game final, in which Los Angeles succeeded in becoming the first team to repeat as NBA champs since the 1968–69 Celtics. Jordan not only led the NBA in scoring and commercial endorsements, but he also paced the Bulls to 50 wins and a spectacular first-round playoff victory over the Cavaliers. Jordan's play was so spectacular that fans across the country tuned in whenever he played, bringing unparalleled exposure to his early playoff opponents. Likewise, the Lakers were stretched to seven games by the Jazz (with Karl Malone) and the Mavericks (with Mark Aguirre) before reaching the finals. The Knicks even made the playoffs. The NBA fan base was growing.

In 1988–89, the Knicks won their division, the Bulls upset the Knicks in the playoffs and lost in the conference finals, and the Pistons won the NBA title over the Lakers. In the spring of 1989, the cities of New York, Chicago, and Los Angeles were going absolutely crazy about the NBA, and the nation pretty much followed suit. The next year Charles Barkley almost single-handedly led the 76ers to a division crown; the Knicks upset the Celtics in the playoffs; David Robinson revitalized the Spurs; Phoenix reached the conference championship for the second straight year (this time they ousted the Lakers to get there); the Bulls battled the Pistons to seven games in the Eastern Conference finals; and Detroit pummeled the Trail Blazers in the finals. By this point, the NBA

An airborne Michael Jordan prepares to drop the ball in the hole with his left hand. Atlanta Hawk rebounding machine Kevin Willis lurks near the basket at Chicago Stadium, the ancient venue that Michael adored. Jordan transformed Chicago Stadium into his personal museum of basketball artistry. During Michael's sabbatical from the NBA, the Bulls abandoned the stadium to the wrecking crews and moved into the adjacent United Center, a brand-new, state-of-the-art facility that Michael despises. Ironically, a monumental statue of an in-flight Michael Jordan adorns the outside of the Bulls' new home.

was recognized as a league of up-and-coming stars spread throughout each division.

From 1990–91 through 1992–93, the whole world watched while Michael Jordan ascended to the pinnacle of the basketball world. Parity continued to spread throughout the rest of the league, but Michael and the Bulls were poised to supplant the Pistons atop the league. To the delight of the league office, no doubt, and the whole sporting world, they did. By the spring of 1993 very few citizens of the United States, it seemed, were not Michael Jordan fans. Jordan's annual drive to the title was followed as closely as any sporting event in the country, and the same was true across the globe. Consequently, the public became well educated about the NBA. In particular, the league's pantheon of stars became veritable household names, especially after the selection of the U.S. Olympic squad— the Dream Team—for the 1992 Games in Barcelona.

The great stars of this era are many, but first mention belongs to Isiah Thomas' running mates on the Pistons, most notably guard Joe Dumars, rebounding and defensive demon Dennis Rodman, and wily center Bill Laimbeer. It took a while, but Patrick Ewing became one of the league's great centers. Although Cleveland's Brad Daugherty is not Ewing's equal, he has often played brilliantly when not injured, which is also true of Cavalier point guard Mark Price. John Stockton of Utah broke Magic Johnson's all-time record for assists. Forward Tom Chambers and point guard Dennis Johnson led strong Phoenix teams. Forward Chris Mullin emerged as a star for the Golden State Warriors, and teammate point guard Tim Hardaway seemed headed for superstardom before a series of knee injuries slowed him down. Guard Clyde Drexler was the spectacular centerpiece of a number of Portland teams that challenged for the league title. Sleek forward Scottie Pippin played in Michael Jordan's shadow on the dynastic Bulls, but he clearly developed into an all-around star in his own right.

Karl Malone, the great power forward of the Utah Jazz, has already had a tremendous career and has been the backbone of a contending team for the past nine seasons. Malone consistently places in the top ten in rebounding and scoring, and is eighth all-time in points scored per game. Karl bangs under the boards and runs the court with equally spectacular effectiveness. However, his place among the NBA's all-time elite is

Clyde "The Glide" Drexler soars to the basket for a rousing two-handed slam. This particular dunk is one of high-flying Clyde's signature moves; usually the product of a fast break, it's over in an instant. When Drexler joined the Blazers he was already a renowned dunker from his days as a charter member of the University of Houston's Phi Slamma Jamma. As a pro, Drexler evolved into a great all-around player with a dangerous outside shot that complemented his explosive drives to the basket and breathtaking in-flight maneuvers. Drexler also had a thief's sensibility on defense that disrupted opponents, caused turnovers, and produced fast breaks that resulted in two-fisted, full-speed Clyde jams. Drexler was a member of the gold medal–winning Dream Team. Drexler rejoined college teammate Hakeem Olajuwon on the Rockets midway through 1994–95, and Houston went on to repeat as NBA champs.

not as secure as that of the irrepressible Charles Wade
Barkley. Malone has carried his team to the confer-
ence finals twice and failed to reach the finals. Sir
Charles has played in two conference finals, but he
lifted the Suns over the top in the Western
Conference in 1992–93, the year in which he won the
NBA MVP Award, an honor yet to be bestowed upon
Karl Malone. Similarly, Hakeem Olajuwon solidified
his place among the NBA's all-time greats with his
spectacular 1993–94 and 1994–95 seasons. Olajuwon
led the Rockets past Patrick Ewing and the New York
Knicks to their first-ever title, won the league and
playoff MVP Awards, and was named the NBA
Defensive Player of the Year for the second consecutive season. In the 1994–95 season, Olajuwon lifted
his team to the NBA title again, besting Shaquille
O'Neal and the Orlando Magic in the finals.
Nevertheless, one player's accomplishments stand out
from the rest in the late eighties and early nineties:
His Airness, Michael Jordan.

RIGHT, TOP: The Detroit Pistons' flamboyant point guard Isiah Thomas
knifes his way through the Atlanta Hawks' interior defense during the
1987 playoffs. Thomas was the most spectacular offensive player on the
great Pistons team of the late eighties and early nineties that won consecutive NBA titles. An exceptionally quick point guard, Isiah was a great
penetrator, flashy passer, and streak shooter. While Isiah was renowned
for his astounding single-game performances, he also suffered off-nights.
However, the Pistons were a very deep team in their prime, and some
of Isiah's quiet games were probably a sign of his egalitarianism.
Thomas was at his best as a free-form improviser, but was an essential
element of a team that achieved greatness by emphasizing selflessness.
RIGHT, BOTTOM: The Cleveland Cavaliers' crafty Mark Price cuts to the
middle against the Milwaukee Bucks. Teamed with the intimidating front
line of seven-footer (213.3cm) Brad Daugherty and six-foot-ten-inchers
(208.2cm) Larry Nance and John "Hot Rod" Williams, Price led the Cavs
to some tremendous records in the late eighties and early nineties.
However, Cleveland was continually victimized by Michael Jordan in the
playoffs and by numerous injuries. Price is the most accurate free throw
shooter in NBA history, making 90.6 percent of his attempts from the
charity stripe. BELOW: John Stockton of the Utah Jazz is one of the
greatest point guards of all time. He broke Magic Johnson's all time
record for career assists during the 1994–95 season.

MICHAEL *Jordan*

Jordan takes a breather in Game One of the 1993 NBA finals versus the Phoenix Suns; he set an NBA finals scoring record in the series, averaging 41 points per game. The 1991 finals was a showdown between Michael and Magic; the 1992 finals was MJ against Clyde Drexler; and 1993 was His Airness versus Sir Charles. Michael reflected, "If they're going to have a chance to judge you as the best player in the game, then give them a chance to see why. My entire career was a progression of developing skills to stay on top. At first they said about me that I didn't pass enough. So I learned from that. Then, they said I couldn't go to my left. And I practiced that, and they stopped saying that. Then, they said I couldn't hit the jump shot consistently, that I was primarily a driver and a dunker. I practiced my jump shot. Eventually, they didn't know where I was going or what I was going to do and that became the most lethal part of my game."

What Michael Jordan offered his fans, as they watched him play Dr. Naismith's game, was not unlike what a great artist or musician offers his audience at the peak of his career. Indeed, many more Americans grow up following sports than studying the arts. In fact, only movies, television, and pop music rival sports as a form of mass entertainment; many more adult American males have played baseball, basketball, or football than know how to play an instrument, let alone make a movie. People watching television on couches across the globe played the game Michael played. In the past decade, increasing numbers watched as Magic, Kareem, Larry, and Isiah awed viewers with their state-of-the-art games. But, in fact, these players were just laying the groundwork for the true master. By the early 1990s, Jordan was playing basketball virtually to perfection. It will never be done any better, and tacitly, the whole world knew this. Within the artificial confines delimited by the rules of the game of basketball, Michael Jordan came as close to pure beauty as humanly possible. Countless men and women around the world loved him for this, and he asked for nothing less.

It seems almost impossible that Jordan's ascendancy took place in such a cynical age. There were controversies concerning Michael, but they never tarnished his image. Not that Jordan was some Teflon-coated media simulation—no, Jordan was absolutely committed to his art. Under the most intense scrutiny,

Michael performed almost nightly in the world's living room. He never failed his millions of fans. Of all sports stars, only Babe Ruth and Pelé have ever achieved such an awesome status.

Then in October 1993, a few months after his father had been tragically murdered, Jordan, perhaps realizing that he had no solitude even when he most needed it, shocked the sports world by announcing his retirement from basketball. His legions of fans never had an opportunity to say thank you and goodbye. Then in the spring of 1995, Michael returned to the NBA, following an ill-conceived, self-imposed exile in minor league baseball. Virtually the whole world stopped to embrace its returning hero. In his absence from the NBA, Jordan's myth had gained greater depth. The public's adoration of Michael, the NBA's top superstar, became colored by respect for Michael the man, flawed as we all are, without whom there would never have been Jordan the artist, the master, the greatest basketball player ever.

• • •

Michael Jeffrey Jordan was born in Brooklyn, New York, on February 17, 1963, to James and Deloris Jordan. The Jordans were a North Carolina family, but Michael, their fourth child, was born while father James was attending a General Electric training school. Shortly thereafter the family returned to the small town of Wallace, North Carolina, where James, a sharecropper's son, was advancing through the General Electric hierarchy from forklift operator to dispatcher and, eventually, to supervisor. Mother Deloris was equally successful at the job she took at United Carolina Bank after her children were in day school; she rose from a drive-through teller to the head of customer service. The Jordans believed in the value of hard work.

The civil rights movement's attack on Jim Crow racism was just beginning to affect rural North Carolina. The society was still largely segregated, but change and social tension were in the air. Nevertheless, young Michael was a happy, if mischievous, child. Michael's parents and teachers tried to tell Michael what not to do, but he rarely heeded their advice. Once, he almost cut off a toe with an ax.

The Jordans moved to the small port town of Wilmington, North Carolina, in 1970. Soon the family's central interest was youth sports. Michael merely followed in the footsteps of his older brothers, James and Larry. Michael first excelled as a baseball pitcher, hurling two no-hitters in Little League. Then he led his team to the Babe Ruth League state championship, batting over .500 with 5 home runs in seven games and pitching a one-hitter in the semifinals. However, baseball was considered to be a white sport in Wilmington, while blacks typically played basketball. Though he was a star, Michael quit baseball after ninth grade.

Michael's older brother Larry was a star on the Laney High basketball team. When Michael selected 23 as his number it was because it was virtually half that of his revered brother's number, 45. Larry and Michael would play hours of one-on-one in the Jordans' backyard. Early in their rivalry, Larry won handily. Then Michael sprouted to five feet eleven inches (180.3cm) in his sophomore year, and the balance of power began to shift.

However, Michael failed to make the final cut for the varsity in his sophomore year. Michael was crushed, convinced that he was passed over for a taller but inferior player. Michael thought of quitting basketball, but instead he used his frustration to strengthen his resolve. He woke up at six each morning for extra practice.

While Michael was a personable child, he struggled a bit with the changes brought about by adolescence. Always mischievous, he was suspended from high school three times his freshman year, he was unwilling to hold a job, and was a flop with girls. He was so convinced he was fated to be a bachelor that he enrolled in home economics classes to learn how to keep house. Such worries aside, Michael's burgeoning competitiveness made him a strong student and a superior jayvee ballplayer.

Entering his junior year, Michael was confident that he would make the varsity basketball team. He had averaged 25 points on the junior varsity and, even more important, had grown to six feet three inches (190.5cm). Indeed, Coach Fred Lynch not only selected Michael for the varsity but also tapped him as a starting forward. Michael responded with an excellent season, though he finished his junior year with little attention from college recruiters. Thus, unlike many high school basketball stars, Michael continued to study hard, since he was determined to attend college.

The summer before his senior year Michael attended some basketball camps in North Carolina. He failed to make much of an impression on many people until Roy Williams, now the head coach at Kansas, noticed Jordan at Dean Smith's prestigious camp at Chapel Hill. Williams recommended him to the top camp in the nation, the Five Star Camp in Pittsburgh. The Five Star had three one-week sessions, and Jordan arrived for the final two, the first being the exclusive domain of the most highly recruited seniors. Michael, however, made his mark, winning camp MVP each of the final two weeks. Coaches from around the country were awed not only by Michael's leaping ability, but also by his skill at putting the ball on the floor and exploding to the basket. The camp was a turning point in Michael's life; he knew he could be a star.

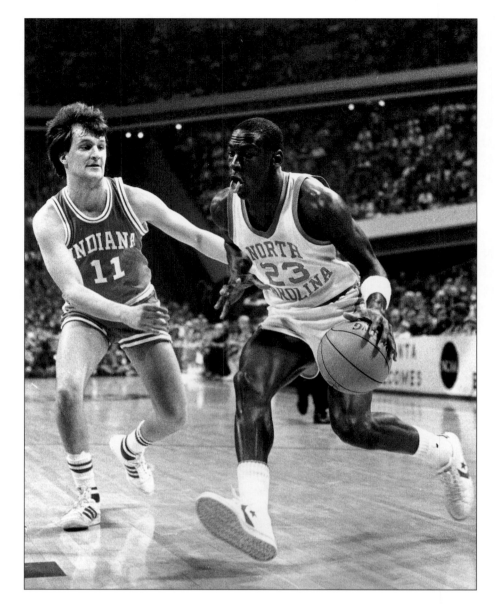

Michael was still not widely recruited outside North Carolina, so in November of his senior year he committed to Dean Smith and the University of North Carolina Tar Heels (even though he grew up a fan of the North Carolina State Wolfpack and had hated the Tar Heels). Smith had recruited Michael actively and his emphasis on education pleased the Jordans. Michael was a solid student and was confident he could pull his weight at such a good university. Michael had a fine senior year on the Laney varsity, was the runner-up for North Carolina Player of the Year, and felt prepared for Chapel Hill.

Dean Smith knew that Michael was talented, but was unprepared for what he saw at autumn practices. During autumn one-on-one drills Smith realized that "we didn't have anyone who could guard him." In these practices, Jordan earned a starting spot on the top-ranked team in the country before ever playing a game. Michael completed a starting lineup that included Sam Perkins at center, James Worthy at forward, Matt Doherty at small forward, and Jimmy Black at point guard.

Coach Smith's system emphasized discipline and teamwork. Players of transcendent talent had passed through Chapel Hill before; like them, Michael was expected to sacrifice individual achievement for the good of the team. When Michael became the NBA's

Michael drives against Indiana Hoosier forward Dan Dakich in what turned out to be Jordan's final college game, on March 22, 1984. Dakich learned that he was expected to guard Jordan on the day before this third-round game of the NCAA tournament. "I went promptly to my room and threw up," Dakich said. The next day the Indiana forward played the game of his life, holding Jordan to 6 field goals and forcing him into 4 turnovers. Jordan fouled out of the game with a little more than a minute remaining; the Hoosiers shot an amazing 64 percent from the field and eliminated the heavily favored Tar Heels 72–68. Ironically, Jordan later played for Indiana Coach Bob Knight on the 1984 U.S. Olympic team that swept to the gold medal in Los Angeles.

Vintage 1987 Jordan: Mike poses, tongue in evidence, as he slams the ball through the hoop against the Clippers; both opponents and teammates are reduced to a blur in the rearview mirror. By his third season, Jordan had established himself as one of the game's all-time greatest scorers and most spectacular players. Rumored to have a four-foot (1.2m) vertical leap, Jordan soared over the entire basketball world. Like the legendary Dr. J, Jordan's dunks would bring down the full houses he attracted everywhere he played. While his "kiss-the-rim" and patented backhanded, behind-the-head, tongue-wagging dunks were showstoppers, nothing in Jordan lore compared to the maneuver he immortalized in the 1988 slam-dunk contest. Taking off fifteen feet (4.5m) from the basket, Michael leaped forward as he elevated; with the ball in front of him, he cocked his arm back slightly and, by bending his knees to lift his feet further off the ground, created the impression that the length of his body was parallel to the floor. After floating in this horizontal position for eight to ten feet (2.4 to 3m), he slammed the ball home and returned to Earth.

most prolific scorer, the joke circulated: "Who's the only man who could hold Michael Jordan under 20 points a game? Dean Smith." Jokes aside, Smith taught Jordan an invaluable lesson about the importance of teamwork, which was the key to Jordan's later development from an NBA superstar to an NBA champion. Furthermore, Michael's scoring totals might not have been astronomical at UNC but his college career was spectacular nonetheless.

In his freshman season, Jordan established himself as the team's third scoring threat, complementing Worthy and Perkins, and contributed further with his unrelenting defense and expanding all-around game. Michael's athletic skills awed everyone, but even more impressive was his commitment to improve. Worthy noted that Michael rarely made the same mistake twice and Matt Doherty observed that "he's thinking all the time on the floor....He's going to be something awesome before he leaves this place."

Off the court, Michael made a smooth transition to college life. Fellow freshman Buzz Peterson, who was named North Carolina's top high school player over Michael the previous year, was Jordan's roommate and the two became best friends. Peterson found Michael to be quite a character; on one hand, Jordan "spoke trash" incessantly on and off the court, telling everyone how much better he was than them; on the other hand, Michael's personal habits betrayed tremendous modesty—he kept his room meticulously neat and worked studiously to fulfill any and all obligations. Most importantly, Buzz learned that Michael was a true friend, one who valued personal bonds more than anything else.

The 1981–82 season had a storybook ending for the Tar Heels, one that Chapel Hill had waited a long time for. Under Dean Smith, the Tar Heels had reached the NCAA Final Four five times and played for the championship twice, but had never won the national title. The team had an excellent regular season, won the ACC tournament, entered the NCAA ranked number one in the country, and advanced to the finals with a string of convincing victories. The Heels' opponent in the finals was Georgetown, led by their freshman sensation, seven-foot (213.3cm) center Patrick Ewing. It was a marquee matchup played in front of a capacity crowd in New Orleans' massive Superdome and attracted a huge national television audience. The contest exceeded expectations, providing unbelievable twists and turns from the opening tip-off until the last second. Jordan said he had a sense going into the game that he was going to do something special, but he was relatively quiet throughout the tight contest until the final 5 minutes. Then—like he would do so many times throughout his career—he took over, scoring 3 of Carolina's final 5 baskets, setting up the other 2, and twice grabbing key offensive rebounds on missed field goal attempts by teammates. Michael's heroics staked UNC to a 61–58 lead with 2:30 left, but Georgetown remained composed and took the lead on Eric "Sleepy" Floyd's jumper with less than a minute left. North Carolina

called time-out with 30 seconds left and Coach Smith decided to cross-up the Hoyas by calling a play for someone besides Worthy, who had been hot throughout the game. Smith figured the Hoyas would pack the middle to crowd Worthy and Perkins, so he called for a play designed to fool the Hoyas into thinking the Heels were looking inside, thus creating an open jump shot for Jordan. Smith whispered "Make it, Michael" at the end of the sideline conference. Smith was taking quite a gamble, as Jordan would not develop a consistent jump shot until his fourth year in the NBA. The Tar Heels inbounded the ball and moved it around the perimeter. Jordan was open the third time he handled the ball, and he let fly a seventeen-foot (5.1m) jumper as two Hoyas rushed at him. The shot had an unusually high arc, but found nothing but net; the Tar Heels led 63–62. A few seconds remained and the Hoyas quickly inbounded the ball and moved upcourt, but in one of sport's all-time gaffes, guard Fred Brown mistook Worthy for a teammate and threw the ball directly to him. The Tar Heels were champions, Dean Smith had his coveted national title, and Michael Jordan was a hero.

While Jordan would have become more of a team leader in his sophomore year anyway because Worthy skipped his senior season to turn pro, the "shot" as Michael's championship-winning shot became known around Chapel Hill, had a transformative effect on Michael's career. For the first time, he was "the man." Michael later observed "that's when everything started, that's when Michael Jordan started to get his respect." In typical Jordan fashion, getting his due did not mean he relaxed his work ethic; he was back at the gym playing hoops two days after the title game. During the summer, Tar Heel greats past and present played with Jordan in casual scrimmages; and Michael, bursting with confidence, dominated everyone who showed up in the summer of 1982, including NBA stars.

Over the next two seasons, Jordan distinguished himself while remaining within Coach Smith's team concept. In his sophomore season, Jordan pulled three games out of the hat in the last second. When he needed to, Jordan stepped up to make steals, block shots, or score points. Jordan's heroics earned him All-American honors, and *The Sporting News* named him College Player of the Year. But all those last-second victories masked the fact that the team was weaker without Worthy, and though they maintained a high ranking throughout the season, they fell to Georgia in the third round of the NCAA playoffs. But Michael was even more spectacular as a junior. Time and again he took over games at key moments. It often seemed that he could score at will, that he could easily beat any defender off the dribble. Driving to the basket more frequently, Michael began to fully exploit his tremendous leaping ability, producing an astonishing array of dunks and midair acrobatics that thrilled fans. Jordan and fellow All-American Sam Perkins led the number-one-ranked Tar Heels through an amazing regular-season, in which they became the first team in eleven years to win all their regular-season ACC games. But Duke upset UNC in the ACC tournament and the Tar Heels fell to Indiana in the third round of the NCAAs.

Throughout the spring of his junior year Michael contemplated whether he would turn pro or play his senior year at UNC. Michael loved UNC, was very comfortable there, and knew life in the pros would be more stressful. Furthermore, his mother was adamant that he complete his college degree, and Michael, who had done well in his classes, felt strongly about this too. But Michael could earn his degree taking summer classes without risking an injury that could cost him the multimillion-dollar contract he would sign as a top draft pick in the NBA. Michael felt he was ready to play in the world's best league. He announced he was eligible for the NBA draft.

Michael had a busy summer in 1984. He played on the U.S. Olympic Team, was drafted by the Chicago Bulls, selected an agent, and signed a shoe contract. Ironically, the U.S. squad was coached by Bobby Knight, whose team had upset UNC in the NCAA tournament. Many wondered if Michael's penchant for improvisation would provoke a clash with Knight, who was even more emphatic about disciplined team play than Dean Smith and had a legendary temper. At training camp, Jordan frequently beat defenders simply by taking to the air and then deciding what to do. Initially, Knight would stop play and explain to Michael why this was wrong, but once Knight saw that Michael's ploy almost always worked because he could stay elevated much longer than anyone else, he allowed Michael this indulgence. Jordan made the star-studded team along with the likes of Patrick Ewing, Chris Mullin, Wayman Tisdale, and fellow Tar Heel Sam Perkins. Because of the boycott of the 1984 Olympics by the Soviet Union and its allies, the U.S. team faced little competition and easily swept to the gold medal.

University of Houston center Hakeem Olajuwon was viewed as the top prospect in the draft, followed by Jordan and University of Kentucky seven-footer (213.3cm) Sam Bowie. There was some question about whether Jordan was better suited to play guard or forward. Houston selected favorite son Olajuwon with the first pick. Portland went second, and in a move their fans would deride for years, they passed over Jordan in favor of Bowie (whose career would be devastated by injuries) because they already had an excellent small forward-guard in Clyde Drexler. Chicago picked next, and in this way Michael Jordan became a Bull.

Earlier in the summer Michael selected David Falk of Proserv as his agent. Proserv was an ambitious company that was in the forefront of landing endorsement contracts for team athletes. Traditionally, these contracts went mainly to the stars of such single-player sports as golf and tennis (which, conspicuously, were dominated by whites) because of their high name recognition. David Falk, Michael Jordan, and Nike were about to change all that.

Michael Jordan drives against Laker Byron Scott. Sometimes Michael's exceptional ballhandling and passing talents were overshadowed by his aerial and overall scoring skills. This was not the case late in the 1988–89 season, when Bulls Coach Doug Collins experimented with Jordan at point guard to ensure that the ball would be in Jordan's hands more often than it already was. Jordan responded to the change in position by scoring as much as ever, posting a few triple-doubles, and averaging more than 10 assists per game.

At that time, most top NBA prospects signed a contract with a shoe company before their rookie season. However, all this entailed was doing a photo shoot and agreeing to wear the shoes in return for a few thousand dollars and, of course, an unlimited supply of custom-made shoes. Falk, however, sought something more ambitious: a new Michael Jordan signature shoe backed by a huge ad campaign that would earn his client a royalty fee for each pair sold. Actually, Falk had made the same proposal for James Worthy two years earlier. The difference this time was one company's response. Nike had reaped tremendous profits in the late seventies and early eighties during the running boom, but in 1984 their stock was plummeting for the first time. Nike executives were trying desperately to turn things around. By chance, they had also failed to sign any major basketball stars in recent years. Nike decided to take a huge risk and, surpassing even Falk's expectations, offered Jordan the most lucrative endorsement contract in NBA history. As it turned out, Nike's gamble reaped huge rewards.

Before Jordan's arrival, the Chicago Bulls were a terrible team; in 1983–84 they compiled the worst record in franchise history, 27–55, one game worse than the previous year. In 1984–85, the Bulls were a terrible team with a brilliant rookie. From the beginning of training camp, word of Jordan's exploits spread throughout the league. Bulls Coach Kevin Loughery was widely quoted as saying that whatever practice squad Michael was on would win. Consequently, expectations were sky-high. But Michael far exceeded anything imagined. Jordan instantly established himself as a first-rate scorer who could rebound, pass, and play ferocious defense. His aerial acrobatics electrified fans, who flocked to see Michael wherever the Bulls played; his spectacular, gravity-defying dunks were frequently featured on the nightly news highlight reels. And amazingly, he single-handedly turned the Bulls around; Chicago began the season 13–9 and was briefly tied for first. By Thanksgiving, Nike began its "Air Jordan" campaign with a series of spectacular commercials. Michael received rave reviews from veterans like Larry Bird, who said, "Never seen anyone like him. He's the best ever. Yep. At this stage, he's doing more than I ever did." Fans elected him to the All-Star team. The Jordan legend was taking shape.

There were, however, growing pains. The Bulls fell back to earth after their fast start and Michael grew impatient with his teammates, who, in turn, often held the wunderkind in disdain. The Bulls finished 38–44 and were trounced by the Milwaukee Bucks in the first round of the playoffs. Michael led the team in points, rebounds, and assists, becoming only the third player (alongside Dave Cowens and Larry Bird) to accomplish such a trifecta. His 28.2 points per game made him third in the league in scoring and he was named NBA Rookie of the Year. Michael had rekindled Chicago's interest in the Bulls. A new ownership group purchased the franchise and brought in a new management staff that hired a new coaching staff, and everyone exuded enthusiasm. The future looked bright, but first it was rocky.

Michael broke a tiny bone in his left foot early in his second season, keeping him sidelined for the balance of the year. Team doctors and management advised Michael to sit out the remainder of the season, but Michael felt the Bulls front office was trying to tank the season in order to get a high draft pick; after secretly playing in some pickup games in North Carolina, he declared himself ready to play. Bulls management said no, and the doctors concurred, but Michael insisted. The result was a bizarre compromise in which Michael was allowed to play toward the end of the season, but only for 7 minutes per half. Finally, Coach Stan Albeck, trapped in an absurd situation, rebelled and began letting Michael play for more minutes. Jordan responded by lofting the Bulls into the postseason and then performing spectacularly against the Boston Celtics in the first round, scoring a playoff record 63 points in Game Two, though the great Celtics team swept the Bulls. When asked about

Michael Jordan floats into the lane, preparing to launch a jumper over Boston's Kevin McHale during Game Two of the 1986 first-round playoff match-up between the number one seed Boston Celtics and number eight Chicago Bulls. The 1986 Celtics set the all-time record for winning percentage at home, losing only once all season. Michael Jordan missed all but 18 regular-season games for Chicago, but rejoined the team, against doctor's orders, for the stretch run and helped lift the team into the playoffs. Jordan had the flu in Game One but still poured in 49 points. In Game Two his fever subsided, but he was on fire, scoring 63 points to set a new all-time playoff scoring record. Even more impressive, he single-handedly extended the Celtics to double overtime. In the end, Boston prevailed 135–131 and Michael sat dejected in the locker room; taking little solace in his record, he couldn't believe he had missed a jumper that would have won the game at the end of the first overtime.

risking his career in order to play, Michael endeared himself to fans and added to his growing myth, saying simply, "Basketball is my dream, my love; I'm not worried about the financial part."

In the autumn of 1986, Michael picked up where he had left off the previous season: on a scoring rampage. Michael's assault on the league's baskets lasted the entire 1986–87 season. In the process he became the only player in NBA history other than Wilt Chamberlain to total more than 3,000 points in a season, averaging 37.1 per game. Michael had numerous spectacular nights, but the most productive stretch came late in the season when he scored 53, 50, and 61 in consecutive games. In the third game, at home versus Atlanta on April 16, Michael set an NBA record by scoring 23 consecutive Chicago points. The 61 points would remain his highest total for a regulation-length game.

In his third season, Jordan's celebrity began to increase exponentially. Fans in Chicago and throughout the league marveled at Jordan's scoring exploits and sportscasters across the country never failed to mention his point total when reporting a Bulls score. Jordan also added to his legend by winning the slam-dunk contest during All-Star weekend in Seattle. And filmmaker Spike Lee contributed to the Michael myth with the first of his celebrated Nike commercials. Part of what made Jordan so appealing to fans was his intensity while playing the game. Whether he was attacking the basket with his tongue waving around, flashing his smile after a score, or scowling at an opponent, Michael was always magnetic and photogenic. Michael's face became ubiquitous in advertisements; he was becoming one of the most famous and recognizable people on earth.

The 1986–87 Bulls maintained a .500 clip throughout the season. Only second-year power forward Charles Oakley provided Michael with quality support. However, Michael was pleased with new coach Doug Collins because Collins favored a fast pace. The Bulls were once again dismissed by the Celtics in three straight games in the first round of the playoffs in the spring of 1987. Michael had to be happy with his spectacular season, but he declared his willingness to share scoring duties if it resulted in more victories. Jordan's scoring total dropped to 2,868 points (35 per game) in 1987–88 and the Bulls won ten more games. Both statistics were probably related to the arrival of two rookies, sleek forward Scottie Pippen and power forward Horace Grant. Neither was a starter but they contributed instantly and added depth to the team. The All-Star Game was held in Chicago and was a veritable coronation ceremony for King Michael; he won his second consecutive slam-dunk contest and also garnered the All-Star Game MVP. For the second straight year Michael led the league in steals with 259 and also blocked more than 100 shots. No one else in NBA history has compiled 200 steals and 100 blocks in the same season. In recognition of this achievement Michael was named Defensive Player of the Year. When Michael

was voted league MVP he became the first player to receive these two awards in the same season. The Bulls won their first playoff series of the Jordan era, defeating Cleveland in the first round in a tightly contested five-game miniseries in which Michael averaged 45 points, but were dismissed by the Pistons in the second round.

Heading into the 1988–89 season, Michael had clearly joined Larry Bird and Magic Johnson at the pinnacle of NBA superstardom. However, Jordan had detractors who claimed that he was a selfish player who did not improve the performance of his teammates in the way that Bird and Magic did. Jordan is fiercely competitive and refused to accept inferiority to anyone else. He would defend himself against such accusations by noting how superior Johnson's and Bird's respective supporting casts were. But in the back of his mind he knew what it would take to erase such doubts—an NBA championship. Michael felt his efforts to achieve that goal were once again sabotaged by the Bulls front office when it traded Oakley for seven-foot (213.3cm) center Bill Cartwright. The media had consistently harped upon the Bulls' lack of a big man, but Jordan felt that Cartwright wasn't the answer and that losing Oakley was too high a price to pay. However, Horace Grant filled in admirably for Oakley, and Cartwright added consistent low-post scoring, though he was clearly unsuited for a fast-paced style. The Bulls exhibited some growing pains during the regular season and fell three games off the previous year's pace. Jordan led the league in scoring for the third straight year, averaging 32.5 points per game. Late in the season, Coach Collins addressed the troubles the Bulls were having at point guard by experimenting with Jordan running the offense. Michael responded with a flurry of spectacular performances, registering 10 triple-doubles in one 11-game stretch.

Collins returned Jordan to his normal guard position (usually called the "shooting guard") for the playoffs, but occasionally used him at the point. Early in his NBA career Michael had been an inconsistent outside shooter, but he had spent his off-seasons practicing. By his fifth season he was one of the league's best outside shooters, which made him even more of a lethal weapon. Michael put his outside shot to full advantage in the 1989 playoffs, hitting spectacular series-ending jump shots to eliminate first the Cavs and then the Knicks. However, the Bulls encountered their nemesis, the Pistons, in the Eastern Conference finals. The Pistons had devised a secret defensive strategy to contain Michael's scoring, which they called the "Jordan rules." Never explained publicly, the Pistons' strategy amounted to playing Michael tight and forcing him into the middle where the defense would collapse and, whenever possible, be rough on him. Other teams must have tried this as well, but the difference was that the Pistons were, in general, one of the greatest defensive teams in NBA history. The Pistons dismissed the Bulls in five games and then swept the Lakers for their first NBA title.

JORDAN'S PLAYOFF WIZARDRY

Three factors transformed Michael Jordan into the brightest star ever to shine in the NBA: his spectacular game, which was on display throughout his professional career; his celebrated media persona, which was ubiquitous in advertisements throughout the world in the late eighties and early nineties; and his role in the rise of the Bulls from cellar dwellers to an NBA dynasty. In the first and third capacities, Michael turned in some unforgettable playoff performances. The three most stunning are described below.

First, there was Game Two of the first round of the 1986 playoffs at the Boston Garden versus the Celtics. The background to this game is the stuff that myths are made of. Jordan fractured a tiny bone in his foot early in the season and grew frustrated as he healed more slowly than expected. Eventually, Jordan's doctors and Bulls management recommended that Michael sit out the remainder of the year. But Michael had secretly been playing pickup games behind everyone's back and, certain that he was ready to play, spurned the advice of the experts and demanded to be reinstated. He returned and lifted the Bulls into the playoffs, setting up a matchup with the league's top team, the Boston Celtics, in the first round. The Celtics had set a record by losing only one home game all year. In Game One, Michael had a touch of the flu but still poured in 49 points in a losing effort. Michael was at full strength two nights later. Throughout the game, Michael blasted to the basket, challenging the entire Celtics defense by himself. Making spectacular moves improvised on the spot, he set the all-time record for points in a playoff game, 63. He also extended the Celtics to two overtimes before Boston emerged victorious, 135–131, from the epic battle. After the contest Michael was inconsolable, for he had missed a short jumper at the end of the first overtime that would have won the game for the Bulls. Celtic superstar Larry Bird commented, "I think he's God disguised as Michael Jordan."

Then there was Game Five of the first round of the 1989 playoffs in Cleveland versus the Cavaliers. The Bulls had eliminated the Cavaliers in the first round of the 1988 playoffs in five games, the Bulls' first playoff win of the Jordan era. But the Cavs improved tremendously in 1989 and the Bulls entered the postseason mired in a slump. However, Jordan carried the Bulls early in the series as they upset Cleveland in Game One and won at home in Game Three. Unfortunately, with an opportunity to close out the miniseries at Chicago Stadium, Jordan and the Bulls choked. With the Bulls ahead late in regulation, Jordan missed 2 free throws that would have clinched the series. The Cavs forced overtime and came away with a season-saving 108–105 win. Two nights later the Bulls led by 1 with less than 10 seconds remaining when the Cavs' Craig Ehlo passed the ball in from out-of-bounds, received a return pass, and buried a jumper; Cavs fans went crazy, but there were still 3 seconds left. The Bulls called time-out. Everyone in the capacity crowd and on both benches expected Michael to take the final shot. Brad Sellars inbounded the ball. Jordan rushed over to the sideline to receive Sellars' pass, dribbled frantically to his left and from near the top of the key—with Craig Ehlo right in his face—he released a jump shot with under a second left. Swish! Jordan repeated similar, if slightly less dramatic, heroics in the next round of the playoffs, drilling a jumper at the buzzer to eliminate the Knicks in six games.

Last but not least was Game One of the 1992 NBA Championship finals at Chicago Stadium versus the Portland Trail Blazers. When Jordan first entered the league, he suffered from an erratic jump shot, but he worked endlessly to try to improve his accuracy. By his fourth season Michael was deadly from middle distance, and as he matured his range improved. He even consistently made shots from behind the three-point arc, though such long-range shooting was not a central part of his repertoire (he averaged just over one three-point effort per game in 1991–92). But in the first half of Game One of the 1992 NBA finals, Michael put on the greatest display of long-range shooting in NBA playoff history, and the whole world was watching. Jordan began by hitting some long-range jumpers and the home crowd responded wildly. Then Michael moved back behind the three-point line, and as every shot continued to fall straight through the basket, the crowd reacted even more frenetically. As the first period ended Michael had 17 points and staked the Bulls to a large lead. He sat out for over 5 minutes to begin the second quarter and then returned more on fire than before. As the long-range bombs continued to hit nothing but net, the reverence of the Chicago Stadium crowd became tangible; no one had ever seen anything like it before. Before the half ended Michael had made a record 6 three-pointers and scored a playoff record 35 points, and the Bulls built an insurmountable lead over the Blazers. Michael had shown conclusively that he could do it all on the court—as well as or better than anyone else.

In the visitors' locker room at the Los Angeles Forum on June 12, 1991, Michael Jordan embraces the 1991 NBA championship trophy, which he and the Bulls just won for the first time, and weeps. "I never thought I'd be this emotional," Jordan said shortly after. "I've never been this emotional publicly, but I don't mind. This is a great feeling, a great situation to be emotional." Two years later, after winning his third straight title, Michael reflected back: "When it got to this point two years ago, I cried in front of everybody. That's when I finally felt that feeling inside—in my chest—the difference between being a winner and not being one."

Bulls Michael Jordan and Scottie Pippen confer on-court during Game Three of the 1993 NBA finals. When Michael first emerged as an NBA superstar, his teammates (with the exception of rebounding specialist Charles Oakley) on the Bulls were roundly disparaged as incompetents. Then, out of the blue, the Bulls added rookies Pippen and power forward Horace Grant for the 1987–88 season. Slowly, Grant matured into a great rebounder and defender, while Pippen evolved into the "second Bull," a player who could do it all, almost as well as Michael himself. When the Bulls won their first NBA title in the spring of 1991, Grant and Pippen chanted "1987, 1987" as they embraced in the locker room. It was a private joke: Scottie and Horace felt that the Bulls began to turn things around with the 1987 draft.

Following their playoff success the previous spring, the Bulls confirmed their status as one of the elite teams in the NBA in 1989–90. Under new Coach Phil Jackson, who emphasized a more disciplined approach than Collins, the Bulls won 55 games. For the first time in three years Jordan increased his scoring average (to 33.6 points per game), to garner his fourth straight scoring title. On March 28, 1990, Michael scored a career-high 69 points in an overtime victory in Cleveland. The Bulls eliminated the Bucks and the 76ers in the playoffs, setting up the rematch with the Pistons. The home team won each of the first six games, and the question was whether the Bulls could produce a breakthrough victory on the Pistons' home court. The answer was a resounding no. Although Michael contributed 31 points, the rest of the Bulls went ice-cold and Detroit advanced to the finals with a lopsided 93–74 win. The Pistons had challenged Michael's teammates to produce by concentrating on stopping Jordan, but the rest of the Bulls shot a feeble .382 for the series. All the old doubts about the Bulls and Jordan resurfaced: some wondered whether Michael could win his coveted title with this supporting cast; others proposed that it was Michael's fault that his teammates performed so poorly in the clutch because he always had to dominate and they didn't know how to compensate when the Pistons shut him down. One thing was certain: after losing to Detroit in the playoffs for three straight

years, everyone in the Bulls camp was haunted by one nagging question during the off-season: how can we beat the Pistons?

The series against the Pistons suggested that two things might help lift the Bulls past their nemesis: earning the home-court advantage with a strong regular season and improving the offensive production of Jordan's supporting cast. These two things became the goals of the Bulls' 1990–91 regular season. The Bulls succeeded in their first goal, finishing 11 games ahead of the Pistons in the Central Division and only two games behind Portland, which had the best record in the NBA. Concerning the other issue, the results were mixed. The Bulls adopted a complex new half court offensive scheme called the triple-post that was intended to open up a variety of options, taking the pressure off Jordan and perhaps allowing other Bulls to develop into better scorers. Still, Jordan, who won his second league MVP Award, collected his fifth consecutive scoring title with a slightly lower average than the previous year (31.5). Scottie Pippen and young point guard B.J. Armstrong became slightly more productive while Bill Cartwright's scoring slipped a little. Overall the Bulls adjusted well to their new offense, averaging 2 more points than the previous year, with Jordan carrying less of the load. Many commentators felt that Scottie Pippen was the key to the Bulls' destiny because he was the only Bull other than Jordan explosive enough to score from anywhere on the floor. Critics of Pippen claimed that he was mentally too weak to produce in the clutch, but his advocates noted that he was showing marked improvement each year. The Bulls swept the Knicks and cruised by the 76ers to set up the showdown with the Pistons. Michael and Company's time had come; behind Jordan and Pippen, the Bulls exorcised their demons with a resounding four-game sweep.

The Bulls' opponents in the finals were the Los Angeles Lakers. The matchup featured the league's two greatest stars, Magic Johnson and Michael Jordan. The hype for the series was intense; media coverage matched that of any sports event in the world. Michael had the perfect opportunity to rebut two of the criticisms most often made about his game: that he could never win a championship and that he was a selfish player who did not use his skills to complement his teammates like Magic did. Game One did not help Michael on either count. Jordan himself was brilliant throughout the game while his teammates were ice-cold. Michael staked the Bulls to a 91–89 lead, but he missed a jumper with seconds left to play. Magic brought the ball upcourt and found Sam Perkins open for a three-point shot, which he buried to give the Lakers a 92–91 lead. The Bulls still had an opportunity to win, and Jordan took it upon himself to take the final shot, which he missed as time ran out. The Michael critics came pouring out of the closets; see, they said, Magic found the open man and the Lakers won while Michael tried to do it all himself and the Bulls lost. Jordan's advocates noted that his Bulls teammates had abandoned him earlier in the game, missing numerous open jumpers.

Game Two was a different story. Jordan was brilliant again, but so were his teammates in a 107–86 rout. The Bulls set a playoff record, shooting almost 62 percent from the field as all five starters—Jordan, Pippen, Grant, Cartwright, and point guard John Paxson—had strong games. The series shifted to Los Angeles, where both teams played unevenly throughout Game Three. The Lakers built a lead in the third period behind Magic's leadership, but then went cold. The teams were neck and neck through the fourth quarter. Michael came through in the clutch this time, sending the game into overtime on a short jumper with 3 seconds left. The extra period belonged to the Bulls, who scored the game's final 8 points to take the lead in the series. Game Three proved to be the key to the series as the Bulls took over in Game Four, led by Jordan's 13 assists and 28 points, and by the perimeter shooting of John Paxson. The Lakers put up a valiant fight in Game Five, but the Bulls responded with a total team effort. Only four games after he was roundly criticized for his selfishness, Jordan was heralded as a consummate team player. In Games Two through Five he had driven the lane, attracting the defense to him, and consistently passed off to the open man, who would bury the shot. In the locker room, Jordan's response to the victory contrasted with the reactions of his teammates or virtually any other American champion in recent memory (though it resembled the passionate response of soccer players to important victories): in front of the international media, Jordan broke down and wept tears of joy. He moved away from the cameras to be alone with his new wife, Juanita, and his father before returning to his teammates. When he was handed the NBA championship trophy, he embraced it as tears of exultation poured down his face.

With Jordan's first NBA championship, Michaelmania reached new heights. His victory was all the more sweet for the adversity he had encountered along the way, including his annual frustration in the playoffs and the criticism he regularly received in the media. Still, Michael's unbending passion made him a hero to most fans. Jordan's image flooded the electronic media like no celebrity before him or since; he endorsed countless products, which was not surprising since market research showed that the public adored him. What was most amazing, perhaps, was the breadth of Jordan's appeal; toddlers, senior citizens, blacks, whites, men, women, Hispanics, Asians, Republicans, radicals, gang members, and yuppies all loved Michael. Jordan's clean-cut, honest, and pleasant demeanor, as well as his physical beauty, contributed to his appeal, but the real reason for the public adulation was simple: Michael's persona both on and off the court remained grounded in his unwavering pursuit of basketball excellence. Simply put, Jordan was the most amazing athlete of his time. In Michael's hands the game of basketball was a vehicle for transcendence.

The Bull's quest to repeat as NBA champions in 1991–92 produced the best regular season, 67–15, in franchise history. Michael's scoring dipped to 30.1 points per game, which still led the league, but his leadership and improving team play earned him his third MVP Award. The playoffs were the real challenge. Along the rocky postseason path, it was evident that repeating as champions would be a formidable achievement for Michael and Company. After disposing of the Miami Heat in the first round, the Bulls encountered the revitalized New York Knicks led by center Patrick Ewing. Ironically, New York had adopted the Pistons' rugged style under Coach Pat Riley, who had led the Lakers during their fast-breaking glory days in the eighties. The Knicks bullied the Bulls and stretched the series to its limit, though Chicago won Game Seven decisively. The Bulls then needed six games to dispose of the feisty Cavaliers. Likewise, the Trail Blazers challenged the Bulls in the finals but Jordan was too much, averaging 35.8 points per game. The Bulls won the series in six games and repeated as champions.

Entering the 1992–93 season, Jordan found special motivation to three-peat as champions. Magic Johnson's Lakers had won back-to-back NBA titles, as had Jordan's old nemesis the Pistons, but only Bill Russell's legendary Boston Celtics and George Mikan's dynastic Minneapolis Lakers had ever successfully won three straight. And Mikan and Russell had played in the NBA when it had consisted of only eight or ten teams; Michael's Bulls were conquering a league with twenty-six adversaries. Michael liked the sound of such historical preeminence. The media, nonetheless, speculated at this time that Michael was grasping for straws to find a challenge that would

Jordan is about to make contact in his first official at-bat for the Chicago White Sox in a spring training exhibition game on March 4, 1994, in Sarasota, Florida. A sign of things to come, Michael hit a slow roller on the right side of the infield and was tagged out at first. Eventually assigned to the AA minor league Birmingham Barons, Jordan never showed much promise as a hitter; in a full season with the Barons he hit a feeble .202, with 2 home runs. He did, however, lead the Southern League in commercial endorsements. After Michael came to his senses (helped along by the nightmare labor relations that plague baseball), he accepted that hitting a baseball thrown by a professional pitcher is best left to baseball players, and returned to basketball. Michael had the good humor and humility to lampoon his baseball odyssey in some hilarious Nike commercials directed by Spike Lee, punctuated by the line "I had this crazy dream."

In the spring of 1995, Michael Jordan returned to the Bulls to the delight of basketball fans across the globe. Michael donned Number 45 (because Chicago had "retired" his legendary 23) and wore it until the second game of the second round of the playoffs, against Orlando. After Orlando won Game One, the Magic's Nick Anderson quipped that Number 45 wasn't the same player as Number 23. When Michael took off his warmups before Game Two, he was wearing his old number. He promptly scored 38 points and led the Bulls to victory, evening the series. Number 45 was erratic in his 17 regular-season and five playoff games, tallying respectable point totals but shooting a low percentage. However, Michael's shooting woes probably had less to do with numerology—or, as was widely speculated, his age—than with his long absence from the game. In the 1985–86 season Michael returned to action a few weeks before the playoffs after missing most of the season with an injury, and shot terribly from the field. Jordan's timing was off on his jump shot and he was out of sync with his teammates. He recovered in time for his record-setting playoff performance against Boston and then averaged a career-high 37.1 points per game in 1986–87. Ultimately, Number 23 couldn't stop Orlando: the Bulls dropped the series in six games. However, fans around the world anticipate Michael—better prepared and ready once again to conquer the NBA—will be back with a vengence in 1995–96.

motivate him on the basketball court. Fiercely competitive throughout his life, Michael began expressing more interest in precision sports like golf and baseball in which he was less than accomplished. Friends and teammates told how Michael's competitiveness sometimes got out of hand, that he couldn't casually accept defeat in games of table tennis or other such friendly contests. Michael's intense drive to conquer was always a large part of his basketball success. Even after he was the NBA's greatest star, if a lesser player beat him for a basket, he would instantly reciprocate with 3, 4 or 5 scores against the overwhelmed foe, just to let everyone know who was king.

The Bulls struggled a bit in the 1992–93 regular season, as Pippen's game fell off slightly and Jordan carried a heavier load. Perhaps Pippen was suffering from fatigue since he and Jordan had played throughout the off-season on the gold medal–winning U.S. Olympic Team. Michael increased his scoring output for the first time in three years, leading the league again with a 32.6 average. It was Jordan's seventh consecutive scoring title, which tied the record set by Wilt Chamberlain. Nonetheless, the Bulls fell to 57–25 and faced the prospect of playing some key playoff games without home-court advantage. However, Chicago exploded out of the gate in the playoffs, sweeping Atlanta and Cleveland in consecutive series to set up a rematch with the rugged Knicks. New York had home-court advantage for the conference finals and they took quick advantage of it, winning the first two games at home in convincing style, but the Bulls bounced back with four straight victories. In the finals, the Bulls faced Charles Barkley and the high-scoring Phoenix Suns. It took six crazy games, in which the home team lost four times; but when the dust settled the Bulls had three-peated as NBA champions. What no one realized at the time was that Michael Jordan had played his final NBA game for a while to come.

On October 6, 1993, Jordan, far and away the greatest basketball player on earth, announced his retirement from the Chicago Bulls. Since the Bulls had won their third consecutive title in June, Michael's world had been rocked by the tragic and senseless murder of his father in the summer. Over the past few years, as Michael's celebrity increased to unprecedented levels, he responded to the pressure by relying on a small circle of close friends and family members. Michael's father had always been Michael's closest confidant and, as Michael would say after his death, his best friend. On October 6, Michael denied that his father's death had led to his decision to retire, but it was clear that the senseless tragedy had had a profound effect on Michael.

By 1993 Michael frequently sounded bitter about the public frenzy he created wherever he went. When allegations arose during the 1993 playoffs that Michael had amassed huge gambling debts—which, since Michael remained extremely wealthy and financially secure, were almost certainly exaggerated—he became indignant toward the media for constantly

investigating every aspect of his life. In retrospect, when Michael announced his retirement, he was looking for a way to reclaim his life.

Around the middle of the 1993–94 basketball season, rumors spread about Michael preparing for a tryout with baseball's Chicago White Sox. The rumors turned out to be true. Jerry Reinsdorf, the managing partner of both the White Sox and the Bulls, assured Jordan a fair trial. The media, the public, and Jordan's former and possible future teammates were all surprised by Michael's unexpected decision; while some felt he could succeed at his new endeavor, others who were more knowledgeable about the difficulty of baseball doubted that Michael could hit well. It turned out that Michael was a few rungs below major league caliber. But he was a huge draw in spring training, and that, combined with his unwavering enthusiasm, led the White Sox to offer him a minor league contract. Thus, the sports world's most renowned superstar became a member of the AA Birmingham Barons, two levels beneath the major leagues. Amid persistent rumors that he would return to the Bulls, which he repeatedly denied, Jordan played a full year with the Barons. He was a consistent outfielder with a decent arm and ran the bases well, but he was a weak hitter, barely managing to bat .200. Jordan showed small signs of improvemen in the winter leagues, and the White Sox were prepared to offer Jordan a AAA contract for the 1995 season, making Michael only one step away from fulfilling his dream of playing in the major leagues.

In the spring of 1995, Jordan, frustrated by the continuing labor strife that plagued professional baseball, left the White Sox spring training camp and returned to Chicago to begin practicing with the Bulls. Speculation about Jordan's return flooded the media. Shortly thereafter, Michael announced that he was, at least temporarily, quitting baseball. As he continued to practice with the Bulls, fans anticipated his return to the NBA. They were not disappointed. Michael announced that he would return to the Bulls to play in the final 17 games of the regular season. The team, which had enjoyed a stellar regular season in 1993–94 before being eliminated by the Knicks in the playoffs, were struggling around .500 but were in position to make the playoffs. On March 19 Michael made his comeback debut at Indianapolis against the Pacers and looked rusty in an overtime loss, but in his fourth game back he hit a game-winning buzzer-beater against the Hawks. In the next game Michael poured in 55 points against the Knicks. Jordan was back and Michaelmania gripped the world like never before. New advertisements featuring Mike debuted, Nike's stock went up, and interest in the NBA reached an all-time high. Media commentators marveled at how one basketball player could have such a tremendous, positive effect on a nation's psyche.

The Bulls responded well to Michael's return, but Orlando eliminated Chicago in the second round of the playoffs. Nonetheless, basketball fans could rest assured that Michael was back.

CHARLES *Barkley*

CHARLES Barkley

Much has been said about Charles Barkley's ability to excel as an NBA power forward at only six foot four inches (193cm). As Sir Charles himself put it, "If I were seven feet tall [213.3cm], I'd be illegal in three states." In fact, Barkley's success stems from a combination of exceptional skill and the unrelenting desire to win that characterizes all NBA superstars. In the paint, Charles uses his wide body, aggressiveness, and court sense to negate his height disadvantage and win rebounds. Of course, when Charles grabs a defensive rebound, the fun is just beginning; if an opening is there, Charles will blast out from under his basket, faking out opponents with the skill of an NFL running back, dribbling between his legs, behind his back, and across the path of would-be defenders, taking the ball full-court for a thundering dunk. Fans marvel at a power forward with such open-court ability, but Charles is no ordinary power forward. As the irrepressible Mr. Barkley will let you know: "There will never be another player like me. I'm the ninth wonder of the world."

• • •

Charles Wade Barkley was born on February 20, 1963, in Leeds, a small town in rural Alabama, where he was raised by his mother and grandmother. A huge, sometimes overweight kid, Charles nevertheless loved playing sports. In high school, basketball was his main interest and he led Leeds High School to its best records ever. Charles attended college at Auburn University and made the varsity basketball team there in his sophomore year. Although just six foot four inches (193cm), Barkley ballooned up to 300 pounds (136.2kg) while at Auburn. But the resourceful young man used his girth to his advantage, blocking out opponents with his wide frame in order to grab rebounds. Dubbed the "Round Mound of Rebound," Barkley led the Auburn Tigers deep into the NCAA tournament in his senior year. Over the next summer, Barkley impressed the media at the tryouts for the 1984 U.S. Olympic Team, but his aggressive style did not suit disciplinarian Bob Knight—who eventually coached a star-studded cast to a gold medal—and Barkley was cut.

Despite Barkley's weight problems and aggressive demeanor, the Philadelphia 76ers made Charles the fifth pick overall in the 1984 draft. Thus Charles joined an aging group of Sixers who had convincingly won the NBA title only two years earlier. However, stars Julius Erving and Bobby Jones were at the end of their careers and Moses Malone was no longer the dominant force he had been for the past few years. Nevertheless, the Sixers remained one of the league's high-profile teams and Barkley made a big splash. Charles' brash, fearless play on the court was mirrored by his sharp verbal wit. Entering the league the same year as Michael Jordan and Hakeem Olajuwon, Barkley made the NBA All-Rookie team and opened some eyes by averaging 14 points and almost 9 rebounds per game, while keeping his weight down around 260 pounds (118kg). The Sixers reached the conference finals, where they were swamped by the Boston Celtics in five games.

The next season Charles really came into his own surpassing Malone as the leading rebounder on the Sixers and scoring 20 points per game. However, Milwaukee, led by Sidney Moncrief and Terry Cummings, ousted the 76ers in seven games in the second round of the playoffs. Milwaukee won Game Seven by 1 point. In the off-season, the Sixers shocked the basketball world and their young star power forward by trading away Moses Malone to the

Washington Bullets. In return, the Sixers got Jeff Ruland, who would play a total of five games for Philadelphia. The Sixers also traded away the rights to the first pick of the draft, which Cleveland used to acquire Brad Daugherty, for a journeyman small forward. Barkley was livid. He was convinced Philadelphia owner Harold Katz cared only about making money and not about winning. Barkley would be an outspoken critic of Katz for the remainder of his stay in Philadelphia. Reflecting back on the Sixers' catastrophic off-season, Charles later pondered that "with a front line of me, Daugherty and Moses, we'd have had a couple of championship rings by now. Who could have stopped us?" Barkley also missed Malone for personal reasons. He reflected on Moses years later: "Moses was the most influential person in my basketball career. Moses taught me not to trust anybody, to work hard, not to worry about the hype, the fans, the media. He said to be my own man because nobody else will be there when push came to shove. I call Moses 'Dad.'" Ironically, Barkley's rebounding prowess was probably instrumental in getting Moses shipped off.

Charles won the rebounding title his third year in the league. Only six foot four inches (193cm), though he is sometimes listed at six foot six inches (198.1cm), Barkley is expert at using his wide frame to secure position under the rim and then using his fantastically springy legs to rocket up for the rebound. In the battle of the trenches, Charles doesn't employ the stoic, heavy form of intimidation of a Moses Malone or a Maurice Lucas; Barkley intimidates with lightning-quick ruggedness. A battle against Charles down in the trenches can result in broken teeth or a busted nose if an opponent is dumb enough to be near Barkley's body or elbows as he explodes toward a loose ball.

Unfortunately, the Sixers began a rapid decline in 1986–87, Dr. J's final season with the team. Eliminated in the first round of the playoffs by the Bucks, Philadelphia failed to make the playoffs the next season for the first time since 1975—though Barkley had the highest scoring average of his career, at 28.3 points per game. Philadelphia bounced back in 1988–89, but was eliminated in three straight games by the Knicks in the first round of the playoffs. The improvement continued into the next season, however, as Barkley almost single-handedly led the 76ers to 53 wins and a division crown. For his efforts, Charles got widespread support for the league's MVP, though the trophy went to Magic Johnson. In the playoffs, the Sixers won their first playoff series since 1986 (over Cleveland) and then went down to Jordan and the Bulls. The next season the Sixers fell off some, but reached the playoffs, where they advanced and were again crushed by the Bulls. Barkley's assessment of his team during these years was often less than flattering. He once declared, "We have so many wimps and complainers on this team." Another time he said, "There's only two people we can't do without and that's me and Hawk

Charles Barkley boxes out a member of the Magic and awaits a rebound during the 1994–95 season. Hampered by a sore back and aching knees, Barkley still managed to pull down over 11 rebounds per game in 1994–95, giving Charles ten consecutive seasons averaging more than 10 rebounds each night. While much of Barkley's legend stems from his rugged play, his success beneath the glass has more to do with finesse and his ability to use his wide frame to keep opponents away from the ball than with his brutal style of play.

[Hersey Hawkins]. Anybody else we can replace." And even more: "There's one reason why the team's been competitive the last six years. The last three or four years—especially with the trades that we've made—there's one reason we've been respectable. You figure it out." The 1991–92 season was a full-on catastrophe for the Sixers. Barkley's name was in lights all season long, for all the wrong reasons. He pummeled someone on the streets of Indianapolis and was charged with assault. The once-proud 76ers failed to make the playoffs. Charles let it be known that he wanted out of the City of Brotherly Love, blasting Katz and Company at every turn. He was traded in the off-season to perennial contender Phoenix.

As harrowing and dark as the 1991–92 season was for Sir Charles, the following off-season was bright. Not only was Charles traded to a competitive, well-run organization, but he was the star of the U.S. Olympic Team. Eight years after he had been cut by Bobby Knight from the 1984 squad, Charles made Coach Chuck Daly's roster. After four consecutive years on the All-NBA first team—preceding the 1991–92 debacle (in which Charles was on the second team)—Sir Charles was a shoo-in. By the time the

Games were over and the gold medals carried home, Barkley was an international household name. In part, Barkley's rise to megacelebrity was due to his excellent play throughout the Olympic tournament, but Charles became a media superstar primarily because of his always unpredictable charm, wit, and wisdom. While other NBA stars remained holed up in their expensive hotel suites, Charles Barkley took to the streets of Barcelona, mingling with the crowds and holding forth for the fourth estate.

By the beginning of the 1992–93 season, the NBA and NBC were thrilled to have the former renegade and newfound pop star in the limelight and playing with a serious title contender. For his part, Barkley was all business: he was playing all-out for the championship. All season long Barkley was spectacular as he lifted the Suns to new heights; the club won 62 games, a club record that earned it home-court advantage throughout the playoffs. In the first round, the Magic-less Lakers won the first two games of the best-of-five series in Phoenix. As Barkley left the court, you could sense that he was fighting back heartbreak. Miraculously, the Suns rebounded and conquered the Lakers in five games, winning the decisive game in overtime. Then Phoenix moved past San Antonio and Seattle to face Jordan and the Bulls, who were trying to become the first team to three-peat since 1966. Barkley had already been named the NBA's MVP, and Jordan was being annointed the greatest player of all time by the media. It was 1993's dream matchup, and Chicago promptly stormed into Phoenix and won the first two games. Once again, the Suns showed tremendous resilience as they won Game Three in triple overtime and captured Game Five in Chicago to bring the series back home. In what proved to be Michael Jordan's last game before his temporary retirement, the Bulls completed their three-peat with a 1-point victory in Game Six.

Charles' magical ride was over for a spell. In 1993–94, Barkley struggled with an injured back and the Suns played inconsistently throughout the season, though they finished with 56 wins. The Suns faced the Warriors in the first round of the playoffs, and in Game Three Charles exploded for 56 points as the Suns wrapped up the series. Charles wasn't full-strength, but he has always been more about heart than anything else. He once said, "Emotion is what makes me what I am today. It makes me play bigger than I am." The Suns then moved into Houston and stunned the Rockets in the first two games at Houston. But in a reversal of the previous season, the Rockets returned the favor in Phoenix and went on to take the series and the NBA championship. Barkley hoped to capture the 1994 title and then retire, but, frustrated, he came back for at least one more try in 1994–95. Although the 1994–95 Suns were loaded with talent and had a magnificent regular season, they suffered another crushing defeat by the Rockets in the second round of the playoffs. After the series Sir Charles underwent knee surgery and hinted at retirement, but his drive to win an NBA ring may again prove too strong for him to resist another attempt in 1995–96.

THE DREAM TEAM: THE 1992 USA OLYMPIC SQUAD

For all intents and purposes, the competition for the Olympic gold medal at the 1992 summer games in Barcelona, Spain, ended in 1989 when the international governing body of basketball voted to allow professional basketballers to compete in the Olympics. College players had always represented the United States before in the summer games and had only lost one game before the 1988 Olympics. At Seoul, the 1988 U.S. team struggled throughout and were forced to settle for the bronze medal. It was clear that the rest of the world was improving and that American amateurs could no longer dominate international competition. Given the opportunity to use pro stars, the USOC readily agreed to send a "Dream Team" loaded with NBA superstars to the 1992 Barcelona games.

The most exciting thing about the Dream Team was the selection of the roster. Tryouts were held in the middle of the summer in Portland, Oregon. Coach Chuck Daly, who had led the Detroit Pistons to two NBA crowns in 1989 and 1990 and then retired temporarily, was chosen to be the choreographer for the greatest team ever assembled, though he would face hairy decisions about who would make the team. Daly and his staff decided on a roster of eleven NBA stars and one collegiate. Daly was an old-school NBA coach who loved tough defense, but also had no compulsion to make controversial selections. Thus, everyone knew from the start that Magic Johnson had a place on the team if he wanted one, even though he was HIV-positive. Likewise, Larry Bird made the team even though chronic back injuries would force him to retire following the Olympics. The other obvious selections for the squad were Michael Jordan, Charles Barkley, Patrick Ewing, David Robinson, Karl Malone, and Clyde Drexler, who had just led Portland to the NBA finals.

The remaining four selections were more difficult. First, Daly chose Duke's Christian Laettner as the token amateur. Daly wanted two more scoring forwards, and many fans assumed he would select high-flying Dominique Wilkins, who had the fifth-highest scoring average in NBA history entering 1994–95 and is among the top ten in points scored. But Wilkins was never much of a team-

player or a defensive stalwart. Thus, the two remaining forward positions were awarded to Scottie Pippin of the champion Bulls, who was just emerging from Michael's shadow and gaining deserved recognition, and Chris Mullin, who was being touted as the game's deadliest outside shooter post-Larry. The other point guard selection was actually made early on, but still sparked some controversy in the media. Daly chose John Stockton, whom the coach felt could be relied on to run the team for an entire game should Magic be unable to compete. Ironically, Stockton was the only Dream Teamer to get injured in Barcelona; a tiny leg fracture forced him to miss a couple of games. The public and media, however, were shocked that Daly had bypassed Isiah Thomas, who was the highest-profile player on Daly's championship Pistons. However, word leaked out that the final guard to be cut was Tim Hardaway, who, before his knee problems, was spectacular at driving through the lane in traffic. Magic apologized to Hardaway, because his inclusion on the team meant that their was no space for the Golden State point guard. After the selection process, the Dream Team still had to qualify for the Olympics from its region. It did so without ever being challenged.

The same was true of the games during the Olympic tournament in Barcelona. The United States cruised to the gold medal. Their closest game was in the championship round, in which Croatia remained close to the Dream Team in the first half before the U.S. pulled away for a typically resounding victory, 117–85. Far more interesting than the competition, which suffered one blowout after another, was the reception of the NBA superstars in Catalonia. Some of the other Olympic athletes complained that the Dream Team was stealing their sole moment of glory. Indeed, since the Dream Team blowouts were not engaging contests, perhaps plans for a Shaq-led 1996 megateam should be scrapped. However, more often than not, other Olympians swooned along with the tourists at the sight of Michael, Charles, Larry, or Magic. The 1992 Olympics proved conclusively that the elite NBA superstars have become the world's most recognizable athletes, surpassing tennis stars, race car drivers, and even soccer greats.

The 1992 U.S. Olympic basketball team, undoubtedly the greatest ever assembled, stands on the winners' podium after receiving their gold medals in Barcelona, Spain. The Dream Team members are, from left to right: Christian Laettner, David Robinson, Patrick Ewing, Larry Bird, Scottie Pippen, Michael Jordan, Clyde Drexler, Karl Malone, John Stockton, Chris Mullin, Charles Barkley, and Magic Johnson.

HAKEEM *Olajuwon*

Hakeem Olajuwon blocks a shot by New York Knick John Starks during the 1994 NBA finals. Olajuwon has always played great support defense, leaving his man to shut down opposing players when they try to drive to the basket. In this case, Starks has beaten his man and blown by Carl Herrera (Number 7) off the dribble. However, Hakeem has shown up to protect the basket even though the man he was assigned to defend, Patrick Ewing, looks on from beyond the three-point line. Plays like this helped make Olajuwon the first player in NBA history to be named league MVP, Defensive Player of the Year, and playoff MVP in the same season.

When most collegiate stars enter the NBA, they're in for a rude awakening; for the first time in their lives they're not top dog. Occasionally, a rookie is an instant impact player; usually there are one or two per year. Great things are expected of these select few. Hakeem Olajuwon was such a rookie in 1984–85. And Hakeem was still learning how to play the game.

Olajuwon did not play basketball at all until he was fifteen and did not participate in competitive organized ball until he was a sophomore at the University of Houston. Still, Hakeem's physical gifts were so great—six feet ten inches (208.2cm) tall, extremely fast and agile with tremendous leaping ability—that he contributed significantly to a Cougars team that reached the NCAA Final Four that year, even though he was still learning the basic fundamentals of the game. Likewise, he led the Cougars to the NCAA finals the next two years though his skills were still rough. As an NBA rookie, Hakeem could dominate games by scoring, rebounding, blocking shots, and making steals; still, it was evident that he was improving day by day. When Michael Jordan left the NBA abruptly before the 1993–94 season, it was clear that, in his tenth season, Olajuwon was the league's premier performer. Hakeem won his first MVP Award in the spring of 1994 and led the Houston Rockets to their first NBA title the same year.

• • •

Hakeem Olajuwon's story is unique within the annals of basketball. He not only grew up unaware of the NBA, he didn't even know what basketball was. Hakeem Abdul Olajuwon was born in Lagos, Nigeria, on January 21, 1963. Hakeem's parents were teachers, and young Hakeem planned to follow in their footsteps. Hakeem grew up in one of the sprawling city's small middle-class neighborhoods. The Olajuwons sent young Hakeem to English-speaking schools and planned to send him to college in America. Hakeem was a good student and America seemed to be in his future as he transferred from the Baptist Academy to the Moslem Teachers College.

Hakeem was a very good athlete, and he was also growing very tall. He excelled in soccer, as a goaltender, and in handball, an extremely popular sport in Nigeria. In Hakeem's sophomore year at the Teachers College (the equivalent of high school), Lagos State Coach Ganyu Otengbade introduced Hakeem to basketball, which was growing in popularity in Lagos. On the city's asphalt courts, Hakeem

began to play in pickup games. The overall skill level was very low compared to similar contests in America, but Hakeem liked the game and found he was very effective grabbing rebounds and blocking shots because of his size and great leaping ability. He also met and played with Nigeria's greatest basketball star, Yommy Sangodeyi. Yommy was trying to head to Houston, Texas, to attend a community college there and play American basketball. Sangodeyi was over twenty-five and thus ineligible for NCAA Division One play, but he helped direct young Hakeem to the University of Houston and Coach Guy Lewis.

Olajuwon had to sit out his freshman year after inadvertently violating NCAA rules by practicing prematurely with the varsity. When informed of the consequences of his innocent mistake, Hakeem just about picked up and returned to Nigeria, but was talked out of it. So he stayed, diligently pursuing his studies and working on his basketball skills. He made the varsity his sophomore year.

The University of Houston Cougars were loaded with talent for the 1981–82 season. Nicknamed "Phi Slamma Jamma," the team included a future NBA superstar, high-flying Clyde "The Glide" Drexler, along with a cast of other superlative athletes. The team had a successful season and then exploded into the national consciousness by upsetting number-one-ranked Missouri to reach the Final Four. Drexler and Company were truly thrilling, but just as much hype surrounded their backup center Akeem "The Dream" Olajuwon. Then known as Akeem, Olajuwon wasn't a starter, but he would come off the bench and swat away opposing players' shots with an athletic ferocity even more intimidating than Georgetown's freshman sensation, Patrick Ewing. However, Olajuwon's offensive skills were unrefined; he was still "learning how to play the game in English," as he would jest (few knew that he spoke English in his homeland). The Cougars lost in the National Semifinal to eventual champion North Carolina, 68–63.

In the off-season, Hakeem worked hard to develop his skills, especially offensively. He scrimmaged daily and often went up against Houston resident Moses Malone. Hakeem arrived back at school ready for his junior season with a soft fadeaway jump shot. Houston raced through the season with a 27–2 record and entered the NCAA tournament ranked number one. They then whipped through the Midwest Regional, disposing of Maryland, Memphis State, and

Hakeem shoots a short jumper over Patrick Ewing. The two great centers finally faced each other in the 1984 NCAA final, Hakeem's last college game. Ewing's Georgetown Hoyas had lost in the finals two years earlier and Hakeem's Houston Cougars had been runners-up in 1983; finally, one of them would win it all. The Cougars jumped ahead 10–2 but the Hoyas stormed back and led 40–30 at the intermission. Hakeem was in foul trouble throughout and had to sit down when he was called for his fourth foul in the first minute of the second half. In his absence Houston made a run, but got no closer than 3 points. Hakeem finished with 15 points and 9 rebounds. Patrick only scored 10 points, to go with 9 rebounds, but played dominant interior defense. Georgetown won 84–75 and Ewing was named tournament MVP.

Villanova. In the semifinals, the Cougars dispatched high-powered Louisville, 94–81, to set up a final against underdog North Carolina State. In the previous three games, Hakeem had served notice to the nation that he had arrived as a player, averaging 21 points, 14 rebounds, and 6 blocks per game. Against North Carolina State, Hakeem had a triple-double (20 points, 18 boards, and 11 blocks), but the Wolfpack pulled a dramatic and stunning upset, 54–52. In Hakeem's senior season, he led the Cougars back to the finals, where they lost again, but this time to a favored, powerful Georgetown team, 84–75. "The Dream" was ready for the next level.

Hakeem was drafted by the Houston Rockets, who had the top pick in the draft for the second straight year. Thus, Hakeem joined Ralph Sampson to form a daunting "Twin Towers." Sampson was seven feet four inches (223.5 cm) but preferred to play away from the basket, so Olajuwon played center. Slowly, Hakeem had developed an all-around low-post game, which featured either turnaround jump shots or spin moves for dunks. With Hakeem, the Rockets improved 19 games and made the playoffs for the first time since Moses Malone had left for Philly. Hakeem averaged over 20 points per game and finished fourth in the league in rebounds. Unfortunately, the Rockets were upset by the Jazz in the opening round of the playoffs.

The next year, the Twin Towers came of age in the NBA. Hakeem's scoring average jumped up to 23.5 and his rebounding remained steady. The Rockets won their division with 51 wins and cruised into the Western Conference finals, where they stunned the defending champion Lakers in five games. In his second NBA season, Olajuwon was in the NBA finals.

However, the Rockets were overmatched and the Celtics won in six. The next season Sampson's legs began to fail him and the days of the Twin Towers were numbered, though the Rockets did advance to the second round of the playoffs. The next three years the team became Hakeem's, but failed to click and advance past the first round of the playoffs. Hakeem won consecutive NBA rebounding titles in 1988–89 and 1989–90 with 13.5 and 14.0 averages, respectively. Houston improved to 52–30 in 1990–91, but suffered the same playoff fate. Then the Rockets had an off-year and failed to make the playoffs for the only time in Olajuwon's career. From such adversity, the club reversed its fate, winning its division in 1992–93 for the first time since 1986 and winning in the first round of the playoffs for the first time since 1987 (before losing in overtime of the seventh game of the conference semifinals at Seattle). Hakeem was voted the NBA's best defensive player for the season and named first-team All-NBA for the fourth time in his career, but the first time in three years.

The small taste of success in 1993 made the Rockets hungrier for the 1993–94 season. The nucleus of the team had been together for a number of years. Hakeem, a lifetime Rocket, had been joined by commanding power forward Otis Thorpe in the 1988–89 season, so the pair were entering their sixth year together. The starting backcourt pair of Vernon Maxwell and Kenny Smith were entering their fourth full season together. This group exploded out of the gates, winning their first 15 games of the regular season. From there, the team coasted to the division crown. Olajuwon had his best overall season, finishing with his highest scoring average, 27.3, and finishing fourth in the league in rebounding and second in blocked shots. He was voted league MVP. In the playoffs, the Rockets got by Portland, then struggled to overcome Sir Charles and the Suns before blasting by Karl Malone and the Jazz to set up a showdown with Patrick Ewing and the Knicks in the finals. Olajuwon outplayed his old college foe in convincing fashion throughout the series and the Rockets triumphed in seven tension-filled games.

The best was yet to come. The Rockets struggled through the 1994–95 regular season, failing to find the proper chemistry after trading Otis Thorpe to Portland for Clyde Drexler. Then Houston, led by Hakeem, came together. In the first two rounds of the playoffs the Rockets fell behind in their series with both the Jazz and the Suns, respectively; Houston won five games in which they faced elimination, exhibiting the fortitude of true champions. Then the Rockets dismissed the Spurs in six games and swept the Magic to complete their unlikely defense of the NBA title. Hakeem shined throughout the postseason, averaging an amazing 33 points per game. In particular, he thoroughly outplayed David Robinson of the Spurs and got the better of Shaquille O'Neal in the finals. Hakeem's play in the 1995 playoffs left little doubt that he has established himself among the greatest basketball players of all time.

Olajuwon slams one home past Ewing. Ten years after they first met in the NCAA title game, the two great centers met in the NBA finals. To protect Ewing from foul trouble, Knicks Coach Pat Riley had his star center guard Hakeem only on occasion. In contrast, Olajuwon defended Ewing throughout, and caused him fits. Patrick, who averaged 24.5 points per game during the season, was held to 18.9 in the finals and shot a horrendous 36 percent from the field. Ewing did win the battle of the boards, outrebounding Olajuwon 87 to 64, and blocked 30 shots compared to Hakeem's 27. However, Olajuwon was the star of the series, proving to be the only consistent scorer that either team had, averaging 26.9 points per game. Most importantly, Hakeem guided his team to victory in the tightly contested seven-game series. Sweeping all the NBA's most significant awards, Hakeem had finally brought the city of Houston, his adopted hometown, its first major sporting championship. Also, leading the Rockets to the NBA title solidified Hakeem's status as the game's greatest contemporary player. For the first time in basketball history, the sport's top performer was a man who was neither born nor raised in the United States, illustrating how basketball has truly become an international sport.

Chapter

THE REGENTS AND FUTURE KINGS OF THE NBA

At the outset of the 1993–94 season the NBA had an unexpected crisis on its hands. The league was left without a premier superstar when Michael Jordan stunned the sports world by retiring from basketball. As recently as 1989, four of the seven greatest players in NBA history—Kareem, Magic, Larry, and Michael—were active. In the autumn of 1993, there was none. As long as Michael was around, the departure of other legends did not constitute a full-fledged crisis. Then suddenly, and prematurely, all the mega-stars who were instrumental in the renaissance of pro basketball were mere memories. A league that relied on its big names to market itself no longer had its leading men. Had the NBA truly come of age or was the boom merely a product of the immense popularity of a few transcendent performers?

In light of Michael's absence and the issues that it raised, the 1993–94 NBA season was a qualified success: fan support of local teams reached a new high, but national interest in the championship finals, which Michael had made into his personal showcase, declined. The early nineties was the first era in which sports fans across America followed their local NBA teams as closely, and as seriously, as their Major League Baseball and National Football League counterparts. The 1993–94 season represented a novel scenario to these fans. With no prohibitive favorite to win the championship, without Michael lurking to crush all challengers, many teams believed they had a legitimate shot at the title. Veteran stars, who had been outshined each spring by the likes of Larry, Magic, Kareem, or Michael, seized the moment. Young greats strived to become the new legend. Thus, more fans followed more franchises more closely than ever before, and there was tremendous excitement in the

early rounds of the 1994 playoffs. But come finals time, Michael was clearly missed. The showdown between Houston and New York was hotly contested, featuring rugged defense, but the games were not spectacular. If one of the teams had not been from the nation's media capital and largest city, the TV ratings would have been meager.

Two rule changes were implemented at the start of the 1994–95 season in order to increase scoring. The three-point line was drawn closer to the basket. Larry Bird scoffed at this change; every year shooters had been making a higher percentage from behind the original line. Similarly, a stringent hand-checking rule was drafted to handicap aggressive defensive teams. The beginning of the season took center stage in the sports world because labor strife paralyzed both pro hockey and baseball. Orlando jumped ahead of the Eastern Conference and remained there for the regular season, while a quartet of teams—Phoenix, Utah, San Antonio, and Seattle—vied for the best record in the West. However, the seminal event of the season took place in mid-March, when Michael Jordan returned to the Bulls from self-imposed exile in minor league baseball. The entire nation and most of the Western

San Antonio Spur David Robinson, the 1994–95 NBA MVP, slams home 2 points over the Houston Rockets' Clyde Drexler Spur rebounding demon Dennis Rodman and Rockets Vernon Maxwell (Number 11), Kenny Smith (Number 30), and Hakeem Olajuwon (the previous season's MVP) watch from nearby. The Spurs and Rockets dueled in the 1995 Western Conference finals. Houston stole the first two games at San Antonio, but the Spurs bounced back to tie up the battle of Texas with two wins in Houston. In the end, the Rockets took the series in six games behind the brilliant play of Olajuwon, leading now-commentator Bill Walton to remark that Hakeem "is a polished gem."

RIGHT, TOP: The Milwaukee
Bucks' great young forward
Glenn "Big Dog" Robinson, out of
Purdue University, dishes off to a
teammate while driving the lane.
The first player selected in the
1994 NBA draft, Robinson started slow in his rookie season (a
lengthy contract dispute kept
him sidelined during the presea-
son), but then picked up steam.
He finished the season averaging
21.9, tenth-best in the league,
and added over 6 rebounds per
game. Still, there's room for
improvement: Big Dog led the
league in turnovers in his inaugural NBA campaign. Once
Robinson learns the nuances of
the pro game, who knows how
far he'll take the Bucks. Robinson
finished third in the 1994–95
Rookie of the Year voting and
led the Bucks to 14 more wins
than they had had the previous
season. RIGHT, BOTTOM: The
Bucks' improvement was a small
step compared to the giant
stride made by the Dallas
Mavericks in point guard Jason
Kidd's rookie season. The
Mavericks improved 23 games
over their 1993–94 record, the
fourth-greatest single-season
increase in wins in league history, behind only the improvement
made by the Spurs (in David
Robinson's rookie season), Celtics
(in Larry Bird's rookie season),
and Bucks (in Lew Alcindor's
rookie season). Kidd plays the
game at breakneck speed, tear-
ing up and down the court, creating havoc on defense and
making unbelievable passes as if
they were second nature to him.
When Kidd, who was named Co-
Rookie of the Year (with Grant
Hill) for the 1994–95 season,
leads the Mavs into the limelight, NBA fans are in for a
thousand thrills.

world took notice; never before had NBA regular-season games received such attention. Jordan's return
instantly transformed the Bulls from first-round can-
non fodder to title contender, though the team lacked
the interior strength they had had from 1990 to 1993.

Nine teams—Orlando, New York, Indiana,
Chicago, San Antonio, Utah, Phoenix, Seattle, and
defending champion Houston—entered the postseason
with serious title aspirations. Utah and Seattle confirmed their reputations as playoff pushovers by losing
in the first round to Houston and the upstart Lakers,
respectively. The second round produced four brilliant
series. The marquee matchup featured Shaq and the
Magic versus Michael and the Bulls—the new,
unproven megastar versus the game's all-time greatest
player, back from the dead, more myth than man.
After six frenzied games, the torch was passed: Shaq
advanced, and to the dismay of NBC, Mike had to
wait 'til next year. The Spurs ousted Los Angeles in
six games, though Laker point guard Nick Van Exel
provided some spectacular late-game heroics.
Olajuwon's Rockets stunned Charles Barkley and the
Suns for the second straight year, becoming only the
fifth team in NBA history to come back from a three-
games-to-one deficit to win a seven-game series.
Ewing's Knicks and Reggie Miller's Pacers met in a
rematch of their classic 1994 Eastern Conference
finals; again it came down to Game Seven at Madison
Square Garden. This time the Pacers nipped the
Knicks by 2 points. Apparently, the shorter three-point
shot did nothing to diminish the domination of the
league's four great centers: Olajuwon, Robinson, and
O'Neal all reached the final four, and Ewing missed
out by only 2 points. In the conference finals,
1993–94 MVP Hakeem Olajuwon schooled the new
(1994–95) MVP David Robinson as he led the
Rockets over the Spurs in six games; the Magic
squeaked by the Pacers in seven tough, and often
thrilling, games. Then Olajuwon and the Rockets
crushed Shaq and the Magic in four straight to repeat
as NBA champions. Up until the lopsided finals, the
1995 playoffs were the most exciting in years; consequently, fan interest was up substantially from the previous season and close to record levels.

With Michael having returned to close out his
career, Charles playing brilliantly when not disabled,
and Hakeem at the top of his game in his early thir-
ties, the NBA's new generation should recognize the
commitment it takes to be great enough to enter the
NBA's all-time pantheon. Before considering today's
young superstars, three Dream Teamers merit special
note: Patrick Ewing, Karl Malone, and John Stockton.
While these three have not distinguished themselves
as spectacularly as Mike and Hakeem (though perhaps
as well as Charles), it is still too early to assess Ewing
and Utah's dynamic duo for posterity; currently, they
straddle the criteria for inclusion in this book.

Jordan, Olajuwon, Barkley, and Stockton were all
rookies in 1984–85, and Ewing and Malone began their
NBA careers the following year. These two rookie
crops dominated the pro ranks through the early

nineties. In the six seasons following 1984–85, only one player emerged whose career earns him a place among the NBA's greatest ever: David Robinson. The sleek seven-foot-one-inch (215.9cm) San Antonio Spur has been a superstar from the moment he debuted in the NBA in the autumn of 1989. A few other stars with exceptional skills entered the pro ranks between the 1986–87 and 1991–92 seasons, but without a couple of rings they won't make it into the NBA pantheon: the New Jersey Nets' sleek guard Kenny Anderson and agile power forward Derrick Coleman; the Seattle Supersonics' floor general, Gary Payton, and acrobatic, slam-dunking forward Shawn Kemp; the Sacramento Kings' clutch shooting guard Mitch Richmond; Phoenix's heir to Charles Barkley, Danny Manning; and the Denver Nuggets' shot-blocking, rebounding giant, Dikembe Mutombo. Finally, there's the Indiana Pacers' scoring tandem of Rik Smits and Reggie Miller. Seven-foot-four-inch (223.5cm) Smits is lethal when he has the ball along the baseline or facing the basket, but his rebounding and defense are mediocre for someone his size. Six-foot-seven-inch (200.6cm) shooting guard Miller, on the other hand, is a first-rate NBA star; his spectacular three-point shooting and legendary playoff performances have made him a folk hero, but he is so committed to being a scorer that his game lacks dimension.

A plethora of talented players entered the league in the 1992, 1993, and 1994 drafts; they are poised to wrestle control of the NBA away from the Dream Team generation. Already each of these three drafts has produced one transcendent player who may one day take a place among the all-time greats: center Shaquille O'Neal; one of his Orlando Magic teammates, point guard Anfernee Hardaway; and the Detroit Pistons' high-flying forward Grant Hill.

Behind O'Neal and Hardaway, the Magic have plans to become the NBA's next dynasty, but other young teams such as the Charlotte Hornets, Los Angeles Lakers, Washington Bullets, Milwaukee Bucks, and Dallas Mavericks have different ideas. If these teams succeed in winning a championship or two, their premier stars may move into the realm of the all-time NBA legends. The Hornets are led by center Alonzo Mourning and power forward Larry Johnson, who has been slowed by injuries the past two seasons. However, Mourning is a rising star. A defensive stalwart, Alonzo plays Shaq well. Charlotte fans hope Alonzo can be to Shaq what Russell was to Wilt. The Lakers' Nick Van Exel, crafty scorer Cedric Ceballos, and guard Eddie Jones form the nucleus of a brash team that can light up the scoreboard. The Bullets feature the 1993–94 Rookie of the Year, six-foot-eleven-inch (210.8cm) adonis Chris Webber, teamed up with one of his college buddies, seven-foot (213.3cm) Juwon Howard, in the low post. The Bucks are led by the dynamic frontline duo of Glenn Robinson, the first pick of the 1994 draft, and Vin Baker, an agile, strong inside player. Robinson is a large forward, who is good on the boards, but exceptional on offense; he has a soft, accurate shot and a

Charlotte Hornet center Alonzo Mourning shoots a short hook shot over Denver Nugget center Dikembe Mutombo on December 17, 1993. College teammates at Georgetown, Mourning and Mutombo quickly became two of the most feared centers in the NBA. Both are ferocious defenders, though Mutombo is even more exceptional in this department: he led the league in blocked shots in 1994 and 1995 and won the NBA's Defensive Player of the Year Award for 1994–95. Mutombo also grabs about 4 more rebounds per game than Mourning, but Alonzo is a much more consistent scorer than Dikembe, averaging almost 10 more points per game. As these two young centers enter the prime of their careers, they stand poised to make their mark on NBA history.

full complement of moves to the basket from either the low post or the perimeter. Lastly, the Mavericks are led by the superflashy point guard Jason Kidd (1994–95 Co-Rookie of the Year), Jamal Mashburn, and Jimmy Jackson. In Kidd's first year, the Mavs improved 23 games, the fourth-best turnaround in NBA history. While Mashburn and Jackson can put the ball in the basket from anywhere on the court, Kidd knows how to get the ball to his teammates from anywhere on the court. Kidd's jump shot began to improve late in his rookie season. When he starts to bury outside shots regularly, he'll be almost unstoppable.

When Michael Jordan retired before the 1993–94 season, he walked away from the game while on top, at the peak of his powers. He also broke the NBA's chain of generational succession. By quitting prematurely he deprived budding NBA stars of an important rite of passage: playing against the previous generation's greatest player in the twilight of his glory. Many young players expressed resentment when Jordan retired; they had wanted a chance to play against him. Jordan's return to the NBA rights the wrong, allowing for a smooth transition from one generation to the next. As Michael tries to capture another NBA scoring title and league championship, he will square off against the likes of Glenn Robinson, Grant Hill, Joe Smith, and Jerry Stackhouse, who in twelve years will be the venerable men of the NBA as they face another litter of rookie stars—just as Michael once competed against Julius Erving and Kareem Abdul-Jabbar, who played against Wilt Chamberlain and alongside Oscar Robertson, who did battle with Dolph Schayes, who was among the first generation of NBA stars.

DAVID Robinson

Seven-foot-one-inch (215.9cm) center David Robinson of the San Antonio Spurs has the scoring skills of a small forward: he can blow by opponents with his quickness and soar above them with his leaping ability; he can take the ball to the basket off the dribble and finish with authority; and he can pivot to the baseline from the low post and elevate for a smooth jumper. When Robinson first entered the NBA, veteran center Caldwell Jones commented that Robinson had "the talent all us big guys only hope and dream for." His slender frame rippling with muscle, Robinson is also a powerhouse near the basket, clearing the boards and shutting down opposing centers with his exceptional shot-blocking skills.

An excellent and disciplined high school student, Robinson was admitted to the Naval Academy in Annapolis, Maryland. He had been a fine high school basketball player and planned to try out for the Navy varsity team. The basketball program at Navy has a severe handicap: no one over six feet six inches (198.1cm) is admitted to the academy because of height restrictions on submarines. David was under six feet six inches when he was accepted to Annapolis but then experienced a phenomenal growth spurt. By his junior year David was approaching seven feet (213.3cm) and becoming a great basketball

player. Single-handedly, Robinson led the Midshipmen to a conference title and through the first three rounds of the NCAA tournament. David led Navy back to the NCAA and was a consensus All-American as a senior. As the NBA draft approached, the big question was whether the navy would require David to do his mandatory four-year, full-time duty or allow him to turn pro. A compromise was reached before the draft: Robinson would be permitted to play in the NBA after a two-year stint in the navy, followed by part-time duty. The San Antonio Spurs had the first draft pick in 1987 and had to decide whether or not to take Robinson, who would not play for two years and would have the option of reentering the draft in either of those two years. The Spurs decided that "The Admiral" was worth the risk; they made the right decision.

When Robinson finally joined the Spurs for the 1989–90 season there was considerable speculation that he would be a bust. Robinson had been the starting center and premier star of the 1988 U.S. Olympic Team that had floundered in Seoul, taking a bronze medal in the worst performance ever by a U.S. basketball team. Critics noted that Robinson seemed to experience lapses on the court; he would be brilliant for five minutes and then invisible the next five.

In his rookie NBA season, The Admiral averaged 24.3 points, 12 rebounds, and almost 4 blocked shots per game, and led the Spurs to a first-place finish in the Midwestern division. The team's 56–26 mark was a record-setting 35-game improvement over the previous season, surpassing both the 32-game improvement made by the Celtics in Larry Bird's first year and the 29-game boost that Lew Alcindor gave the Bucks in his rookie season. However, both Larry and Lew led their teams to an NBA title in their second seasons, while Robinson's Spurs faltered in his. After losing an epic seven-game series to the Trail Blazers in the second round of the 1990 playoffs, the Spurs seemed destined to become the Western Conference's next dominant team. Robinson's strong supporting cast included promising rookies forward Sean Elliot and point guard Rod Strickland, as well as mature veterans power forward Terry Cummings and guard Maurice Cheeks. Robinson continued to improve in his second NBA campaign, winning the rebounding title and leading the Spurs to another division title. However, Golden State stunned San Antonio in the first round of the playoffs. In a brilliant strategic maneuver, the undersize Warriors forced Robinson to play perimeter defense by having their center dribble the ball upcourt and, in effect, play point guard.

The next three seasons were tumultuous in San Antonio. Coaching mastermind Larry Brown departed in the middle of Robinson's third season, and the Spurs managed only 47 wins before getting swept in the first round of the playoffs by Phoenix. Then, in an ill-advised move, the Spurs hired college coaching legend Jerry Tarkanian to turn things around. Tarkanian was not cut out for the NBA, however, and stepped down after just 20 games. Tarkanian's assistant, John Lucas, took the reins and guided the Spurs back on course, though they lost to Charles Barkley and the Suns in the second round of the playoffs.

Things looked even brighter in 1993–94 as the Spurs revival continued through the regular season. The Spurs made a key acquisition in the off-season: free agent power forward Dennis Rodman, a great defender and even better rebounder. Rodman had won two consecutive rebounding titles with the Pistons, averaging 4 more rebounds per game than any other player in the league. Rodman's presence on the offensive glass allowed Robinson to concentrate more on scoring. Consequently, the Admiral averaged 29.8 points per game, an increase of more than 6 points over the previous season. On the last day of the season Robinson needed a big performance to remain ahead of Shaquille O'Neal for the scoring title. Coach Lucas instructed the Spurs to feed David the ball throughout the game and The Admiral responded with an amazing 71-point outburst, only the ninth time in NBA history that someone reached the 70-point plateau. The effort clinched the scoring title for Robinson. Rodman won another rebounding title. It was the first time in league history that teammates won the scoring and rebounding titles in the same season. The Spurs finished with 55 wins, and just when it seemed they were back on track, Utah upset them in the first round of the playoffs. Shortly thereafter, Coach Lucas quit to take over the 76ers, and the Spurs were again in disarray.

The 1994–95 season started out similarly when Rodman, a notorious rebel whose body is covered in tattoos and who dyes his hair different colors throughout the season, would not comply with the team's new etiquette code and went AWOL. In his absence the team began the season 7–9. However, when Rodman returned, the Spurs caught fire. The Admiral anchored a team that was as deep and talented as any in the league. The Spurs' starting five of Robinson, Rodman, Elliot, Vinnie Del Negro, and point guard Avery Johnson was supported by an astounding bench featuring veterans J.R. Reid, Terry Cummings, Chuck Person, Doc Rivers, and Willie Anderson. Nevertheless, everyone expected the Spurs to stumble when Rodman was sidelined for a few weeks in March after a motorcycle accident. Instead, Robinson elevated his game and the Spurs went on a winning streak that catapulted them to the best record in the league. In the playoffs, San Antonio overcame the resurgent Lakers, but then succumbed to the eventual champions, the Houston Rockets, in the Western Conference finals.

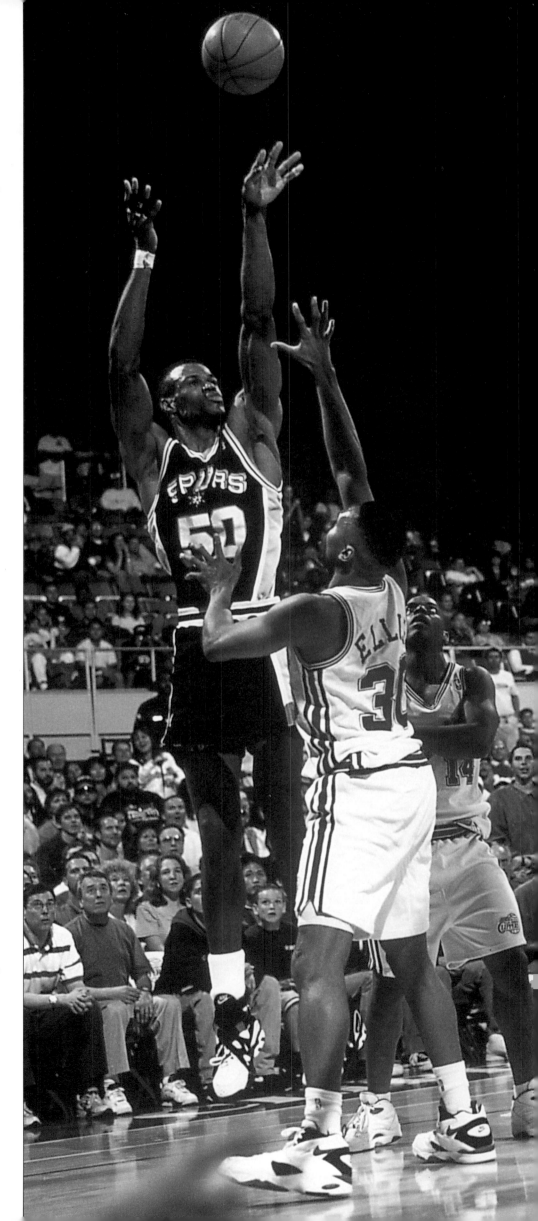

SHAQUILLE O'Neal

The one and only Shaquille O'Neal gives the people what they want as he powers home a bone-jarring slam dunk. Warrior Latrell Sprewell, the Magic's Anthony Bowie, Orlando Coach Brian Hill, and a sellout crowd at the "O"rena all watch in awe. In his first NBA campaign, Shaq's attacks on the rims and basket supports throughout the league grabbed headlines; however, by his third season, in which he led the league in scoring and finished second in the MVP voting, it was Shaq's well-rounded game and ability to lead the Magic to victory that kept him in the spotlight.

Shaquille O'Neal is the real deal. Shaq is an awesome physical specimen, possessing everything necessary to dominate the game of basketball. He's seven feet one inch (215.9cm) tall, weighs 300 pounds (136.2kg), is well coordinated, and has a rock-solid body, soft hands, and spring in his legs. With the development of his baby hook and short jumper, he is almost unstoppable in the low post. He controls the boards like an adult playing against children. Shaq has improved each of his three years in the NBA and in that time transformed an expansion team into a championship contender.

Shaquille Rashan O'Neal was born in Newark, New Jersey, on March 6, 1972, to Lucille O'Neal. He was raised by his mother and Staff Sergeant Phillip Harrison of the U.S. Army. An army brat, Shaq lived wherever Harrison happened to be was stationed. Louisiana State Coach Dale Brown happened upon Shaquille, then a six-foot-six-inch (198.1cm) high school sophomore, playing a pickup game at an army base in West Germany. Two years later, after Shaq had gone to San Antonio and led his high school to a 68–1

record, O'Neal committed to play for Brown at LSU. After sharing the spotlight in his first year with fellow seven-footer (213.3cm) Stanley Roberts (now an injury-plagued Clipper) and point guard Chris Jackson (now Denver Nuggets star Makmoud Abdul-Rauf), O'Neal took center stage in his sophomore year. He got rave reviews but was a one-man show, and the Tigers never went far in the NCAA tournament. After three years in Baton Rouge, O'Neal declared himself eligible for the NBA draft and Orlando won the Shaquille lottery.

Shaq exploded onto the NBA scene in the autumn of 1992 with a cavalcade of commercial endorsements and a devastating array of power slams. Shaquille studied the rims and basket supports around the league, sizing up their vulnerability, and, to the delight of fans, managed to tear a few down. He also scored 23 points and grabbed 14 rebounds per game. The Magic improved by 20 games over the previous season, though they missed the playoffs by a game, and Shaq was a consensus Rookie of the Year. Orlando made the playoffs the next season, as Shaq's scoring production increased to over 29 points per game. With Michael Jordan temporarily retired, O'Neal became the NBA's leading celebrity and a ubiquitous presence in television advertising throughout the world. Shaqmania continued during the 1994–95 season, in which O'Neal won his first scoring title and the Magic finished with the best record in the Eastern Conference. The Magic won the first and second rounds of the playoffs (overcoming the Jordan-led Bulls in the second) and beat the Pacers to take the Eastern Conference title. However, the defending champion Rockets schooled the young team by sweeping the finals.

When Kareem Abdul-Jabbar saw O'Neal play during Shaq's sophomore year at LSU, he quipped, "Don't call Shaquille the next anybody. Let him be the first Shaquille." However, through three pro seasons, Shaquille's career bares a striking resemblance to Wilt Chamberlain's. Like the Big Dipper, O'Neal is not only a giant but also a great athlete, agile and preternaturally strong. Shaq developed a full range of low-post skills by his third pro season, just like Wilt. Neither man could shoot free throws well. Most significantly, Shaq has been frustrated so far in his quest for a championship, like Wilt was so often during his career. Of course, the Magic are still young and improving; the challenge before them is to evolve into a truly great team. Shaq, in particular, has to perform better in the clutch. If he does so, and leads the Magic to an NBA title, then he really will be the "first Shaquille."

PATRICK EWING, JOHN STOCKTON, AND KARL MALONE

A persuasive case can be made that the New York Knicks' Patrick Ewing or the Utah Jazz's Karl Malone belong on the short list of all-time NBA greats. The Knicks and the Jazz have built winning teams around Ewing and Malone; Ewing was among the league's top centers and Malone one of its preeminent power forwards for an entire decade. In virtually every season in the late eighties and early nineties, both Ewing and Malone were among the leading MVP candidates (though neither ever won) and the Knicks and Jazz contended (in vain) for the league title. Through the 1994–95 season, most commentators agree that Hakeem Olajuwon deserves the nod over Ewing as the greatest center of his generation and that Charles Barkley has a more impressive resume than Malone; however, the margin of difference in both cases is so small (and open to question) that it seems possible that Ewing and Malone's achievements in the remainder of their careers could catapult them into the upper echelon of the NBA pantheon.

Patrick Ewing was born in Jamaica on August 5, 1962, and his family moved to Cambridge, Massachusetts, where Patrick became a high school basketball phenomenon. Patrick was an overnight sensation at Georgetown as he led the Hoyas to the NCAA championship game in his freshman year. Georgetown Coach John Thompson had played for Red Auerbach during the Celtics dynasty of the sixties as Bill Russell's backup. Clearly influenced by Auerbach's scheme, Thompson used the awesomely athletic seven-foot (213.3cm) Ewing as his "Russell." Thus, Patrick's primary role was defense, and he developed low-post skills on offense that were meant to complement his teammates' abilities.

Ewing had one of the greatest college careers ever, leading the Hoyas to the NCAA finals three times and capturing the title in his junior year. The jewel of the 1985 draft—Patrick was the first choice overall—he was selected by the New York Knicks, who had won the draft lottery. Built around two injury-plagued stars, Bernard King and Bill Cartwright, the Knicks were an aging and awful team in the mid-eighties. In Ewing's first two years, the Knicks were terrible, and it wasn't until some other high draft picks joined the squad that things turned around. Under new coach Rick Pitino, the Knicks made the playoffs in Patrick's third year and then won the Eastern division the next year; over this period Ewing established himself among the NBA's elite stars. His defense was exceptional (especially his skill at blocking shots when opponents drove the lane) as was his rebounding. His offensive skills were increasingly impressive, in particular his signature turnaround baseline jumper, which Patrick can still swish with uncanny frequency. However, wunderkind Pitino returned to college hoops and the Knicks struggled for two years, though Patrick's offensive output increased. Then in the autumn of 1991, former Lakers Coach Pat Riley took over the Knicks and the

Utah's Karl "The Mailman" Malone delivers 2 points past Denver's Dikembe Mutombo while teammate John Stockton (Number 12) looks on. In the eight seasons that Stockton and Malone have played together in their prime, they've led the Jazz to victory in an amazing 64 percent of their regular-season games. Unfortunately, success has been more elusive in the playoffs, where they are a sub-500 team that has won only six playoff series.

team took off, winning three straight division titles and finally reaching the NBA finals in 1994, where they lost a heartbreaking seven-game series to the Houston Rockets in a matchup that featured Patrick going head-to-head with Rocket center Hakeem Olajuwon. Throughout the first ten years of his career, Ewing has established a level of excellence that has rubbed off on the Knicks, who call Patrick "the franchise." Ewing's legacy to date is that of a ferocious competitor whose considerable offensive and defensive skills have made him the backbone of good, but not great, Knicks teams; if Patrick's supporting cast had been slightly stronger he probably would have won a few championships.

Unlike Ewing, Karl Malone was an unknown coming out of college. Malone attended Louisiana Tech University in his home state, where he led the varsity basketball team to an appearance in the NCAA tournament. An agile and massive six-foot-eleven-inch (210.8cm) center/forward, Malone was an attractive prospect to NBA scouts, but the 1985 draft was loaded with top-flight, high-profile talent and Karl slipped to the middle of the first round, where he was selected unceremoniously by the Utah Jazz. Utah had made the playoffs the previous season and was not a weak team. The team featured high scorers Adrian Dantley and Darrell Griffith, shot-blocking giant Mark Eaton, and young point guard John Stockton from tiny Gonzaga College, a late first-round selection in the 1984 draft. Malone became a starter in his first season.

For the next few years Utah showed gradual improvement, and Karl became a fixture near the top of the NBA leader boards in scoring and rebounding. A power forward who runs the floor as well as a guard, Malone has an accurate outside shot and is a terror in the paint and off the boards. Karl is also among the league leaders in free throws attempted—and made—every year. By the end of the eighties the Jazz ranked among the NBA's elite teams and has been in the upper echelon ever since. Unfortunately, the team advanced to the conference finals only twice (1992 and 1994), and has earned a reputation for being a playoff patsy. Still, Malone and teammate John Stockton make up one of the great tandems in NBA history. The six-foot-two-inch (187.9cm) Stockton has already shattered the all-time record for career assists and is simply one of the best point guards ever. Likewise, Malone, the beneficiary of many of Stockton's assists, plays the large forward position as well as anyone in NBA history. It has often been noted that had Malone and/or Stockton played for New York or Los Angeles, they would be as renowned as Jordan, Bird, and Johnson. But alas, Utah's dynamic duo has displayed its brilliance in the relative obscurity of Salt Lake City and in recent years has been saddled with a weak supporting cast. Nevertheless, before they hang up their sneakers, Malone and Stockton will be at or near the top of some prestigious categories in the record books.

ANFERNEE Hardaway

The Orlando Magic's fleet-footed six-foot-seven-inch (200.6 cm) point guard Anfernee Hardaway encounters Houston's Pete Chilcutt on his way to the basket after leaving Vernon Maxwell (Number 11) in the dust during a 1994–95 regular season contest. Shortly before the 1995 playoffs, David Robinson assessed Hardaway: "If he's not the best all-around player in the league he's awfully close. I mean, the man can make some plays that only a few people can see, let alone make." Hardaway, for his part, is not bashful about where he feels he and Shaquille will lead the Magic: "I know what I can do. I know what this team can do. It can set the standards for the NBA of the 1990s."

When the Orlando Magic missed the playoffs by one game in Shaquille O'Neal's rookie season, the consolation was that they entered the NBA draft lottery. Since the lottery is structured to give the weakest teams a better chance, the Magic were long shots to win their second consecutive lottery. However, Orlando bucked the odds. On draft day, the Magic conformed to expectations and made Michigan's great power forward Chris Webber the number one choice. Philadelphia took seven-foot-seven-inch (231.1cm) beanstalk Shawn Bradley second. The Golden State Warriors selected six-foot-seven-inch (200.6cm) Anfernee "Penny" Hardaway, a brilliant swingman from Memphis State being touted as the "next Earvin Johnson," and then announced they were trading him, along with some future draft picks, to the Magic in exchange for Webber. In short, the Orlando Magic's lottery-day magic brought the "next Magic" to the Magic Kingdom.

Orlando fans were not so thrilled. The congregation of Magic faithful watching the draft at Orlando's Arena booed when they heard the announcement of the trade. Since the lottery, they had anticipated watching O'Neal and Webber wreak havoc on opponents in the paint. Furthermore, Hardaway was being touted as a point guard, and the Magic's current point guard, Scott Skiles, was a fan favorite. Thus, young Anfernee Hardaway was going to have to prove himself to his new hometown fans.

Acceptance was never a problem for Anfernee in college. A huge high school star in Memphis, Tennessee, Hardaway decided to stay home and play college ball at Memphis State. The decision almost backfired tragically when, during his sophomore year, Anfernee stumbled upon an armed robbery in his neighborhood. The assailant opened fire on Hardaway. Luckily, Anfernee was only hit in the foot and recovered fully. On the basketball court, Penny thrilled the hometown fans and impressed the scouts. A lithe player with exceptional ballhandling skills and court vision, Penny preferred an up-tempo game and wasn't shy about trying spectacular plays, most of which worked. Hardaway carried Memphis State into the NCAA tournament in his second season and then declared himself eligible for the NBA draft.

Hardaway further endeared himself to Orlando fans when he held out for a long time in a contract dispute before his rookie season and then got off to a shaky start. But by the end of his first season in Orlando, however, Penny was beginning to click. Midway through his second NBA campaign, Hardaway's picture adorned the cover of *Sports Illustrated*. The Magic were playing exciting, racehorse basketball with Penny taking the reins. Often compared to Magic Johnson because he is a tall point guard, Hardaway differs considerably from Earvin. Much slighter than Johnson, Hardaway can post up occasionally, but overall he doesn't have the inside potential that Magic did. Anfernee is a better scorer than Magic was at this stage of his career, though Penny's three-point shot still needs work. Hardaway has not yet developed Magic's brilliant tactical sense of the game, but few players have ever matched Earvin in that regard. Alas, Penny is an amazing and rare player in his own right: he is just as comfortable throwing an alley-oop pass as he is jamming one home, and he is equally skilled at making no-look passes on the fast break as he is at sweeping down the baseline for a flying dunk over an opposing center. An instinctive player, Hardaway summed up his game by saying, "I like to entertain. Most of all, I want to win, but when I do something special, I can feel the vibe from the crowd. I live for the 'ooh,' the 'aah.'" And alongside Shaquille O'Neal in Orlando, Anfernee Hardaway is ready to transform the Magic into the next NBA dynasty.

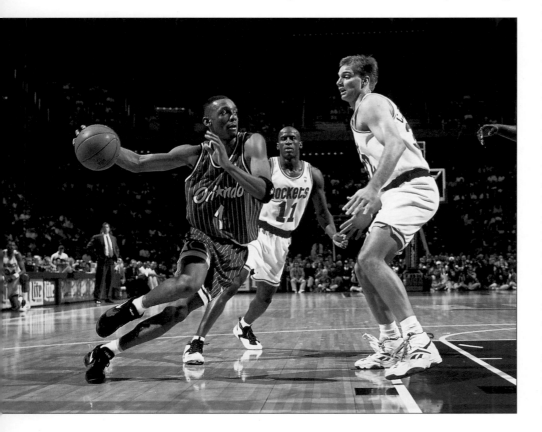

GRANT Hill

Within the first few weeks of his NBA career, Grant Hill was declared the "next Michael Jordan" by the media. Like His Airness, Hill was capable of sensational, gravity-defying maneuvers on the way to the basket; like Mike, Grant could effortlessly beat any defender off the dribble; and, like Mike, Grant's exploits made the highlight reels almost nightly. However, Grant Hill is not Michael Jordan; he is Grant Hill and that's more than enough.

Grant Hill is the scion of an amazing family. Father Calvin was a legendary football player at Yale and then in the NFL with the great Cowboys team of the 1970s and later with the Washington Redskins. Mother Janet was a suitemate and friend of Hillary Rodham (Clinton) at Wellesley. The Hills were intent on raising their son right, and emphasized discipline. The house rules were so rigid that in high school Grant was allowed to use the phone on weekends only. While an NBA rookie, Grant reflected that his childhood was "like being born into a royal family and being raised like a prince, being taught one day to become king. Not just how to be an athlete, but how to do things right." The Hills' strict regimen paid off as Grant became an exceptional athlete and student, earning a scholarship to Duke University.

In his freshman season Grant earned a starting spot on a Duke team that had lost to UNLV in the NCAA finals the previous season. Led by stars Christian Laettner and Bobby Hurley, the Blue Devils returned to the Final Four, where they stunned heavily favored UNLV and then defeated Kansas for their first national title. Hill's outstanding defense made a huge difference in the Blue Devils' rematch with UNLV. The next year Duke became the first college team to repeat as national champions in nineteen seasons. In his first two seasons at Duke, Grant was primarily a defensive specialist. Almost all his scoring came on layups and slam dunks; he had no outside shot to speak of and was a horrendous free throw shooter. But Grant worked arduously and his shooting improved. By his senior season, Grant was a lethal offensive threat. Grant led Duke back to the NCAA finals, where they lost to Arkansas on a last-second shot.

By the autumn of 1994 only Joe Dumars remained from the champion Pistons of 1989 and 1990. All the other Bad Boys had retired or moved elsewhere. The Pistons were committed to rebuilding and were bottoming out when they landed the third pick in the 1994 lottery; their reward was Grant Hill.

Before the 1994–95 season was a month old it was clear that the Pistons, behind their sensational rookie, were on their way back. Away from the zone defenses allowed in college ball, Hill was able to beat any defender off the dribble. Grant could then drive for a spectacular slam, pass off to an open teammate if double-teamed, or use his leaping ability to spring over the defense for a short jump shot (which still needs work, but continues to improve).

Grant instantly became a favorite among fans, and was the first rookie ever to receive the most votes in balloting for the All-Star Game. The public's adoration of Hill stems not only from his on-court brilliance but also from the perception of him as a hard-working, intelligent, upright young man who stands in sharp contrast to the apparent laziness and arrogance of many NBA stars. Grant may be a model citizen, but his politeness does not impede his competitiveness: "I don't show it, but I'm very cocky and confident underneath," says Hill. "When I show up on the court, I feel I'm the best player out there, and no one can stop me. I want to beat you and embarrass you….But I don't want people to know that. It's like a little secret I keep to myself." In his first year in the NBA, Grant averaged 19.9 points, 5 assists, 6.4 rebounds, and numerous spectacular plays per game.

Detroit Piston Grant Hill (who shared Co-Rookie of the Year honors with Jason Kidd) floats above the baseline past some astounded New Jersey Nets to deposit the ball in the basket during his rookie season. In his second season, Hill will play for the new Pistons head coach Doug Collins, who coached the Chicago Bulls during Michael Jordan's most prolific years as a scorer. Collins favors a wide-open offense that allows for a lot of individual creativity; it should be exciting to see what Hill produces in this new system. Jordan's average increased almost 10 points per game in his first year playing under Collins; like Grant, Mike had not yet perfected his outside shot at that point in his career.

AFTERWORD

Michael Jordan participates in the official ceremony commemorating the retirement of his number on "Michael Jordan Day," November 1, 1994, at Chicago Stadium. Of course, Michael would once again wear Number 23 for the Bulls before the end of the 1994–95 season after a brief stint (22 games) as Number 45. During his abbreviated retirement, Michael was almost unanimously heralded as basketball's all-time greatest player. However, after his shaky play during the spring of 1995, some commentators speculated that Jordan will compromise his historical standing unless he returns to his preretirement form. Michael's detractors pointed to Kareem Abdul-Jabbar as an example of a great player who was able to integrate his skills onto championship quality teams throughout his twenty-year career and questioned whether Michael could do the same as he entered into the twilight of his career. However, Jordan's 1994–95 season lasted only 27 games and, overall, will have little bearing on how fans remember him. Furthermore, Michael Jordan is not only one of the fiercest competitors ever to lace up hightops, he's also acutely aware of his historical stature; barring injury, fans can expect Michael to rebound with an exceptional 1995–96 campaign and, if the Bulls provide him with any support, can expect to see him playing in June.

When Larry Bird was in his prime in the mid-eighties, *Time* magazine ran a cover story declaring Bird the greatest basketball player of all time. Only a few years later, when NBA career scoring leader Kareem Abdul-Jabbar made his final tour of the league, American pundits bestowed the same title upon him. By the early nineties, when Michael Jordan was leading his Chicago Bulls to three straight titles, fans and journalists almost unanimously anointed Michael "the best ever." Nonetheless, throughout this period, Wilt Chamberlain was still commonly referred to as the single most dominant player in the sport's history, and Bill Russell as the game's greatest champion. The two legends provided the standard against which the newer generation was compared. Of course, there is no way to determine who deserves the appellation "the greatest basketball player of all time," but it is every fan's right to have an opinion.

Since *Kings of the Court* provides ample background on the greatest players of all time (excluding playground legends), this is as good a place as any to raise the question "Who was the greatest basketball player ever?"—and answer it. As a warmup, however, let's first consider who deserves a place on the all-time NBA Dream Team and then the all-time NBA starting five. The problem with choosing such a team is whether to select players strictly according to their positions or simply to select the league's all-time top twelve performers, while only vaguely acknowledging the need for a balanced distribution of forwards, guards, and centers. Using the latter method the twelve players selected would be Robertson, Johnson, Jordan, Bird, Baylor, Jabbar, Chamberlain, Russell, Moses Malone, West, Erving, and Pettit (Olajawon and Barry barely miss out). Mikan fails to make the list (but not by much) because he played before Russell's defense revolutionized the sport. It is immediately evident that there is a dearth of power forwards (only Pettit played there among this group) and an excess of centers. Thus, if the guideline for selecting the team required the selection of a career power forward to fill that position, Malone would be cut and Elvin Hayes brought in to back up Pettit. But that would probably make the team weaker overall, and anyway, Malone played center like a power forward and more effectively than any so-called power forward in history. Thus the all-time NBA Dream Team is set with the twelve players listed above.

So, which five get to start? Once again the selection problem is whether to tap "the best five players," the best at each of the five positions, or select the five players from NBA history who would jell together as the best possible unit. Clearly, the starting backcourt consists of Jordan at the shooting guard position and either Johnson or Robertson as the starting field general. West begins the game on the bench. While in terms of offense it seems Magic would complement such a high-powered group better than Oscar, the Big O has a substantial edge on the defensive end of the court, so the starting nod goes to Robertson. The coaching staff of Auerbach-Riley-Daley would encourage Robertson to run the show as he did late in his career at Milwaukee—more as a distributor than a scorer (though a few of his patented back-in moves would be allowed). Larry Bird starts at the small forward position, Baylor backs him up, and Erving takes the floor when a running game is emphasized. The power forward and center positions are split among the four centers. Basically, Jabbar and Chamberlain are cast as pure centers, while Russell and Malone are competing for the power forward job. The rationale for this is simple: Jabbar and Chamberlain rank higher as centers than Russell and Malone because Kareem and Wilt have more complete offensive skills. The question becomes which pair deserves to start (Pettit comes off the bench, getting playing time

Michael slams one down against the Knicks in Madison Square Garden. Michael Jordan is as physically gifted as any basketball player, but what separates him from other great athletes is that he possesses an abundance of two things that the NBA's greatest players have had: on-court intelligence and an intense drive to win. As Michael put it: "When I step onto the court, I'm ready to play. And if you're playing against me, then you'd better be ready too. If you're not going to compete, then I'll dominate you." Nowhere was Michael more impressive than in basketball's largest arena, New York City. For three straight years, from 1991 through 1993, the Jordan-led Bulls eliminated the up-and-coming Knicks from the postseason. Michael transformed Madison Square Garden, New York's hollowed hall of roundball, into Chicago Stadium—East with one spectacular performance after another. The Knicks finally broke through and beat the Bulls in the 1994 playoffs, when Michael was in retirement, In his only appearance in New York during the spring of 1995, Jordan lit up the Garden for 55 points and led Chicago to a 1-point victory.

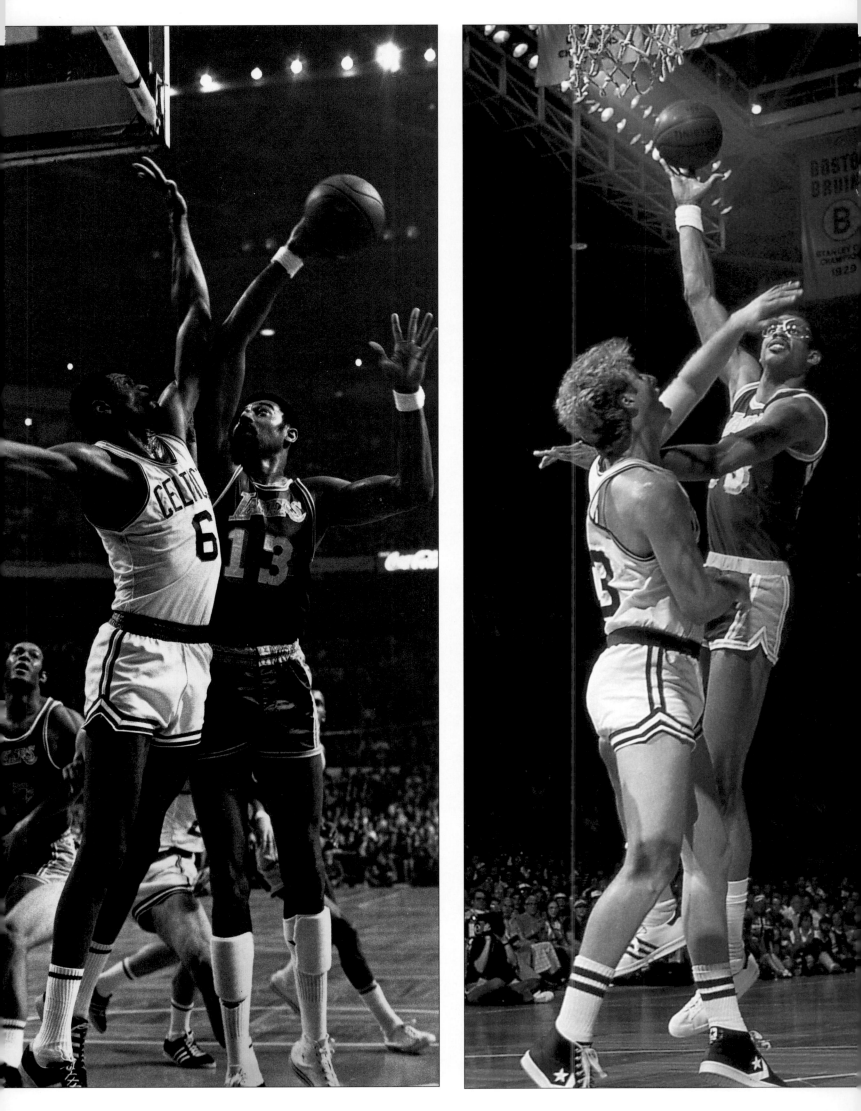

against rough opponents who play a slow-tempo half court game). Kareem has passing and free throw shooting over Wilt, but Chamberlain provides a stronger presence in the middle. At power forward, Malone's strength is his scoring ability off the offensive glass, while Russell's strength is his support defense, which could come in handy since Bird is a weak link defensively and Larry's man could blow by him and penetrate the lane. So a conundrum emerges: in almost every way, Malone's game is more suited to the role of power forward than Russell's, but Bird's slowness of foot makes Russell seem the obvious choice to start. Both offensively and defensively Jabbar and Malone complemented each other well. Kareem preferred to play away from the basket and shoot skyhooks as well as challenge any opponent's drive to the basket away from the hoop. Malone always liked to stay near the paint on both ends of the court. On the other hand, if Russell, only six feet nine inches (205.7cm) and thin, is at power forward, it seems the more physical Chamberlain should start at center. So a generational division emerges: Malone and Jabbar versus Russell and Chamberlain. It's a toss-up: Russell provides a defensive edge that Chamberlain's free throw shooting negates on the offensive end; Chamberlain rebounds better than Jabbar, but Malone possesses much more refined offensive skills than Russell. Let Bill and Wilt start the first game (because of seniority), and Moses and Kareem the next game; then decide which unit deserves to start. For the first game, the starters are Chamberlain, Russell, Bird, Jordan, and Robertson.

On to the main event: "Who is the greatest player of all time?" Borrowing from baseball analyst Bill James, there should be two categories: the top player at the peak of his career and the top player in terms of overall value throughout the course of his entire career. James then blends consideration of the two categories to determine the best player of all time. The need for the two categories becomes evident when considering the huge difference in Jabbar from 1974 to 1988 and, even more significantly, the difference between Bill Walton in 1977 and his career value.

The discussion of the NBA's all-time starting five, while inconclusive, did establish some things for our present query: namely that the top players of all time are Robertson, Johnson, Jordan, Bird, Chamberlain, Jabbar, Russell, and Malone. Of these eight, Robertson was given a nod over Magic, while Kareem and Wilt were selected over Moses and Russell. Bird falls out because of his defensive liability. This leaves Jordan, Robertson, Jabbar, and Chamberlain, even though Russell ends up ranked ahead of Robertson overall because Bill was the greatest team player in the history of the game in spite of his offensive inadequacy.

The four finalists include two centers, a point guard, and a scoring guard. Oscar had a complete all-around game, but he's open to the criticism that he dominated his own team too much. The Royals improved rapidly during Oscar's first four seasons, then stagnated and declined. Perhaps Oscar's absolute control of every game's tempo impeded the growth of his teammates. A similar criticism was made of Jordan, yet the Bulls improved into champions. And Michael improved as well, perfecting a deadly long-range jumper by his fourth season in the league. Jabbar made an astounding initial impact on the league and then modified his game for the long haul, playing at a virtually unparalleled level for almost two decades. Kareem's rapid decline in the twilight of his career can be excused because he remained an integral part of a championship team. Initially, Chamberlain was an unbelievable soloist, shattering individual records like clockwork in his early years. He later metamorphosed into a great low-post team player, but poor free throw shooting plagued Wilt throughout his career.

The thing that ultimately separates Jordan from Jabbar and Chamberlain is that he developed into a player who would not lose. Opponents could not deny Jordan the ball, and once he got it, he would use one of the weapons from his seemingly infinite arsenal to score—and win. At crunch time, opponents could double- or triple-down on Kareem or Wilt, frequently forcing one of their lesser teammates to take the clutch shots. Not so with Michael: with his speed and leaping ability, Jordan would almost always get, and sink, a good shot—against the whole world if necessary. His offensive prowess and defensive savvy negate any rebounding advantage held by the centers. When all is said and done, Michael Jordan ranks as the greatest basketball player of all time.

OPPOSITE PAGE, LEFT: The immovable object versus the unstoppable force: Bill Russell tries to stop Wilt Chamberlain during the 1969 NBA finals. OPPOSITE PAGE, RIGHT: Kareem Abdul-Jabbar launches a skyhook over a mismatched Larry Bird. Who was the greatest center of all time: Russell, Chamberlain, or Jabbar? After the 1995 playoffs, many NBA pundits wondered whether Hakeem Olajuwon belonged alongside the immortal three. However, Russell, Chamberlain, and Jabbar dominated the league for more than a decade that began with each player's first season; Olajuwon only became thoroughly dominant in his eighth season.

PEAK VALUE	CAREER VALUE	OVERALL
Michael Jordan	Kareem Abdul-Jabbar	Michael Jordan
Wilt Chamberlain	Bill Russell	Kareem Abdul-Jabbar
Kareem Abdul-Jabbar	Michael Jordan	Wilt Chamberlain
Oscar Robertson	Wilt Chamberlain	Bill Russell
Larry Bird	Magic Johnson	Oscar Robertson
Bill Russell	Oscar Robertson	Magic Johnson
Magic Johnson	Larry Bird	Larry Bird
Elgin Baylor	George Mikan	Elgin Baylor
Hakeem Olajuwon	Jerry West	Moses Malone
Moses Malone	Bob Pettit	Jerry West
Bill Walton	Moses Malone	Bob Pettit
Julius Erving	Elgin Baylor	Julius Erving

APPENDIX: STATISTICS

CAREER STATISTICS

Player	Yrs.	Games	Mins.	FGM	FGA	Pct.	FTM	FTA	Pct.	Rebs.	Assts.	PFs	Pts.	Avg.	Career
Kareem Abdul-Jabbar	20	1,560	57,446	15,837	28,307	.559	6,712	9,304	.721	17,440	5,660	4,657	38,387	24.6	1970–1989
Charles Barkley	11	819	30,300	6,813	12,285	.555	5,062	6,888	.735	9,490	3,233	2,602	19,091	23.3	1985–1995
Rick Barry*	14	1,020	38,153	9,695	21,283	.456	5,713	6,397	.893	6,893	4,952	3,048	25,279	24.8	1966–1980
Elgin Baylor	14	846	33,863	8,693	20,171	.431	5,763	7,391	.780	11,463	3,650	2,596	23,149	27.4	1959–1972
Larry Bird	13	897	34,443	8,591	17,334	.496	3,960	4,471	.886	8,974	5,695	2,279	21,791	24.3	1980–1992
Wilt Chamberlain	14	1,045	47,859	12,681	23,497	.540	6,057	11,862	.511	23,924	4,643	2,075	31,419	30.1	1960–1973
Bob Cousy	14	924	30,165	6,168	16,468	.375	4,624	5,756	.803	4,786	6,955	2,242	16,960	18.4	1951–1970
Julius Erving*	16	1,243	45,227	11,818	23,370	.506	6,256	8,052	.777	10,525	5,176	3,494	30,026	24.2	1971–1987
John Havlicek	16	1,270	46,471	10,513	23,930	.439	5,369	6,589	.815	8,007	6,114	3,281	26,395	20.8	1963–1978
Elvin Hayes	16	1,303	50,000	10,976	24,272	.452	5,356	7,999	.670	16,279	2,398	4,193	27,313	21.0	1969–1984
Magic Johnson	12	874	32,287	6,074	11,657	.521	4,788	5,649	.848	6,376	9,921	2,002	17,239	19.7	1980–1991
Michael Jordan	10	684	26,510	8,245	16,051	.514	5,205	6,161	.845	4,336	4,025	1,991	21,998	32.2	1985–1995
Moses Malone*	21	1,455	49,444	10,277	20,750	.495	9,018	11,864	.760	17,834	1,936	3,477	29,580	20.3	1974–1995
George Mikan	9	520	8,350	4,097	8,783	.404	3,570	4,588	.778	4,167	1,245	2,162	11,764	22.6	1947–1956
Hakeem Olajuwon	11	828	31,184	7,905	15,306	.516	4,081	5,749	.710	10,233	2,135	3,204	19,904	24.0	1985–1995
Bob Pettit	11	792	30,690	7,349	16,872	.436	6,182	8,119	.761	12,849	2,369	2,529	20,880	26.4	1955–1965
Oscar Robertson	14	1,040	43,886	9,508	19,620	.485	7,694	9,185	.838	7,804	9,887	2,931	26,710	25.7	1961–1974
Bill Russell	13	963	40,726	5,687	12,930	.440	3,148	5,614	.561	21,620	4,100	2,592	14,522	15.1	1957–1969
Dolph Schayes	16	1,059	29,800	6,135	15,427	.380	6,979	8,273	.844	11,256	3,072	3,664	19,249	18.2	1949–1964
Jerry West	14	932	36,571	9,016	19,032	.474	7,160	8,801	.814	5,376	6,238	2,435	25,192	27.0	1961–1974

* Includes ABA statistics

NBA MOST VALUABLE PLAYER

1955–56 Bob Pettit, St. Louis	1969–70 Willis Reed, New York	1983–84 Larry Bird, Boston
1956–57 Bob Cousy, Boston	1970–71 Kareem Abdul-Jabbar, Milwaukee	1984–85 Larry Bird, Boston
1957–58 Bill Russell, Boston	1971–72 Kareem Abdul-Jabbar, Milwaukee	1985–86 Larry Bird, Boston
1958–59 Bob Pettit, St. Louis	1972–73 Dave Cowens, Boston	1986–87 Magic Johnson, Los Angeles
1959–60 Wilt Chamberlain, Philadelphia	1973–74 Kareem Abdul-Jabbar, Milwaukee	1987–88 Michael Jordan, Chicago
1960–61 Bill Russell, Boston	1974–75 Bob McAdoo, Buffalo	1988–89 Magic Johnson, Los Angeles
1961–62 Bill Russell, Boston	1975–76 Kareem Abdul-Jabbar, Los Angeles	1989–90 Magic Johnson, Los Angeles
1962–63 Bill Russell, Boston	1976–77 Kareem Abdul-Jabbar, Los Angeles	1990–91 Michael Jordan, Chicago
1963–64 Oscar Robertson, Cincinnati	1977–78 Bill Walton, Portland	1991–92 Michael Jordan, Chicago
1964–65 Bill Russell, Boston	1978–79 Moses Malone, Houston	1992–93 Charles Barkley, Phoenix
1965–66 Wilt Chamberlain, Philadelphia	1979–80 Kareem Abdul-Jabbar, Los Angeles	1993–94 Hakeem Olajuwon, Houston
1966–67 Wilt Chamberlain, Philadelphia	1980–81 Julius Erving, Philadelphia	1994–95 David Robinson, San Antonio
1967–68 Wilt Chamberlain, Philadelphia	1981–82 Moses Malone, Houston	
1968–69 Wes Unseld, Baltimore	1982–83 Moses Malone, Philadelphia	

TOP NBA CAREER SCORERS

Kareem Abdul-Jabbar	38,387
Wilt Chamberlain	31,419
Moses Malone	27,409
Elvin Hayes	27,313
Oscar Robertson	26,710
John Havlicek	26,395
Alex English	25,613
Dominique Wilkins	25,389
Jerry West	25,192
Adrian Dantley	23,177

ALL-TIME NBA LEADERS: HIGHEST SCORING AVERAGE

Michael Jordan	32.2
Wilt Chamberlain	30.1
Elgin Baylor	27.4
Jerry West	27.0
Bob Pettit	26.4
George Gervin	26.2
Karl Malone	26.0
Dominique Wilkens	25.8
Oscar Robertson	25.7
Kareem Abdul-Jabbar	24.6

ALL-TIME NBA LEADERS: MOST REBOUNDS

Wilt Chamberlain	23,924
Bill Russell	21,620
Kareem Abdul-Jabbar	17,440
Elvin Hayes	16,279
Moses Malone	16,212
Nate Thurmond	14,464
Robert Parish	14,323
Walt Bellamy	14,241
Wes Unseld	13,769
Jerry Lucas	12,942

ALL-TIME NBA LEADERS: MOST ASSISTS

John Stockton	10,394
Magic Johnson	9,921
Oscar Robertson	9,887
Isiah Thomas	9,061
Maurice Cheeks	7,392
Len Wilkens	7,211
Bob Cousy	6,955
Guy Rodgers	6,917
Nate Archibald	6,476
John Lucas	6,454

COMBINED NBA/ABA ALL-TIME SCORERS

Kareem Abdul-Jabbar	38,387
Wilt Chamberlain	31,419
Julius Erving	30,026

Moses Malone	29,580
Dan Issel	27,482
Elvin Hayes	27,313
Oscar Robertson	26,710
George Gervin	26,595
John Havlicek	26,395
Alex English	25,613

TOP SCORERS IN NBA PLAYOFF HISTORY

Kareem Abdul-Jabbar	5,762
Jerry West	4,457
Michael Jordan	4,165
Larry Bird	3,897
John Havlicek	3,776
Magic Johnson	3,640
Elgin Baylor	3,623
Wilt Chamberlain	3,607
Kevin McHale	3,182
Dennis Johnson	3,116

HIGHEST SCORING AVERAGE IN NBA PLAYOFF HISTORY

Michael Jordan	34.4
Jerry West	29.1
Hakeem Olajuwon	28.3
Karl Malone	27.5
Elgin Baylor	27.0
George Gervin	27.0
Dominique Wilkins	25.8
Bob Pettit	25.5
Rick Barry	24.8
Bernard King	24.5

MOST REBOUNDS IN NBA PLAYOFF HISTORY

Bill Russell	4,104
Wilt Chamberlain	3,913
Kareem Abdul-Jabbar	2,481
Wes Unseld	1,777
Robert Parish	1,761
Elgin Baylor	1,724
Larry Bird	1,683
Paul Silas	1,527
Magic Johnson	1,431
Bill Bridges	1,305

MOST ASSISTS IN NBA PLAYOFF HISTORY

Magic Johnson	2,320
Larry Bird	1,062
Dennis Johnson	1,006
Isiah Thomas	987
John Stockton	980
Jerry West	970
Bob Cousy	937

Maurice Cheeks	922
John Havlicek	825
Bill Russell	770

MOST POINTS IN NBA FINALS

Jerry West	1,679
Kareem Abdul-Jabbar	1,317
Elgin Baylor	1,161
Bill Russell	1,151
Sam Jones	1,143
Tom Heinsohn	1,035
John Havlicek	1,020
Magic Johnson	971
James Worthy	754
George Mikan	741

HIGHEST SCORING AVERAGE IN NBA FINALS

Rick Barry	36.30
Michael Jordan	36.29
Jerry West	30.5
Bob Pettit	28.4
Hakeem Olajuwon	27.5
Elgin Baylor	26.4
Julius Erving	25.5
Joe Fulks	24.7
Clyde Drexler	24.5
Andrew Toney	24.4

MOST REBOUNDS IN NBA FINALS

Bill Russell	1,718
Wilt Chamberlain	862
Elgin Baylor	593
Kareem Abdul-Jabbar	507
Tom Heinsohn	473
Bob Pettit	416
Magic Johnson	397
Larry Bird	361
John Havlicek	350
Sam Jones	313

MOST ASSISTS IN NBA FINALS

Magic Johnson	584
Bob Cousy	400
Bill Russell	315
Jerry West	306
Dennis Johnson	228
John Havlicek	195
Larry Bird	187
Kareem Abdul-Jabbar	181
Michael Cooper	178
Elgin Baylor	167

BIBLIOGRAPHY

Abdul-Jabbar, Kareem. *Giant Steps*. New York: Ballantine Books, 1985.

Barkley, Charles, with Rick Riley. *Sir Charles: The Wit and Wisdom of Charles Barkley*. New York: Warner Books, 1994.

Berkow, Ira. *Oscar Robertson: His Best Season*. Engelwood Cliffs, N.J.: Prentice Hall, 1964.

George, Nelson. *Elevating the Game: Black Men and Basketball*. New York: HarperCollins, 1992.

Halberstam, David. *The Breaks of the Game*. New York: Ballantine Books, 1981.

Johnson, Earvin, with William Novak. *My Life*. New York: Fawcett Crest/Ballantine Books, 1992.

Lazenby, Roland. *The Official Los Angeles Lakers Yearbook: Ninety to Ninety-One*. Dallas: Taylor Publishing, 1990.

May, Peter. *The Big Three*. New York: Simon & Schuster, 1994.

Naughton, Jim. *Taking to the Air: The Rise of Michael Jordan*. New York: Warner Books, 1992.

Pluto, Terry. *Loose Balls: The Short, Wild Life of the American Basketball Association—As Told by the Players, Coaches, and Movers and Shakers Who Made It Happen*. New York: Simon & Schuster, 1991.

———. *Tall Tales: The Glory Years of the NBA, in the Words of the Men Who Played, Coached, and Built Pro Basketball*. New York: Simon & Schuster, 1992.

Russell, Bill. *Second Wind*. New York: Ballantine Books, 1980.

The Sporting News NBA Guide. St. Louis: The Sporting News, 1994.

PHOTO CREDITS

INDEX